CW01653670

Will
Maclean

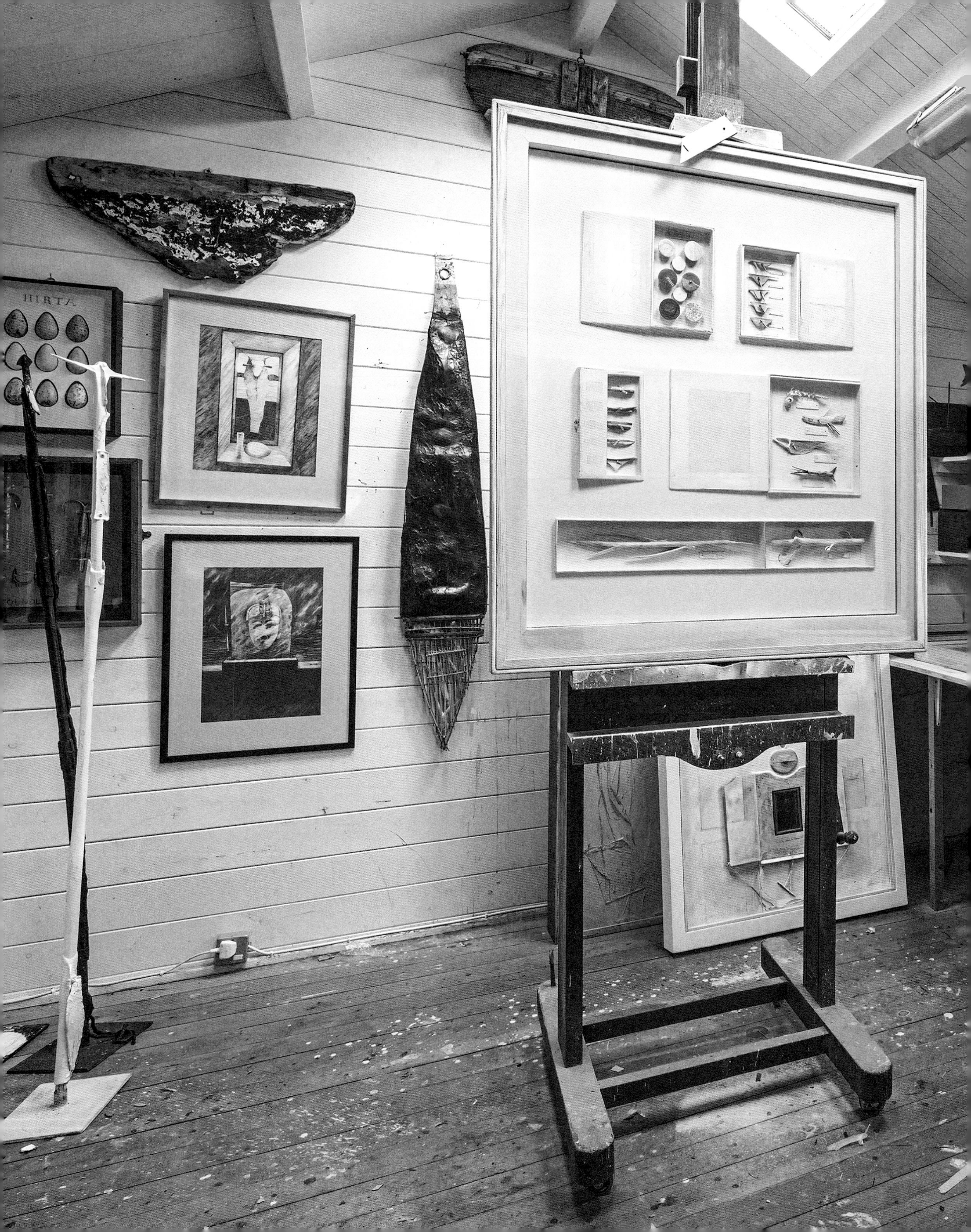
HIRTA

Will Maclean

Points of Departure

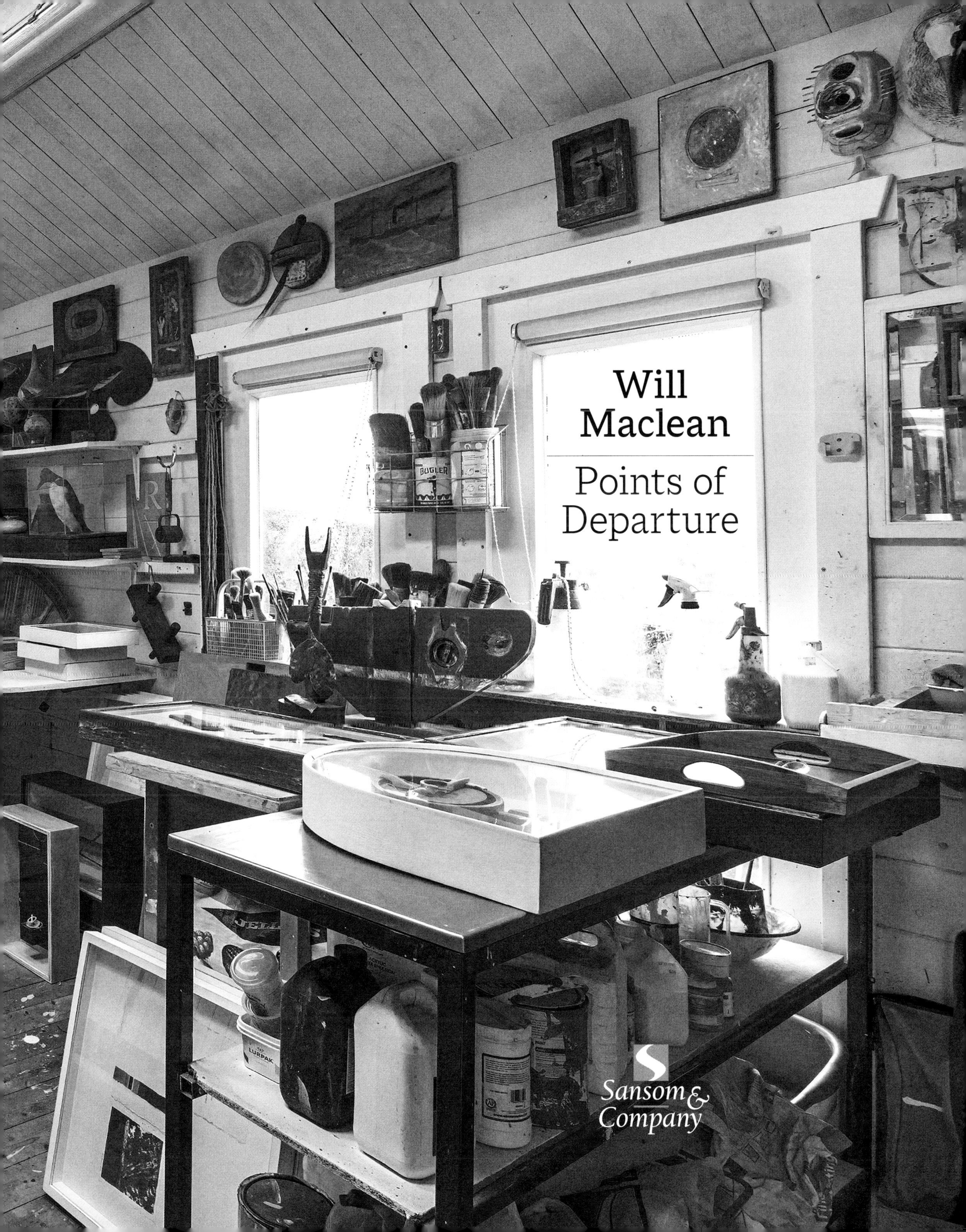

Sansom & Company

First published in 2022 by Sansom and Company,
a publishing imprint of Redcliffe Press Ltd., 81G Pembroke Road, Bristol BS8 3EA
www.sansomandcompany.co.uk · info@sansomandcompany.co.uk

Published on the occasion of the exhibition *Will Maclean: Points of Departure*,
City Art Centre, Edinburgh, 4 June–2 October 2022 · www.edinburghmuseums.org.uk

Will Maclean is represented by Art First, London · www.artfirst.co.uk

ISBN 978-1-911408-98-7

British Library Cataloguing-in-Publication Data:
a catalogue record for this book is available from the British Library.

Commissioning: Paul Deaton · Copyediting: Ann Kay
Design and Typesetting: E&P Design, Bath
Printed and bound by Zenith Print Group

MIX
Paper from
responsible sources
FSC® C010353
FSC
www.fsc.org

This book is made from Forest Stewardship Council® certified paper.
Sansom & Company is committed to being an environmentally friendly publisher.

Front cover: *Mariner's Museum/Taxonomy of Tides*, 2014
Back cover: Will Maclean; photograph Antonia Reeve
Frontispiece: Will Maclean's studio workshop; photograph Antonia Reeve

Contents

Foreword

My first encounter with a 'real' work by Will Maclean was in the unusual context of a job interview. Not long out of University, I'd applied for a junior post at the Scottish Arts Council (before it became Creative Scotland), which tells you how many years ago it was! I don't recall what the position was, but I do recollect that part of the interview involved asking each candidate to talk about a range of artworks laid out on long tables. There, amongst the others, was Will's *Trap No. III*, now in the collection of the Stirling Smith Art Gallery and Museum. I don't remember what I said about it, but evidently it wasn't good enough, for the job went to someone else. Nonetheless, that I can clearly remember the artwork well over thirty years later is, in itself, testimony to the impression it made on me.

Fast forward to 1992 and I'm now working as an assistant curator at the City Art Centre. That year we purchased for the City's collection a portfolio of 10 etchings by Will entitled *A Night of Islands*. These prints, each inspired by Gaelic poetry or prose, are full of imagery that touches upon Scottish history and folklore. They are exquisitely printed — some pale and delicate, others dark and brooding. I still regard them as one of the finest suites of prints by a Scottish artist.

Will's work has always intrigued me. Having been born in Northern Ireland, I knew little about the histories he investigates in his work. Yet it seemed to me that the themes which he was exploring, while specific to the peoples and cultures of Scotland and further afield, still had universal resonance. As we look around the globe today, Will's concerns seem even more relevant.

We have human migration on a scale never witnessed before, we watch as whole cultures and people groups are systematically displaced or eradicated, and there is environmental devastation that threatens to engulf us.

It is therefore a tremendous privilege to be working with Will on this major retrospective of his work at the City Art Centre. Every exhibition project has a starting point. This one came about as a result of a discussion between staff at the gallery as we considered a range of senior Scottish artists who we thought were long overdue a reappraisal. I volunteered to contact Will, asking if he would consider working in partnership with us with the intention of staging a major survey of his work. As it happened, Will told me later, my email arrived the day after he had confided to his wife Marian that he thought his exhibiting days were over — a fortunate stroke of serendipity indeed!

Now, several years later, and the exhibition will grace the walls of the gallery during the summer and early autumn months of 2022. To see it come to fruition after such a long period is down to the efforts of so many people. On behalf of the City Art Centre, I'd like to pay special tribute to Will himself. Trying to distil such a long and distinguished career into a few gallery floors was always going to be the biggest challenge. To help me, Will provided folders of information, separating his work into categories (constructions, prints, drawings, sculpture and so on) as well as into groups — some of which (such as pieces inspired by St Kilda) have survived the selection process. Not only that, but he had a record of where most of the works had ended up, which made the task of bringing everything together for the exhibition a lot easier.

Of my colleagues at the City Art Centre, Louise Williamson deserves a special mention for helping with the early administration of the show. I'm also indebted to many other museum and gallery staff who have contributed to different aspects of the project.

Finally, I would like to reserve a special thank you to Clare Cooper of Art First, and to the many private and public lenders involved. Through their generosity, we have been allowed the privilege of seeing in one place constructions, drawings, sculptures and prints which normally take pride of place in their homes, offices, galleries or museums. Their support is greatly appreciated.

David Patterson
Curatorial and Conservation Manager
Edinburgh Museums and Galleries

Points of Departure

Duncan Macmillan

In Iona of my heart, Iona of my love,
Instead of the voice of monks shall be lowing of cattle,
But ere the world come to an end
Iona shall be as it was.

Patrick Geddes cites these beautiful lines attributed to St Columba near the end of his essay, 'The Scots Renascence', published in *The Evergreen* periodical's Spring edition of 1895. They are a poignant mix of sadness and prophetic optimism, the note Geddes strikes in his discussion of Scotland's identity and future. Then, in the following century, the title of his essay was adopted by the poets and artists who sought to bring about just that, a Scottish renaissance. Hugh MacDiarmid was the acknowledged leader. Following Allan Ramsay and the good old bards, the makars of the first Renaissance whose memory Ramsay had preserved, MacDiarmid wrote in Scots, which, almost defunct as a literary language, he had to revive. Among the other poets, however, Sorley MacLean wrote in the living language of Gaelic, which gave his work a very different dynamic, and it became a vital link between Will Maclean and these great predecessors. In the visual arts, MacDiarmid was associated with William Johnstone and J.D. Fergusson, both leaders in their generation, but others were also inspired by this ambition. Among them, Ian Fleming was principal of Gray's School of Art in Aberdeen when Will Maclean was a student there.

It was not just the general idea of a Scottish renaissance that was launched by Geddes and then taken up by these cultural leaders, however. Central to his thinking was the idea that for a healthy and forward-looking society to be modern it has to know its past, but, equally, to be international it has first to be confidently national and that all of this is an imaginative process. Following Ruskin, Geddes argued that, even more than it needs its history books, a nation needs the arts to articulate its imaginative life and to ground its self-esteem and this, as important in nations as it is in individuals, was at its nadir for Scotland during the first decades after the Second World War. In those years the nation's cities committed terrible acts of self-harm, just as an individual might have done in such a crisis of self-worth. This was the background to Will Maclean's teenage years, as it was to my own. We may not have articulated it then, but nevertheless we knew somehow that we had either to surrender to collective depression, leave, as many did, or dig our way out of the hole we were in — and if the last option was our choice, the leaders of the Scots Renascence were there as an inspiration.

Consciously or otherwise, this was the challenge Maclean's art has met. Those were also the decades, however, that saw in much of the mainland Highlands the last generation born into a Gaelic-speaking world, and with their passing the end of their distinctive way of life and the final shift from Gaelic to English. Perhaps it was this more than the broader story of the cruel depopulation of the Highlands that was Maclean's starting point. Certainly the older, Gaelic-speaking generation of his boyhood are commemorated in such beautiful and very personal works as *Abigail's Apron* [p. 50], a memorial to the vivid personality of a Highland aunt who, as all such women did, always wore a full-length apron. *Memories of a Northern Childhood* [p. 11] and

Nostalgic Locker [p. 48] also celebrate with exquisite poetry his own Highland background.

In these and other works dating roughly from between 1976 and 1980, Maclean also moved away from painting and began to use assemblage and construction. This has been his principal way of working ever since, although by no means his only one. He also often incorporated quite precious things with strong associations into his earlier constructions. Later, as well as using found objects, which can be bits of boat (the beautiful *Rudder Requiem* [p. 61], for instance, is made of an actual rudder), driftwood or all sorts of other things, he has frequently cast more significant objects in various materials. This allows him much more flexibility. Always, however, he achieves the same exquisite and wholly distinctive quality of finish. His craftsmanship is such that its subtlety somehow suggests that time works on memories and reflective thoughts like water over pebbles in a burn, slowly polishing and refining them. By some mysterious alchemy, this makes time seem part of the image.

It was while still at art school in Aberdeen that Will Maclean's ambition was born to find a visual equivalent to the achievement of the Gaelic poets, not as something narrow and imitative, but as a vehicle for a particular perspective on the world, past and present: a modern art but one rooted in identity and the memories that shape it, very much as Geddes had proposed. As Sorley MacLean created something that is modern and of international significance in the medium of the Gaelic language, so Maclean eventually matched this in the visual language he developed. More particularly, too, there are several beautiful works inspired directly by Sorley MacLean's poetry. *Sabbath of the Dead* (1978, present whereabouts unknown), for instance, takes its text from 'Hallaig', the poet's great lament for the Highland villages left empty by the Clearances. Works like *Death Fish* and *Inner Sound*, both from 1984, also echo the poet's invocation of the menacing sight of nuclear submarines cruising in Highland waters, a sinister new embodiment of the same cruel pursuit of 'progress' that had emptied the glens.

But Maclean's exchange with the poets has not been limited to one individual, however important. He has also been inspired by the poetry of a good many others, both past and present. His great suite of prints, *A Night of Islands* [p. 69], for instance, is a visual anthology of Gaelic poetry. Complex and rich in imagery, the suite of 10 etchings was produced at Peacock Printmakers in Aberdeen and is an outstanding achievement of Scottish printmaking. *A Catechism of the Laws of Storms* is an equally striking combination of his own images with the poems of John Burnside. These dramatic compositions, which grew out of a dialogue between poet and artist, also appear to be based on collages of old printed material and part of their effect is the intriguing time shift this suggests, a homage perhaps to Max Ernst, pioneer of the Surrealists' use of collage.

A key early work, *Symbols of Survival* from 1976 [p. 46], records Maclean's childish wonder at a US Navy survival kit given to him by an uncle when he was a boy. Its evocative and mysterious contents were

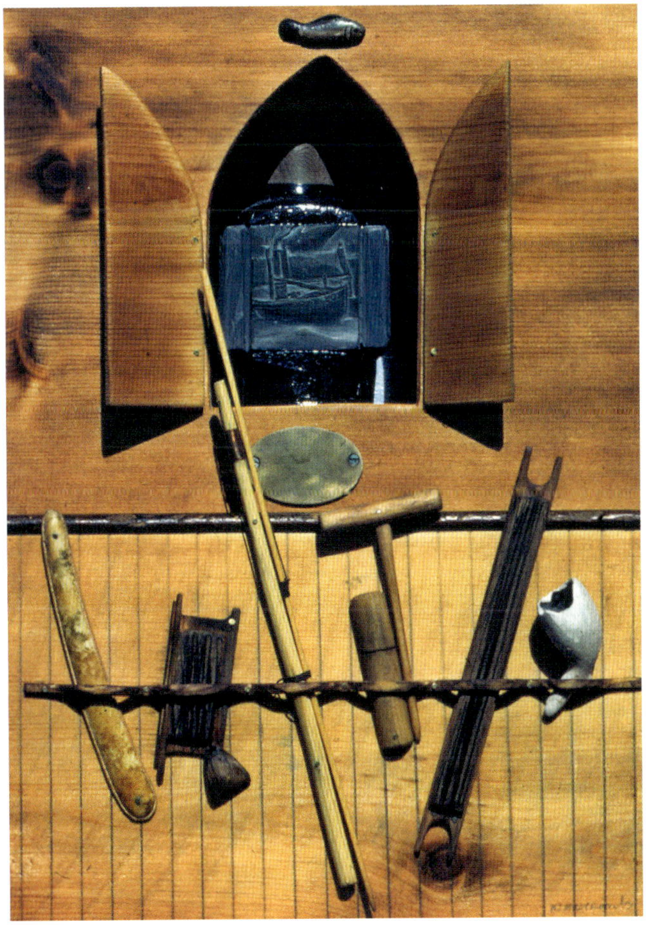

Memories of a Northern Childhood
1987, wood, slate and found objects, 48 x 35 x 15 cm
private collection

like the epitome of a museum. This is an idea that has stayed with him and since then he has frequently included the word museum in the titles of his intriguing assemblies of real and invented instruments and tools, as he does, for instance, in *New World Museum, Navigator's Museum: Instructions for Coastwatchers I* [p. 93] or *Mariner's Museum No. 1/Fictitious Sun* [p. 102]. He also often makes variations on the museological idea of objects of unknown use, witnesses to lifestyles and technologies, whether forgotten or imagined.

For a child, however, such a survival kit could also have had another very special aura. It was a witness to a wider world, to brave deeds and the dangers of the age-old relationship of humanity with the sea whether in peace or war; and in the west and in the isles, the sea is a constant. It is a paradox, but the islands are by no means insular. Set in the ocean, the people have always been ocean-going. To be able to navigate, they needed to understand the tides and long ago knew that it was the moon that commanded their diurnal movement. Correspondingly, the standing stones of Calanais, near Stornoway, appear to measure the lunar year, and so it seems they may be a 5,000-year-old temple of the moon. A work like *Mariner's Museum/Taxonomy of Tides* [p. 105] reflects on this continuity — John Maclean, the artist's father, was a sailor in this long tradition. His life at sea and later as Harbour Master in Inverness is beautifully commemorated in *Requiem Construction (John Maclean)* [p. 42].

The artist sought to follow his father and go to sea himself, but although he did serve an apprenticeship

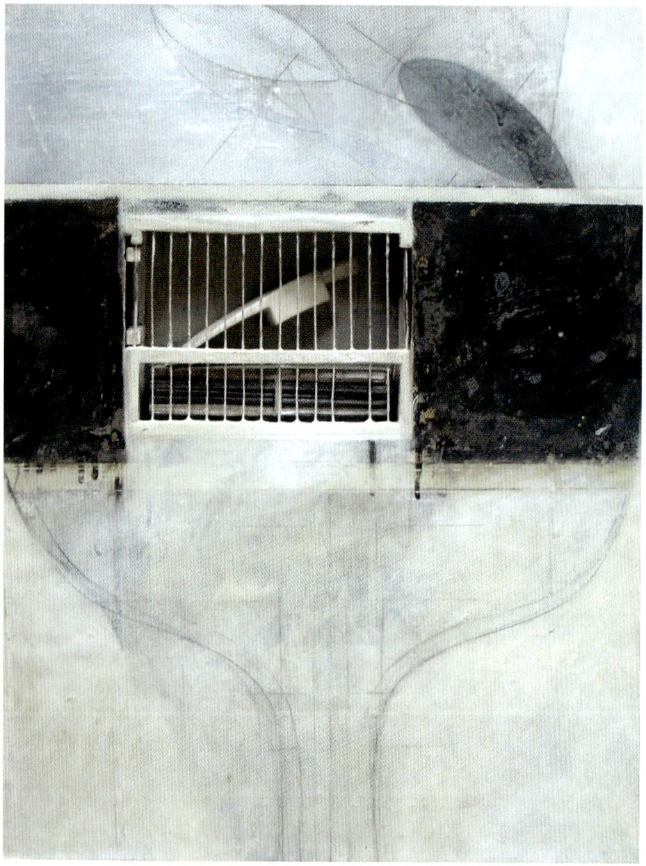

Voyage of the James Caird/South Georgia
2012, mixed-media construction, 67 x 52 x 9 cm
private collection

at sea, he had to abandon this ambition. We are the beneficiaries of that change of destiny, but the sea and sailors have been a constant in his work ever since. Later, too, he served a second apprenticeship studying the ring-net fisheries. The result was a body of work that is astonishing in its comprehensive detail, and often very beautiful. It also turned out to be a precious record of a technology and way of life that had been created by the dispossessed people of the Highlands, but which then vanished almost as Maclean completed his study. This historical coincidence gave poetic resonance to something that set out simply to be documentary and in a way his work has kept that character. It is often pinned, if only by its title but nevertheless quite specifically, to people, places and events, like *A Candle for Lübeck* [p. 106], for example, which commemorates the tragic death of concentration-camp survivors under Allied bombing, but then the work opens out to invite wider poetic reflection.

Throughout his work, whether as fishermen, whalers, explorers or the Celtic monks who made their pilgrimages into the unknown in flimsy leather boats, Maclean celebrates the courage of those who, like the anonymous figure of the *Skye Fisherman, in Memoriam* [p. 68], navigated the seas and made their living from the wide waters. As *Composition from High Latitudes* and other similarly titled works make clear, it is almost always the dangerous northern seas that they navigate — even up to the frozen Arctic when, in works like *North West Passage, Arctic Route* [p. 74], *Ice Log* [p. 75] or *Franklin's Second Journey to the Polar Sea* [p. 92], he celebrates the polar explorers. In the case of Shackleton,

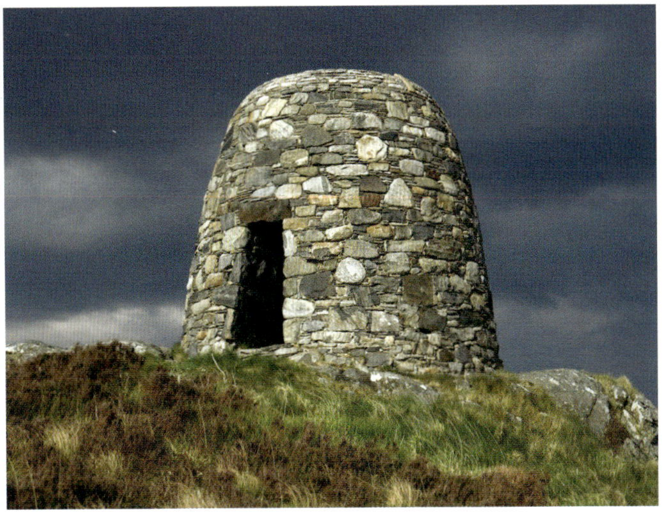

Balallan Memorial
Isle of Lewis; in collaboration with stonemason James Crawford, 1994
photograph Robin Gillanders

however, as he is remembered for instance in the *Voyage of the James Caird/South Georgia* [opposite], Maclean turns south to the Antarctic, but he rarely seems to spend time with the intermediate latitudes. (It is a focus he shares with his teacher at Gray's, Frances Walker. Her work has dealt almost exclusively with the landscapes of Scotland and further north. When she did go south, it was all the way to Antarctica.) He gives an enduring presence to the countless anonymous sailors and fishermen of the northern maritime tradition. More than the simple but undoubted courage of these people, however, it seems to be their endurance that has fascinated him. Shackleton, for instance, sailed the *James Caird*, an open boat (named after a Dundee jute magnate), eight hundred miles over the roughest seas in the world to find help for his ship, *Endurance*, and her stranded crew. She was appropriately named, but in addition, endurance, I suppose, really means courage extended over time and time is certainly always implied in Maclean's work.

Patrick Geddes dealt with time in the landscape in an essay called 'The Megalithic Builders', also published in *The Evergreen* (Winter 1896–7). In it he wrote memorably about the dark side of progress and the depopulation of the Highlands by greedy and inhumane land lords: 'the story of a passing race, a megalithic people, the utter winter of their disappearance seemingly nigh at hand'. It is a sentiment to which William McTaggart had earlier given memorable expression in his great painting *The Sailing of the Emigrant Ship*. Indeed, in what he writes Geddes might well be commenting on McTaggart's painting, which, much later, was also to find a direct echo in Maclean's own work, *The Emigrant Ship* [p. 21].

Three of the monuments on Lewis for which Maclean has been primarily responsible, although always working collaboratively, are also a reflection on this same tragic history, but their stark grandeur and manifest energy clearly reflect a more positive view than Geddes's bleak pessimism about the future of the Highlands. There are five of these monuments altogether. The three that were first carried out celebrate the 'heroes of the land raids' [above, pp. 78–81]. Each monument is set in the landscape where these land raids took place as the defiant people confronted the authorities and successfully fought back against clearance and dispossession. The two later monuments were *An Sùileachan* [p. 109], a more contemplative memorial to the same events, undertaken with the artist's wife Marian Leven, and the *Call na h-'Iolaire'* (The Loss of the *Iolaire*) [p. 108]. Again undertaken with Marian Leven, but also with Arthur Watson, this last piece commemorates the wreck of the *Iolaire* off Stornoway in 1919 with the loss of two hundred lives. Compounding the tragedy, the lost were demobbed servicemen returning home to Lewis.

Just as in the first three monuments he celebrated the success of the people of Lewis in reclaiming their own, Maclean also shares Geddes's, and indeed Sorley MacLean's, condemnation of the cruelty of the eviction and consequent forced emigration of the Highland people. This tragedy of dispossession is a frequent theme for him. It is clearly the subject of *The Emigrant Ship*, for instance, or of a small work like the *Emigrant's*

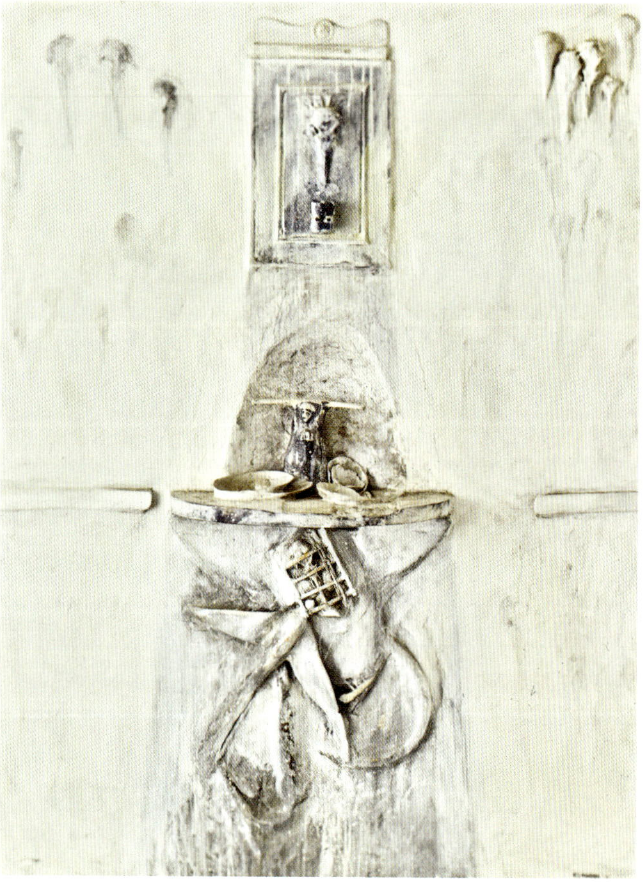

Bird Altar
1988, acrylic and wood on board, 138 x 103 x 28 cm
Sabhal Mòr Ostaig, the National Centre for the Gaelic Language and Culture, Isle of Skye

Garden Box, while *Strathnavar*, site of a notorious clearance, is the title of one of the most striking prints in the suite *A Night of Islands*. There are many other works, too, like *Canada Composite Memory (Vessel)*, for instance, or the small Newfoundland works, that relate to the emigrants' journeys but also to their sometimes tragic arrival in Canada.

Maclean, however, also shares Geddes's sense of the continuity and great antiquity of the people in the land of chambered cairns and megaliths. There are direct references to the megalithic builders and their imagined tools in works like *Alignment Receiver/Calanais* [p. 86] or *Alignment Frame Paradox* [p. 51]. Other works, like *Bird Altar* [left] with its reference to what seems to have been a Neolithic bird cult uncovered by archaeologists in Orkney, suggest the forgotten rites of these ancient people. Indeed echoing this mystery, while also suggesting continuity, delicately beautiful bird skulls, bleached white by time, are a frequent motif in his work. The Lewis cairns really are megalithic, too. Geddes would have loved them and among them, perhaps most telling of all in this context, is the arch in the monument, *An Sùileachan*. It is built from stones found nearby that had clearly been prepared thousands of years earlier for some Neolithic monument — planned, unbuilt then, but now completed. It is a stunning and entirely fitting claim to continuity.

Even when working on a very different scale, however, Maclean's art has an aesthetic affinity with these Neolithic monuments. They represent immemorial time and are also at once plainly significant and deeply

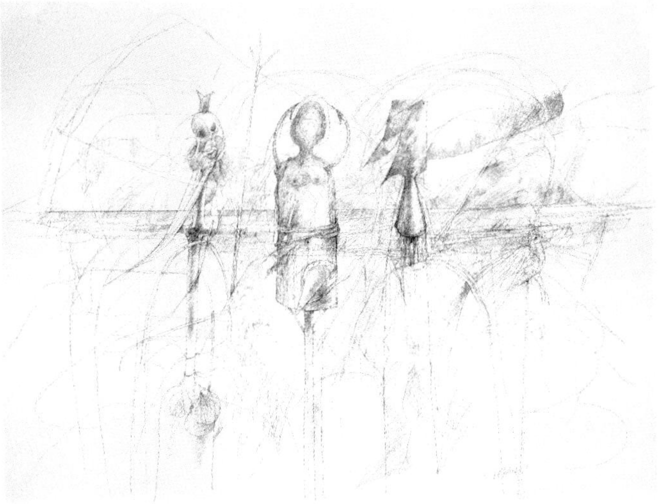

Three Totems Badentarbert
2014, graphite and gesso on paper, 57 x 75 cm
private collection

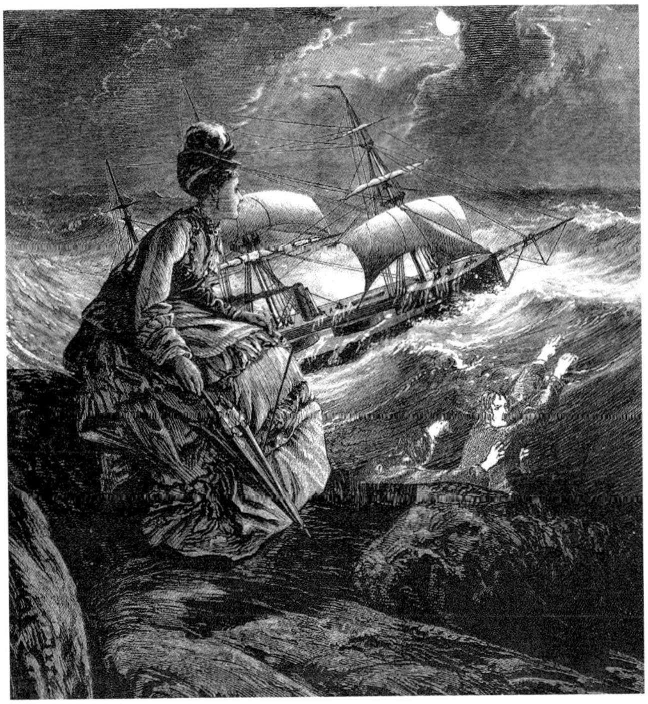

A Catechism of the Laws of Storms
in collaboration with John Burnside, 2014; screenprint from a suite of 12
private collection

mysterious. His art frequently sits between those qualities. It intrigues us by its complexity and its beauty while hinted references invite us into the mysterious, liminal place between significance and mystery, between a question and its elusive answer. This is the distinctive quality of a totem, too. While Maclean uses that word specifically in the title of his drawing *Three Totems Badentarbert* [above], for instance, and also in other works, his art more generally does often seem to achieve the aura of mystery invested with meaning that is the essence of the totem's power. In this he is not out of tune with modern art. Indeed he is actually succeeding where others have failed. From Duchamp's ready-mades onwards, even if unspoken, it has been a frequent ambition of modern artists to endow the things they make, however unpromising they may seem, with this mysterious quality, but too often the result simply remains inert. By itself, an act of will is not enough; such works need to have some association and with it the power of suggestion, however imprecise, to lift them into an imaginative realm. This was the gift of the Surrealists. It was also they who saw the imaginative possibilities of collage and assemblage. Maclean clearly belongs in that tradition, as his illustrations to John Burnside's poems, with their implied homage to Max Ernst, bear witness [left].

It is also part of this imaginative tradition — although perhaps leaning more towards Jung than to Freud, who was the particular hero of the Surrealists — that seers, shamans, bards and other spiritual figures are invoked in works like *Shaman Board, Herring Caller* [p. 101] or *Diviner's Wall* [p. 73], for instance, or the wonderful

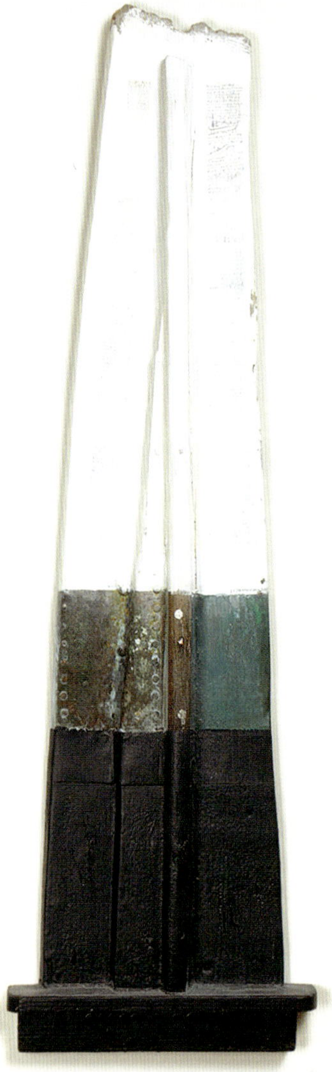

Memory Board
2012, mixed media and found materials, 109 x 24 x 6 cm
private collection

Bard Macintyre's Box [p. 57]. These all suggest openings to forgotten spiritual traditions, to what Eduardo Paolozzi called the lost magic kingdoms, but with them also perhaps to a collective unconscious, a shared imaginative realm whose territory in turn borders folk memory. One striking example of this latter idea is *Blue Men of the Minch* [opposite]. A confused mass of figures in the lower part of the work suggests that the mythical blue men were a faint folk memory of sad victims of the Viking slavers, captured in the warm south and dumped shivering on some bleak island entrepôt in the Minch before being traded on across the North Sea.

Words are the vehicle of such folk memories and Maclean regularly uses them in his work. In the exquisite *Memory Board* [left], for instance, what seems to be a fragment of boat is adorned with two tall columns of script. They are neatly close-written in pencil, but are nevertheless scarcely legible. Nor it seems are they meant to be, but the artist frequently uses text like this. In the same way, he also incorporates fragments of graphics, bits of charts and maps, of compass roses, or of the plans and layouts of ships and boats. At best only half-legible, but nevertheless adding to the subliminal poetry of the work, these written or graphic elements are like votives, messengers to the gods perhaps, to be read by them, not us, or simply messengers from another time or place. After all, the traditional wizards' spell, Abracadabra, is just a, b, c, d, the alphabet; their wizardry was the magic of letters.

A most beautiful example of the artist using this same magic is the three-part work, *Atlantic Messengers*

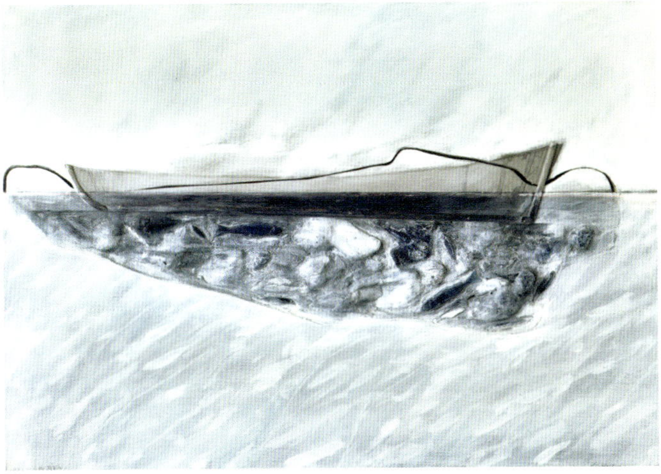

Blue Men of the Minch
1998, acrylic and wood, 70 x 102 x 6 cm
private collection, London

[pp. 36–7]. Having no regular contact with the outside world, to communicate beyond their group of islands the people of St Kilda once resorted to entrusting their letters to flimsy little boats or to bottles in the hope that if they should reach the mainland on the tide, someone would find them and post them on. The work is a homage to the resourcefulness, but also to the faith in humanity, of people living in extremis. In the work itself, hints of these messages are visible in casts of the eggs of St Kilda guillemots. The transparent material of these casts is a synthetic resin, perhaps inviting comparisons with amber, a natural resin but transformed by the passage of time, by a kind of transformative endurance, into something precious.

The root of that word, endurance, is the same as the French *durée*. A flexible word meaning roughly a period of time, or time elapsed, it was adopted by the French philosopher, Henri Bergson, to describe time lived as opposed to time intellectually understood. Bergson occupies a significant place in the history of modern art. Cubism itself may have been in part at least an attempt to accommodate visually his ideas about time. Much influenced by Bergson, Patrick Geddes enthusiastically adopted the idea of *durée* as the unifying dimension of his idea of the web of life: time as we share it with all creation. It is measured beyond counting by the movement of the tides that in turn transported these fragile vessels from St Kilda at the world's edge. The messages incorporated into *Atlantic Messengers* are exactly like the insects we see trapped in amber: messengers, not just across oceans but across time. It is an epitome of art itself. Umberto Eco once said of his own life and work: it is like 'leaving a message in a bottle'. This three-part work is a metaphor for the whole remarkable enterprise of Will Maclean's art, but also a demonstration of how clearly it belongs in the wider creative tradition of modern art.

Informed by Place

Murdo Macdonald

Will Maclean has transformed the way we think about Highland culture, but always with the focus of a Highland seafarer, with a keen awareness of both local and global. That broad vision is informed equally by history and by oral tradition. So many of his works bring those together. An example is from 1992, *The Emigrant Ship* (present whereabouts unknown) [p. 21], in which he evokes the loss of people and culture resulting from Highland clearance, and such concern with the imbalances of Highland land use is a core theme of his work.

When I interviewed him at his home in Tayport, Fife, in November 2021 we explored his key role. Will Maclean was born in 1941 and grew up in Inverness, where his father was Harbour Master. His father was a native Gaelic speaker from the crofting village of Polbain in Coigach, and his father's family in Polbain was, through the 1940s and '50s, entirely Gaelic speaking. Maclean feels his own loss of Gaelic as being deeply personal. It was back in Polbain that Will Maclean learned the disciplines and rituals of small-boat fishing for food, peat cutting and croft work — work in a landscape. That is reflected in drawings in the exhibition, in his notebooks and in *Memories of a Northern Childhood* from 1987 [p. 11]. His knowledge of those productive rituals of land and sea is balanced, or rather unbalanced, by the atrocities committed against Highland communities in the name of progress and improvement: 'I learned about the Coigach evictions; my father's great grandfather was two years of age when the family were cleared.'

With great warmth he tells me more of the formative period of his life spent on visits to family and places of ancestral connection on Skye or in Coigach, but mainly on Skye. His grandmother was a native Gaelic speaker from Portree and she would tell him of Skye in former times: 'of clearance and land struggle, the Battle of the Braes and her aunt's defiance of the bullying Sheriff Ivory, at the village post office in 1882, or when the marines were ashore in Portree'. Will Maclean was an only child, and he talks about growing up in Inverness 'in a Highland bubble', meaning that 'all the people coming from Skye and Coigach, for trains or to hospitals or anything else, all came through the house'. And again, 'we were very much a West Coast Gaelic-orientated community within the family'. His father was a huge influence on him as a child, not least through his storytelling. Will remembers being driven over to Coigach by his father, and 'as we passed through the various places, he would tell me stories about what happened there and things that were related to that journey'. That was crucial for how he developed as an artist, and he remembers that when he eventually came to art school 'I just decided that I should make art about things that were important to me culturally and emotionally, a lifelong interest in the history and folklore of the Highlands.'

Another incident from Maclean's childhood illuminates this. It was time spent in North Uist recovering from childhood illness that gave Maclean his first sight of the distant islands of St Kilda. His grandmother gave him the Gaelic Bible used to preach the last Gaelic service before the evacuation in the autumn of 1930. His aunt in Lochmaddy gave him a box of sea birds' eggs that had been brought from Hirta at the turn of the century, and he was also shown a 'St Kilda

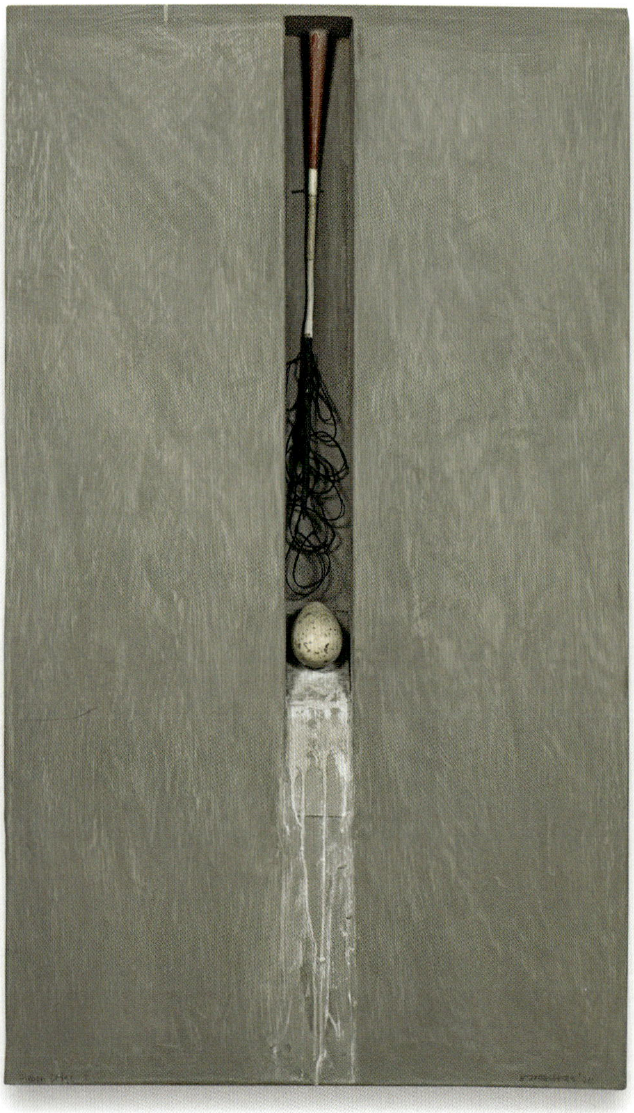

Giben Ledge 2
2020, mixed-media construction, 106 x 60 x 10 cm
private collection; photograph Antonia Reeve

Mailboat'. That image of a message carrier, consigned to the ocean but retrievable through knowledge of time and tide and currents, recurs in *Atlantic Messengers* from 1998 [pp. 36–7]. Related work includes *Homage to Hirta* from 1977 [p. 45] and *Window Visitation, North Uist* from 1980 [p. 52]. More recently, *Giben Ledge 2*, 2020 [left]. With such significant but serendipitous juxtapositions of objects it is no surprise that when Maclean discovered the art of Joseph Cornell, it became a key influence. That the Cornell scholar Lindsay Blair is keenly interested in Maclean's work is of a piece.

Alongside his understanding of the local conditions of the Highlands, Will Maclean has always been a passionate internationalist. As a child in Kyleakin, Skye, he would spend rainy days with Rebecca Matheson, who had been governess to a wealthy Glasgow family in the years between the wars. She had accompanied them on their grand tours of Europe and the near east. Rebecca owned a large collection of postcards of her travels and she would tell Will about Pompeii, the Parthenon and the Holy Land. He recalls vividly 'these pre-television images of the outside world'. They fuelled in him an interest in travel, and 'In 1966 a postgraduate travel scholarship allowed me to follow in her footsteps.' Other wider cultural insight came from two of his mother's sisters, who were arts graduates of Glasgow University: 'it was from them that I was introduced to poetry and the world of books. The edgy world of Walter de la Mare: *Peacock Pie* still sits on my bookshelf.' Other influences included Andrew Lang storybooks and R.M. Ballantyne. 'Perhaps [Ballantyne's]

The Emigrant Ship
1992, mixed media on board with slate and wood, 120 x 240 x 12 cm
private collection

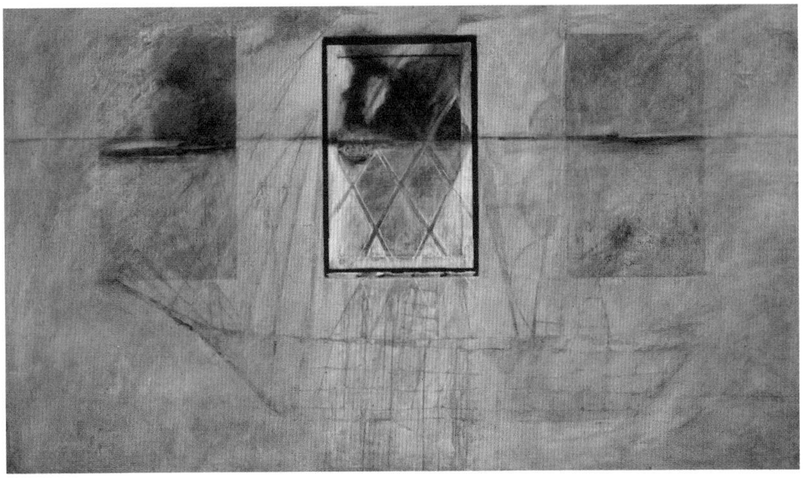

Ungava and *The World of Ice* contributed to works in the current [CAC, 2022] exhibition such as *Pole Marker*, from 1987 [p. 66], *Ice Log*, from 1998 [p. 75], and *Franklin's Second Journey to the Polar Sea* [p. 92], from 2003.'

I ask Will how he made the transition to art school, suggesting to him that few of his peers would have been headed in that direction. His answer is illuminating. It was, in short, a bit of an accident; indeed he calls it 'completely fortuitous', for he had only ever wanted to go to sea:

> *All the male members of my family were seamen, merchant mariners, fishermen, crofter/fishermen, naval reservists or national servicemen. They were my role models; my only thoughts were to follow in their footsteps and go to sea.*

In 1957 he left school at the age of 15 and went to the Merchant Navy college in Wales, located on HMS *Conway*, as a cadet. In 1959 he signed as a midshipman for Liverpool's Blue Funnel line, but after two years at sea was advised that he would not pass the Board of Trade sight test. So, Maclean resolved to retrain as a teacher and then return to sea as a deckhand when he wished. To that end he studied in Edinburgh at Skerry's College for a year to get more certificates. In Edinburgh there was a crucial moment when he fell in with another former *Conway* student who had left the sea and was attending evening classes at Edinburgh College of Art. So, Maclean went along and through the winter months drew from a life model. In 1961 he enrolled for formal study at Gray's School of Art in Aberdeen. He is extremely complimentary about his time at Gray's, regarding himself as very fortunate to be accepted, because looking back on his work 'it was just so poor'. He remembers the staff being very patient with him in his first year, and then managing to 'scrape through and into the painting department'. Thanks to that staff support one of Scotland's most significant artists began to develop. During holidays from art school, he went back to sea and in his own words 'wandered around the Mediterranean'.

The two-year general course at Gray's offered a broad range of skills from woodcarving and silversmithing to calligraphy and printmaking. In retrospect Will Maclean feels that this broad training provided a creative platform for his future career as an artist and teacher. Among the staff, David Fowkes and Frances Walker were a huge influence. He particularly notes Fred Stiven, both as a teacher and a mentor. He remembers struggling with oil painting and the academic rigour of life painting, and it was the relative freedom of the composition class that led him to begin to explore the subject matter of Highland history and culture. But this was still at a time when the current thinking was that, as Edward Gage put it, 'any vernacular is normally anathema or dismissed as incomprehensible'. To that deeply educative experience at Gray's was added a scholarship in the summer of 1964 to Hospitalfield House in Arbroath. David McClure was his tutor, and that time was, he recalls, 'the real breakthrough'. Building on that was a year of scholarship travel in 1966, which included a period of study at the British

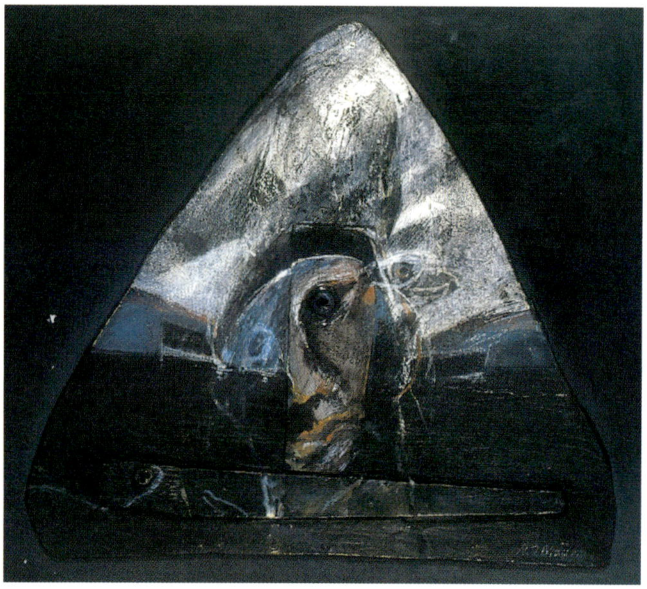

Fisherman Listening for Herring
1988, found objects and acrylic on board, 34 x 39 x 3 cm
M&S Strobel

School at Rome where 'the archaeology students took me on their field trips to Apulia and introduced me to the world of the Etruscans'.

As his ideas developed, Will Maclean's direct experience of the sea became crucial, in particular his knowledge of fishing. After art school he taught at Bell Baxter high school in Cupar, Fife, and was keen to take a break from teaching to pursue his art. The opportunity came through the educational trust set up by Sean Connery and chaired by Richard Demarco: 'I applied to this trust for funding to make a visual record of ring-net herring fishing', explaining that from a young age, when he was on Skye, his uncle would take him out for 'the odd day or the odd night or a few days'. After he left art school he worked as a ring-net fisherman for several months. Maclean thus emphasises that he was not some artist being parachuted in: 'I knew the structure of it, and ring-netting at that time was so much part of the community of Kyleakin.' He points out that Kyleakin village life revolved around the ring-net herring fishing fleet. His uncle and cousins were at sea during the week and came home at the weekend to 'repair and bark the nets, play in the football team and sing in the church choir'. The influence of those years can be seen not only in his remarkable *Ring Net* documentary-exhibition project of 1973–8, but also in works such as *Nostalgic Locker*, from 1976 [p. 48], *Fisherman Listening for Herring*, from 1988 [left], and *Skye Fisherman, in Memoriam*, from 1989 [p. 68]. And what was true of Kyleakin was true right up and down the coast: 'so many of these communities had one, two, three ring-net boats, six of a crew, supporting the community'.

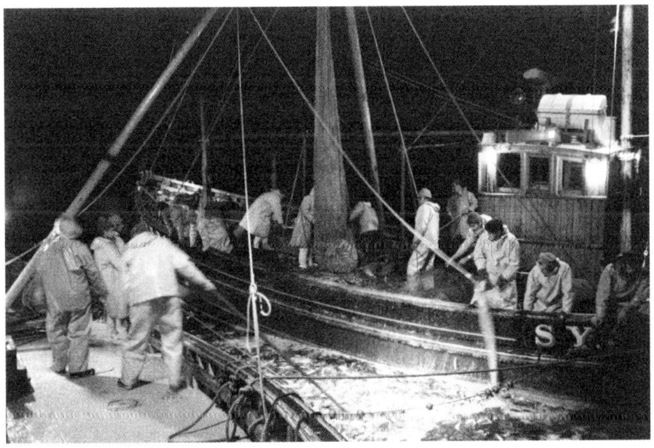

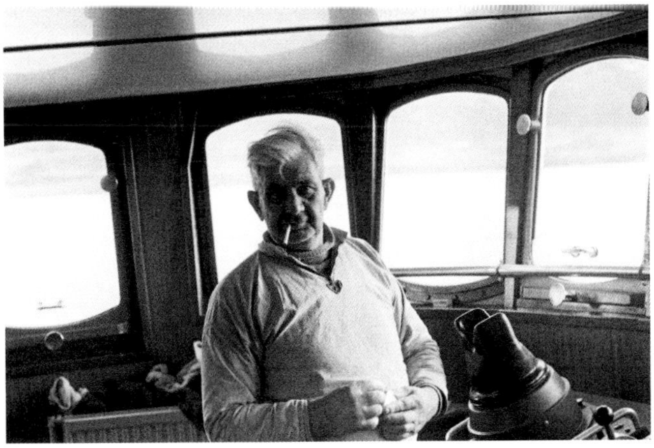

Boarding Herring, Score Bay, Skye, November 1973 [*top*]*, and Mr Manson, Skipper, in the wheelhouse of 'Crystal Sea 2', Mallaig, 23 October 1973* [*above*]*; from 'The Ring Net' exhibition*
private collection, photographs Will Maclean

At that time, he had no thought that this would ever change, because he had known it all his life. But, at the same time, he had a keen sense of its importance and visual and technical fascination. So, with his funding, he spent the next year on and off the boats drawing and taking photographs.

When he returned to teaching, Maclean had a mass of material to sort out, and in what proved to be a crucial collaboration, he teamed up with a poet from Campbeltown, Angus Martin. 'Angus did all the recordings and collecting of material from the Campbeltown area, which was where ring-netting began.' And, 'For two or three years we just wrote back and forth, and I drew things and sent them to him, and he sent me drawings.' Will Maclean refers to this as 'a quiet, wonderful kind of relationship between us, of information passing back and forth'. In 1978 the Third Eye Centre in Glasgow put on Will Maclean's *Ring Net* exhibition [left], and Angus Martin's book, *The Ring-Net Fishermen*, with illustrations by Will Maclean, was published in 1981. Maclean underlines to me that 'the genesis of it was getting that time off, getting that money through the Trust, that was the important thing'. I ask him how the work entered the collection of the Scottish National Gallery of Modern Art, and he answered that when Douglas Hall, the Director, went down to see the exhibition at the Third Eye Centre he bought six pieces. 'Then he phoned me up and said, "look I think we should have the rest"', but with a chuckle Will Maclean notes that 'at the end of the conversation, he said, "How many pieces are there?" I said, "five hundred"'. Thanks to Douglas Hall that work is where it should be and has been studied in particular by the historian and curator Patricia Allerston. Perhaps it is time now for a new full-scale exhibition of it at the Scottish National Gallery of Modern Art.

Maclean's first solo exhibition had been 10 years before, in 1968, at the New 57 Gallery in Edinburgh. This came about partly thanks to the agency of Marian Leven, Maclean's wife. The two had met at Gray's. She is now, like Will Maclean, a distinguished member of the Royal Scottish Academy of Art and Architecture (RSA), and has been a critical friend to his work throughout his career. In 1967 she was training as a teacher at Moray House in Edinburgh, and she brought Maclean's work to the attention of Gordon Bryce, who was the New 57 Gallery Chair. Another key supporter makes a notable appearance in 1972:

> *I had a joint show at the New 57 Gallery, with Ian McLeod. Richard Demarco came to see it and then offered me a show in what was then the Melville Crescent gallery.*

Demarco's support came at a crucial time and continues to this day. When Maclean left art school and started to show in Edinburgh, the friendship of other artists was very important to him. Among them were Sandy Moffat, Barbara Rae, Stephen Lawson and Ian and Mary McLeod. Also important was inclusion in group exhibitions such as Jack Knox's *A Choice Selection*, of 1975, and Paul Overy's *Inscape*, of 1976, both supported by the Scottish Arts Council and held at Edinburgh's Fruitmarket Gallery. Another was Cordelia Oliver's *Painters in Parallel*, of 1978. The support of critics was crucial; in addition to Cordelia Oliver were Edward Gage, Marina Vaizey and Duncan Macmillan. He remembers that the first review he ever had was from Edward Gage, for work shown at the New 57 Gallery, 'and I read it on a ring-net boat'. Gage described him as 'working poetically, dauntlessly, pursuing the telling metaphor' and included his work in the book, *The Eye in the Wind: Scottish Painting since 1945*, published in 1977, one of the first survey publications on modern Scottish art.

Will Maclean also mentions the support he had from Cyril Gerber at the Compass Gallery in Glasgow and remembers his first contact with Duncan Macmillan, in 1980. In due course Macmillan would write the key book on Maclean's work, *Symbols of Survival: The Art of Will Maclean*, published in 1992 to coincide with a retrospective, curated by Macmillan, at the Talbot Rice Gallery, University of Edinburgh. By that time Maclean was himself teaching in higher education, and his work at Duncan of Jordanstone College of Art and Design at the University of Dundee was an inspiration to generations of students and, indeed, to fellow teachers such as myself. During Maclean's time at Dundee he was a strong supporter of the establishment of Dundee Contemporary Arts, and for its opening in 1999 he worked with his colleague Mary Modeen and the poet John Burnside on *A Tayside Inventory*. Based at DCA, Dundee University's pioneering Visual Research Centre was crucial to the success of the rethinking of Highland art made possible by Maclean's advocacy of the *Window to the West* project from 2005 to 2013.

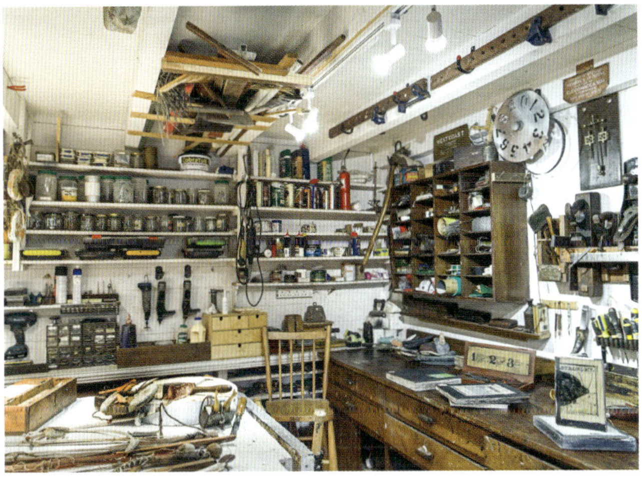

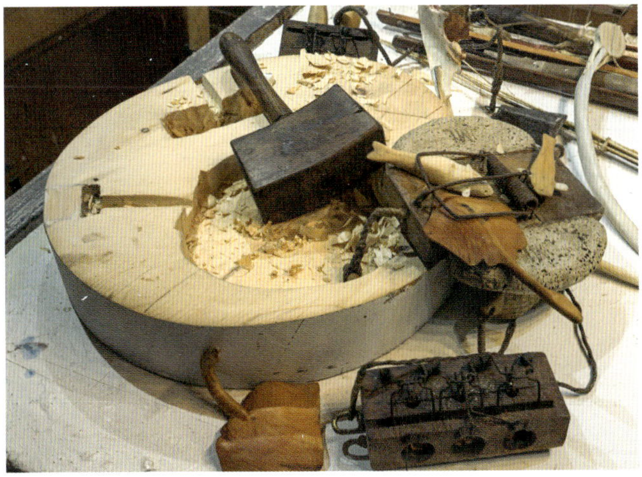

Will Maclean's studio workshop
photographs Antonia Reeve

The Scottish art collector, Sylvia Stevenson, came across Maclean's work at his mother's home in Skye, and that led to his productive association with Art First in London. But at this point in our conversation Maclean reflects on how he is only too aware of what we will not be able to cover in any detail. For example, collaborations with Kenneth White, Douglas Dunn, John Burnside, Ian Stephen and Alec Finlay. And work with key institutions like Peacock Printmakers in Aberdeen, the Scottish Sculpture Workshop in Lumsden, Aberdeenshire, and the Fleming Collection in London. And we are both aware that there is no time to fully explore the work created with Marian Leven for *Waterlines* (2012) at the Sir Duncan Rice Library, University of Aberdeen, or the Cairngorm work with Arthur Watson (2008), or the collaboration with both Watson and Leven on the *Iolaire* centenary memorial on Lewis (completed 2018, to mark the 2019 centenary [p. 108]). One factor that helps one to understand these networks of cooperation is Maclean's election as Associate of the Royal Scottish Academy in 1973, becoming a full member in 1991, and the fact that he refers to the Academy not as an institution, but as an artists' collective. In due course Maclean, along with Arthur Watson, became one of the driving forces behind rejuvenating the Academy's role as a support for students and artists beginning their careers. His reference to the Academy as a collective tells you, of course, what a real academy should be. As such, the Royal Scottish Academy has been central to Will Maclean's life as an artist.

I ask him about contacts made in the 1970s when Richard Demarco was bringing so many artists

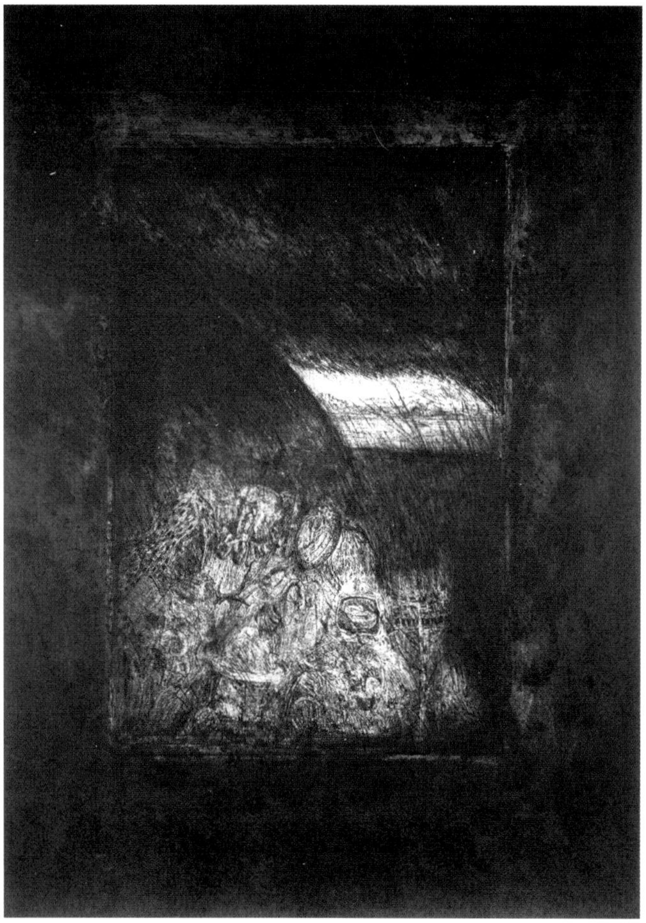

The Loss of Gaelic
1991, coloured etching on paper, 80 x 55 cm;
from ***A Night of Islands****, suite of 10*
Royal Scottish Academy of Art and Architecture

and writers together. He remembers that Demarco brought Paul Neagu over to meet Marian and himself at their house. Demarco also introduced Maclean to Jon Schueler, the outstanding American painter who spent a significant part of his career in Scotland. 'Jon Schueler was very supportive, in fact I kept up with him; he had a place in Mallaig when I was ring-net fishing, so I used to go and see him in his studio.' Arthur Boyd, the Australian artist, was another who Demarco introduced him to. 'I was a great admirer of Boyd's work. Then of course Beuys, who Ricky had first brought to Scotland in 1970, was important too.'

I want to get a bit more insight into the cultural rootedness of Maclean's work, so I ask him about the importance to him of the poet Sorley MacLean, to whom I know he is related. But he surprises me by saying that his first meetings with Sorley were through the teaching profession, for his aunt was head teacher in Kyleakin when Sorley was teaching in Plockton. Maclean remembers that the head teachers had a group, and he was invited to speak to them. Sorley came along. In due course Sorley would write the introduction to Duncan Macmillan's *Symbols of Survival* book about Will Maclean's work. Sorley's poetry has been a fundamental reference point for Will Maclean: 'when I started to read his poetry, I was struck in particular by poems like "Hallaig" — so visual', and again: 'Sorley set the groundwork for literature, and I just had this ambition to try and do something in the visual arts to complement what he was doing in poetry.' In his print series *A Night of Islands*, of 1991, Maclean unites poetry in both Gaelic and English with etched responses. Emblematic is the print from this series called *The Loss of Gaelic* [opposite], which responds to Meg Bateman's eponymous poem. Wider Highland history of importance to Maclean includes the collections of folklorists J.F. Campbell, R.C. Maclagan and Alexander Carmichael. A book 'that my father said should always be at my bedside' was Alexander Mackenzie's *History of the Highland Clearances* (first pub. 1880s). Other key works were Donald MacLeod's *Gloomy Memories* (1800s) and James Hunter's *The Making of the Crofting Community* (first pub. 1976).

One thing that struck me when I first encountered Will Maclean's work was the way it brought out ideas and practices that I was completely unaware of, like fishermen listening for herring. So, I ask him how different the techniques had been when the boats were quieter. He replied that 'you were dependent upon what was called appearance, which is what happens with the type of sea at night, with phosphorescence, and in the daylight with the gannets'. He tells me about trailing piano wires 'and from the feel of the fish striking on the wires you could tell the density of the shoals', and again that fishermen could tell when they looked at the phosphorescence what type of fish were there:

> *they'd bang the anchor, and you could tell by the reaction ... if it was mackerel they'd burst out like a star. If it was herring it was a sort of ball. And when I was first standing on the deck at night looking, staring into a moving sea, I was amazed at the old boys' ability to understand.*

Maclean calls it 'a privilege to be at the end of that particular cycle before it all finished'.

Such technical, traditional-cultural insights run deep in Maclean's work and extend to his interest in traditional cultures throughout the world. At the heart of those cultures are communities, their lives made harder by the need to struggle for land. Among Maclean's most well-known works are the land-struggle memorials on Lewis. I ask him how he got involved and he tells me how, in the early 1990s, he had got a call from Roddy Murray of An Lanntair arts centre in Stornoway, suggesting that he might design a plaque: 'I said, maybe we could do something more than a plaque.' Roddy introduced Will to Angus 'Ease' Macleod and Will tells the story of their first contact:

> *Angus phoned me up and said, are you Will Maclean, and I said yes, and he said, where are you from boy? And I said, well my people are from Skye and Coigach, but then I said my forefathers were from Uig. And Angus said, when can you start?*

Maclean's admiration for Angus is evident in every word, describing him as 'an amazing man who had been collecting material culture virtually all his life, and he had the most astonishing collection'. He continues:

> *He brought me into this group in which I became simply 'the artist'. Everybody had their place. For the first time ever, I had a place in a group of people as a functioning artist. And probably what was*

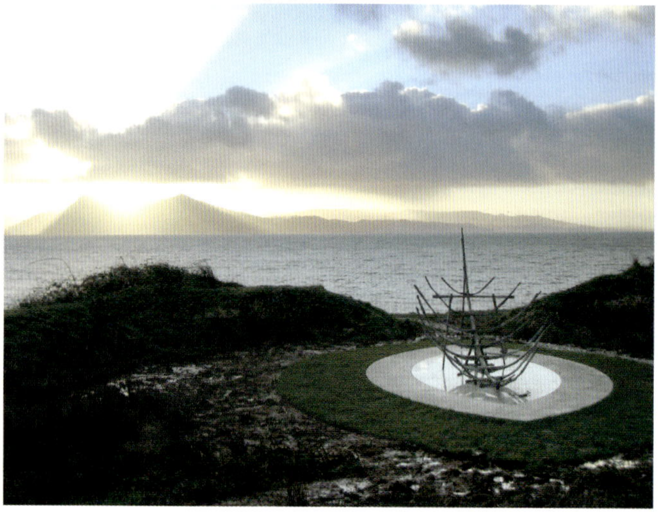

Crannghal
Sabhal Mòr Ostaig, the National Centre for the Gaelic Language and Culture, Isle of Sky; in collaboration with Arthur Watson and Eden Jolly, 2006, bronze and granite, 220 x 339 x 580 cm
photograph Murdo MacDonald

most astonishing of all from my point of view was when they opened the memorial at Balallan, Angus asked me to open it. When was an artist ever asked to open such a work? It's usually the Lord Lieutenant or somebody.

For the other Lewis memorials, Maclean talks of being 'moved, as the artist, to the next community ... each community had its own identity and its own committee and its own ideas', explaining how he went back to the genesis of what happened in the land struggle at that place, what it was about, the particular circumstances.

I ask about the monument, *An Sùileachan* [p. 109], at Reef on the Valtos Peninsula, designed in collaboration with his wife, Marian, and completed in 2013. Maclean immediately notes that he didn't know at the time they began the work that some of those involved in that land struggle were his Uig relations. The aim of the memorial was to look forward as well as back: 'each rock knoll could be the past or future or a link through to it'. He reflects that 'the main thing that holds the piece together is down to Jim Crawford, its builder, who discovered – when he was up and down in his boat – these amazing stones that were lying under the water'. At low tide, Crawford discovered that these stones had been obviously chipped out and chopped up at some time and then abandoned. The finding of those stones was crucial to the way the central arch of the monument was put together. But Maclean also notes that the joining technique was a nod to Inuit buildings that were put together in that particular way. That is again a reminder of how important other traditional cultures have been to Maclean. He reflects on working with Marian, and how they wanted the work to look to the future, so they asked the distinguished Gaelic writers Finlay and Norma MacLeod about a name for it 'and Finlay and Norma came up with *An Sùileachan*'. The meaning is 'the eye-opener, the warning, the lesson'. Will Maclean explains how that strongly visual referencing word 'lifts it outside itself and gives it a name to do with the eye. It's all things to all men but it is specific at the same time. A wonderful ingenious title that holds it all together.'

I ask about that other ingeniously named sculpture, *Crannghal*, of 2006 [above], which Maclean made with Arthur Watson and Eden Jolly for the new campus at Sabhal Mòr Ostaig, the Gaelic college on Skye. He recalls that it was like working on the Lewis pieces, with none of the hoops of Arts Council applications or preliminary drawings. Instead, 'the trust was there'. 'I came up with the name *Crannghal* through Dwelly's dictionary. Dwelly had this definition of a wooden skeleton or latticework or rigging that for me evoked a creature or a boat ... It was a great experience and an amazing relationship with Sabhal Mòr Ostaig. A lightness of touch. It wasn't really until the last minute we decided which way up it would be.' That reminds me of a later 'remaking' of it in willow, made on the spot by Maclean and Watson, and indeed hung the other way up. It was an installation for the exhibition *Window to the West: The Rediscovery of Highland Art*, held at the City Art Centre, Edinburgh over the winter of 2010–11 [opposite].

Will Maclean comments 'I think *Window to the West* was incredibly important; it established a given that

Crannghal
'Window to the West: The Rediscovery of Highland Art' exhibition installation, City Art Centre Edinburgh, 2011; in collaboration with Arthur Watson, 2011, mixed-media construction, based on 'Crannghal' sculpture (facing page)

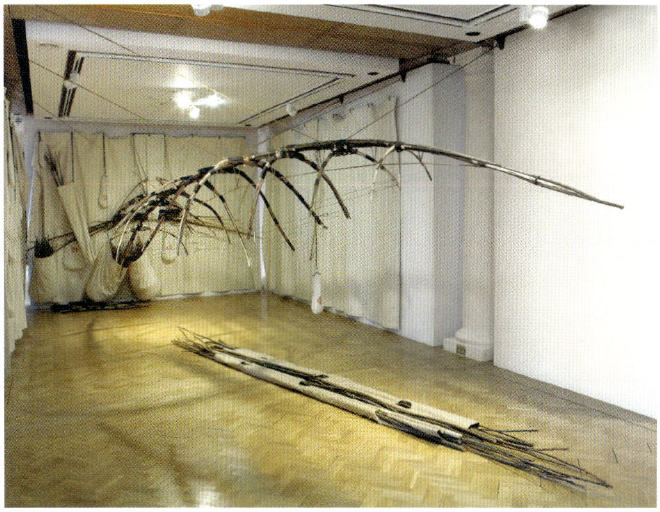

there is a visual thing as well as the oral one in the Highlands.' Would that exhibition have happened without Will Maclean setting the agenda for Highland art since the 1970s? Probably not.

There are many other points Will Maclean wants to make to me: key influences he mentions include Giorgio de Chirico, in particular his Surrealist novel *Hebdomeros*, published in 1929, which Maclean describes as 'a constant', along with the collages of Max Ernst. Another influence he cites as an early inspiration is Ben Shahn, both his graphic work and his Charles Eliot Norton Lectures, given in 1956–7 and published as *The Shape of Content*. Such balance of verbal and visual is typical of Maclean. Again, he notes with respect to Joseph Cornell that 'he was influential on me not just because of the box constructions but also his ability to transfer a narrative to the visual'. Also important were the works of H.C. Westermann, who drew on his own experiences in the US Navy, and the American sculptor Jimmie Durham, whose work explored Native American identity.

Will Maclean concludes his conversation with me with more appreciation of galleries and gallerists. Richard Demarco, of course, but crucially at a later stage the late Claus Runkel, publisher of his first catalogue raisonné, and Leinster Fine Art, which represented him in London and Washington. He notes Laurel Reuter of North Dakota Museum of Art, who showed and toured his work in North America and published a key catalogue, *Will Maclean: Cardinal Points*, in 2001. And he mentions Karin and Rainer of Galerie Herold in Hamburg, Germany as collectors of both his own work and Marian's, culminating in their joint show at that gallery in 2012, *Scottish Connections: The Art of Marian Leven and Will Maclean*. But acting as a backbone to his representation for 25 years has been Art First in London. He mentions Geoffrey Bertram and Benjamin Rhodes, and, in particular, Clare Cooper, who supported and promoted his work and publications in *North Sea Archives*, 2005, *Will Maclean: Different Meridians*, 2008, and *Gleaned and Gathered*, 2014.

On that note of gleaning and gathering – and from that gathering a weaving of memories of place and planet – we say our farewells.

Pentimenti
Interconnectedness in the Art of Will Maclean*

Kim Ness

**First published to accompany the exhibition 'Driftworks', Dundee Contemporary Arts, 24 November 2001–3 February 2002. Reproduced here, with minor edits, by kind permission of the author.*

During the period of Will Maclean's *Driftworks* exhibition at Dundee Contemporary Arts [overleaf], the Innu children of Davis Inlet, Labrador were returned to their homes following an extensive period of rehabilitation for substance abuse. Their removal from Davis Inlet to St John's and other more urban centres of Newfoundland had been formally requested of the Canadian federal government by the community elders and the children's parents. The continued erosion of the vestiges of indigenous culture, combined with the dearth of resources, finally prompted the resort to external intervention. By early January 2002, within a matter of weeks of their return, the majority of the children from Davis Inlet had resumed sniffing petrol, an act that can only prove to be fatal. Sadly, their story is in no way isolated.

What possible connection could this current North American news story have with the work of Scottish artist Will Maclean? For a Canadian, commonalities or points of conjuncture abound. Inherent in Will Maclean's physically beautiful, moving art is the capacity for a multi-faceted response. Individual created elements are imbued with specific reference points, yet they are not exclusive. Personal experience and therefore associations made by the viewer connect with the allusions contained within the work in the creation of another actuality. In this regard the plight of the children of Davis Inlet coexists on a non-literal level with that of once thriving communities that have disappeared through the imposition of one culture on another. In Will Maclean's work it is as if partial layers of time, of place or material have eroded to reveal a palimpsest, in which the original has not fully faded so that the historical is ever present in the contemporary, the personal conjoins with the communal. Never didactic, but subtle and poetic, the content unfolds in a manner not unlike the process of ebb and flow.

Over the course of the last three decades Will Maclean has continually developed particular themes as well as his practice of creation. This refined evolution has achieved fruition in the new body of work presented as *Driftworks*. Gaelic culture and history, the Highlands and Islands of Scotland, individual memory, land clearances, forced emigration, aspects of coastal or maritime life, the hardships encountered by immigrants in a new, different environment, sea travel, Arctic exploration, loss, the fusion, transmutation and endurance of many cultures, attributes of the original inhabitants of North America — these references comprise aspects of the framework that has progressively informed Will Maclean's art. Equally, the artist's own background, his varied interests and experiences, travel, museum visits, even his own work have served as starting points of exploration.

An exceptional and deceptive artifice is paralleled in Will Maclean's art with a sophistication of conception and execution. Collage, assemblage, utilitarian and found materials, sophisticated simulations and re-creations of 'artefacts', painting, sculpture and most recently sound and digital animation are among the devices and methods that have been and continue to be utilised. Carefully phrased titles serve as guides for contemplation and reflection.

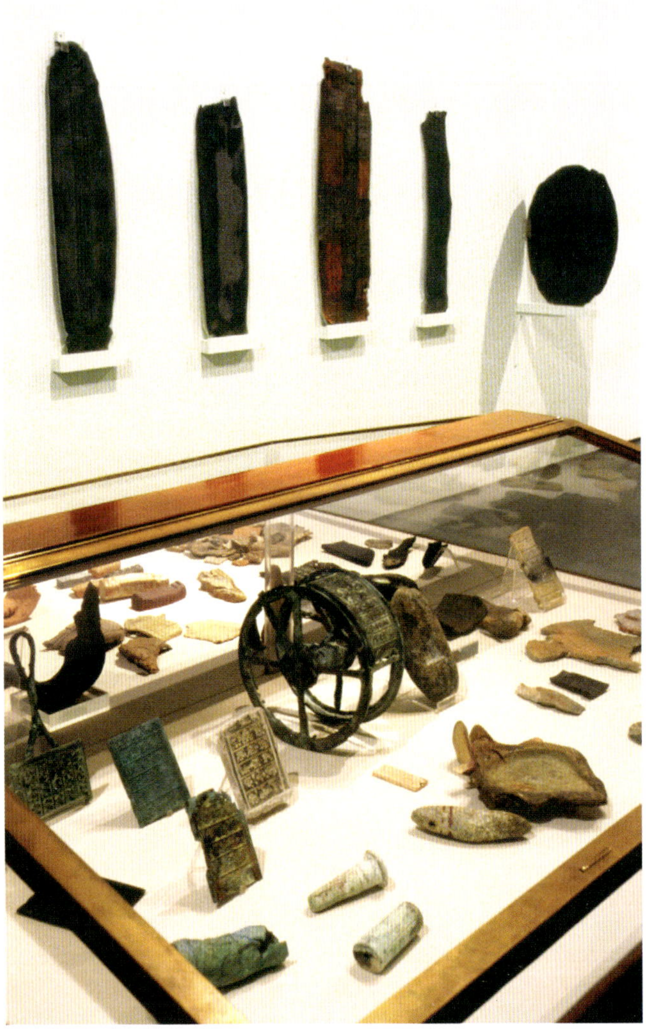

'Driftworks' exhibition installation, Dundee Contemporary Arts, 2001

Above all, it is the exploitation of the associative potential of objects that achieves the metamorphosis or transformation of the mundane that is so powerfully strong in Maclean's body of work. Precise selection, additive layering, focussed juxtaposition and careful ordering reveal new meaning and function as catalysts for memory and imagination. The further utilisation in *Driftworks* of museological devices such as the antique display vitrine combines with the ironic adaptation of pseudo-systematic classification techniques to invite reflection on how knowledge and communication are affected. Rarely is information received solely as the presenter intended. Nowhere is this more evident than in the museum. The process of making meaning is as much bound up with mythologies (whether societal or personal), interconnectedness, fiction and the talisman-like properties of things, as it is with objectivity.

The ambitious *Cod Requiem* work (2001) [opposite], is indicative of the rich complexity of Will Maclean's practice. The installation is comprised of a digital animation and sound collaboration with Andy Rice, sculpture, and museo-graphic shelves that suggest the display of precious, obsolete implements or specimens. Between 1973 and 1978, Will Maclean participated in a documentary project about ring-net fishing off the coast of Skye. Fishing in general had developed out of necessity in the 1830s as an alternative to crofting, following the Clearances. By the 1980s ring-net fishing had been superseded by purse-netting, a more efficient method. While the visual survey of drawings and related materials from Maclean's *Ring Net* project is now held in the collection of the Scottish National Gallery of Modern

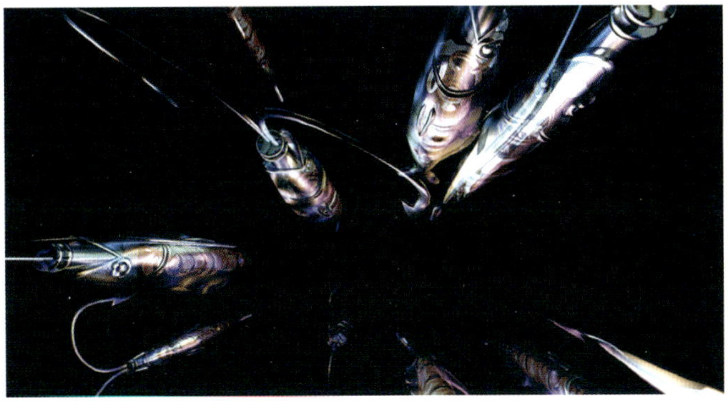

Cod Requiem
in collaboration with Andy Rice, 2001, digital animation projection

Art, recordings of cod sounds and other ambient boat noise now feature in the highly atmospheric soundtrack for *Cod Requiem* and offer a connection to one of Maclean's most important early series.

Cod-jiggers are a type of baitless fishing hook, once again developed out of necessity, but in this instance by cod fishermen in the now defunct cod fishery of Newfoundland. In the 12-minute video projection, they become animated and drift down to the ocean bed. Rather than dancing to entice fish as they were originally intended, the lures become reunited with a construction from 1986, *Log Book II — Winter Voyage* [p. 65]. In itself it evokes transatlantic or Arctic passage, the thrill and terror of exploration and navigation, hardship, the transmutation of one culture into another, of scientific technology as well as ethnographic materials. The original cod-jiggers, found in 1999 by the artist's wife, the painter Marian Leven, at a junk shop in St John's, are installed alongside four bronze and four porcelain casts of the 'true' jiggers on a softly lit glass shelf [overleaf]. The equivalence of presentation, the adoption of an anthropological device, confuses the perception of what is original and what is new. Together with the animation and sound there is, in the combination of these elements, an excavation-like atmosphere to the installation and a conflation of time which is reinforced by the references to cultures and ways of life now lost. Maclean is himself the archaeologist or curator, also selecting as he does from the strata of his own work.

A longstanding interest in museums is also apparent in the mixed-media constructions that have been ongoing since 1987, for instance the *Objects of Unknown Use* [series] as well as the *New World Museum* (2000). Exquisitely rendered, the boxed elements are convincingly deceptive. Not what they initially seem to be, found objects are combined with newly created pieces, such as tools or Inuit carvings, that simultaneously engage and confound the deductive process. The lustre or patina achieved in fabrication, contrasted positioning and the composite of new meaning from old confer these cases with their own integral reality. The memory latent in objects, their hidden meanings, emerge like *pentimenti*, evidence of what has been before, even when the objects are from the hand of the artist. Just as the architecture, the physical context, lighting, the systems of codification, isolation and arrangement of artefacts by a subject-expert influence our acquisition of knowledge in the museum and combine with the prior experience of the visitor in the formulation of story, so does Maclean effectively adopt these conventions in the formulation of myth and metaphor. In *Rudder Shaman* (1989) and *Rudder Guardians* (1999) [p. 82], elongated totemic figures, redolent of other civilisations or eras, stand protectively or as guides for as yet unknown quests that can unfold in a varied, self-conditioned manner.

An ongoing interest in displacement, emigration, adaptation and memory are alluded to in *Cod Requiem*, but provoke essential undulating motifs in several key series from the *Driftworks* exhibition. With the six collages *Journey 1–6*, made in 2000–1, the Highland Clearances and consequent relocation of coastal communities and the forced exodus to other lands are the

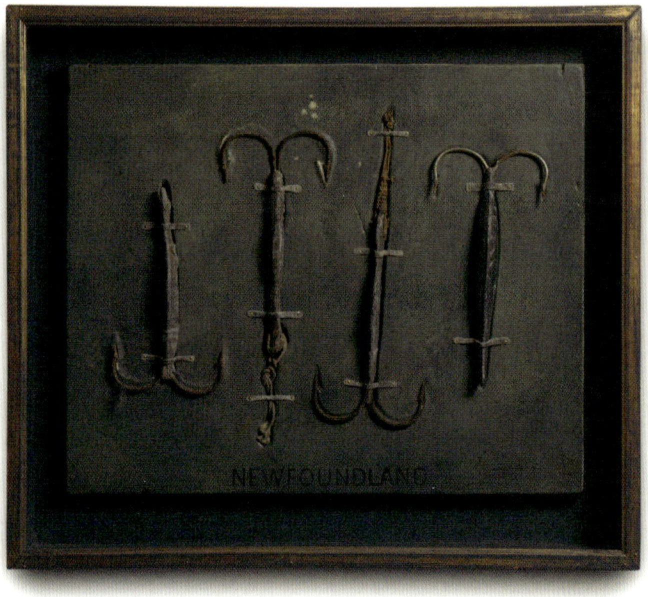

Cod Jigger Box
mixed media, 50 x 60 x 7 cm
private collection; photograph Antonia Reeve

source for multiple associations. These poetic, delicate combinations of found, anonymous photographs, postcards, images of ships, resin and wax possess a melancholy that transcends historical precision. The loss of place, a longing for and remembrance of what has been relinquished that the visual images connote, are further extended by the suggestion of places unseen and life unknown. Settlement in Canada and America by Scots and other nationalities brought hardship, but also new opportunities. In some cases, the possibility for tradition, language and culture to endure, albeit in an evolving format, was actually enhanced. Simultaneously and ironically, the emigration that evokes loss for Europeans precipitated dramatic change and even outright disappearance for the original inhabitants of the Americas. The Beothuk of Newfoundland are an example. Maclean's work fosters reflection on the broader implications of such imposed change.

Particularly poignant are the corresponding citations to the St Kilda saga that informs constructions such as the *St Kilda Song* (1997), and the three *Atlantic Messengers* sculptures (1998). References to the now vanished community of the islands of St Kilda in the Outer Hebrides point to the demise of a once flourishing, self-sufficient, mutually supportive society and the impact of external contact as seen, for example, in the introduction of diseases such as smallpox and influenza. Exacerbated by missionary forays and the rise in visitors and tourism, the indigenous culture was increasingly eroded. By 1930, in spite of the fact that there had been evidence of continuous habitation on St Kilda since the Bronze Age, the deterioration was

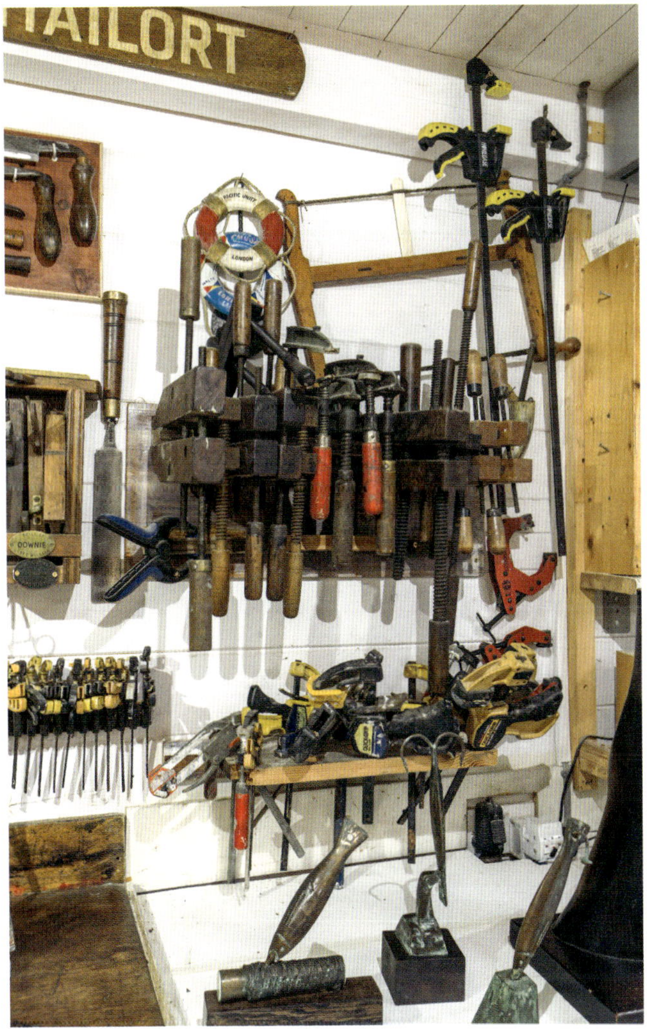

Construction tools, Will Maclean's studio workshop
photograph Antonia Reeve

so extensive and the population so diminished that the last islanders decided at a community meeting to request that they be evacuated. St Kilda was abandoned, later to become a bird sanctuary.

Neither the constructions nor the sculpture present literal accounts of these events. The images adopt the lyrical potential of chosen objects, conscious order and juxtaposition. There is an aching quality, a yearning that infuses these pieces. Related to works like the *Rudder Shaman* and *Rudder Guardians* sculptures, the *Atlantic Messengers* sculptures are totemic, altar or shrine-like in form. Abstracted shapes and mysterious elements, familiar, but not immediately specific, are strung from black frames to subtly reference Island and Hebridean culture. Generalised, dark forms such as the egg or boat in *Atlantic Messengers/Fulmarus* [overleaf] intimate the all-important bird, the fulmar, which had been so central to life on St Kilda. With *Atlantic Messengers/Sula Sgeir* [p. 37] these dark shapes are repeated, but, in this case, evoke the tiny island, Sula Sgeir or 'Rock of the Gannets', which lies north of Lewis, a site in the early Christian era where the penitents chose to suffer extreme conditions. Once again the work is non-literal, symbolic on a much broader level of sacrifice, human endurance and transformation. With *Atlantic Messengers/Hirta* [p. 37], there is a persistent echo of the brooding forms as well as an allusion to the main island of the St Kilda group, Hirta, from which the islanders would travel to the cliffs where birds would nest. New elements also appear such as egg shapes and a partially obscured fragment of text: 'the best of my grandfather's gear'.

In tandem they evoke 'The St Kilda Waulking Song', a traditional love song which would have been sung by women as they pummelled the stiff tweeds they had spun.

Feathered slippers, birds' eggs, vessels for oil, constructed altars, these symbols of St Kilda are equally typical of coastal cultures across a broad geographic range. Will Maclean's consistent transcendence of the local fosters an open-ended process of interconnection and reflection. This capacity to initiate a progressive, associative meditation through the presentation of richly composed objects and images comprise the outstanding attributes of Will Maclean's art. The layered references to the life and fate of the residents of St Kilda are like markers for a transposition to the collective and universal. Isolation, hardship, suffering, loss, the interdependence of community — these attributes of human endeavour are in no way exclusive. A *pentimento* from one culture then, unbound by place or era, can be synchronistic. And so it is that the former inhabitants of St Kilda become comingled with the children of Davis Inlet.

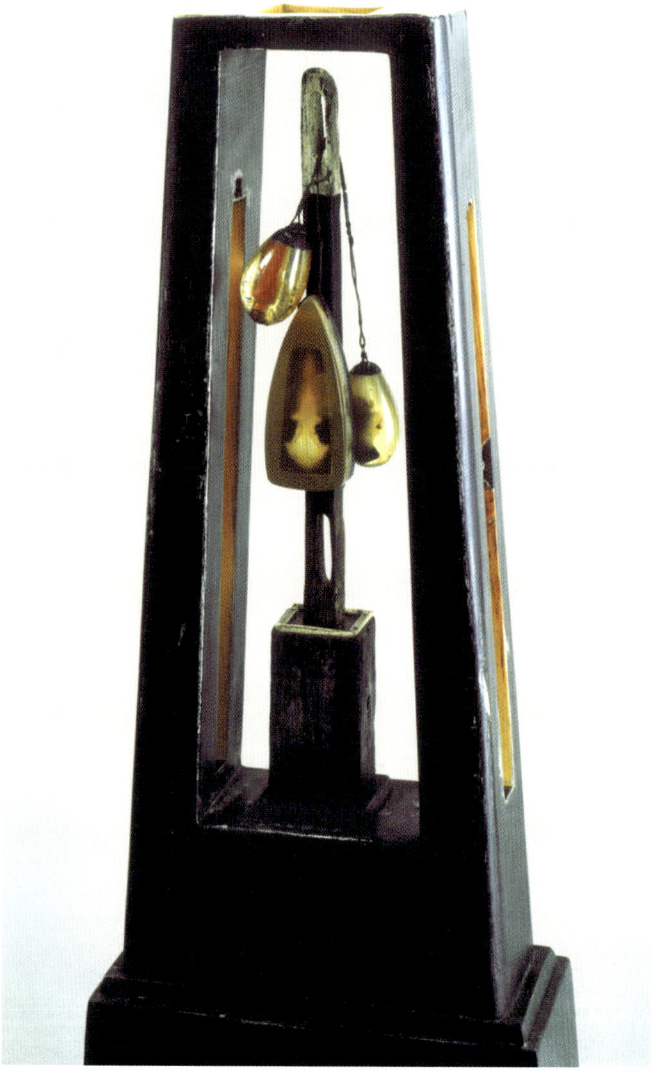

Atlantic Messengers/Fulmarus
1998, mixed-media sculpture, 104 x 30 x 15 cm
private collection

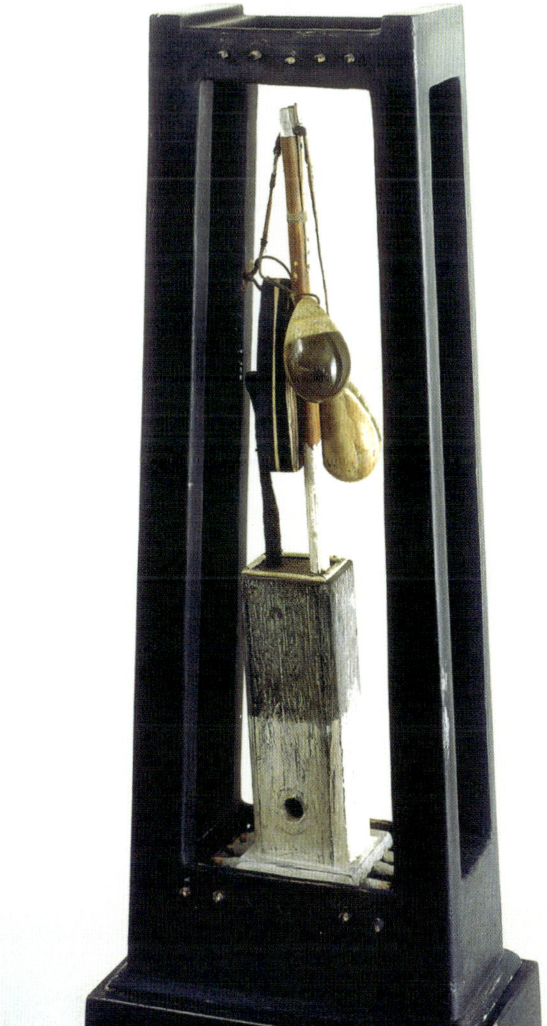

Atlantic Messengers/Sula Sgeir
1998, mixed-media sculpture, 104 x 30 x 15 cm
private collection

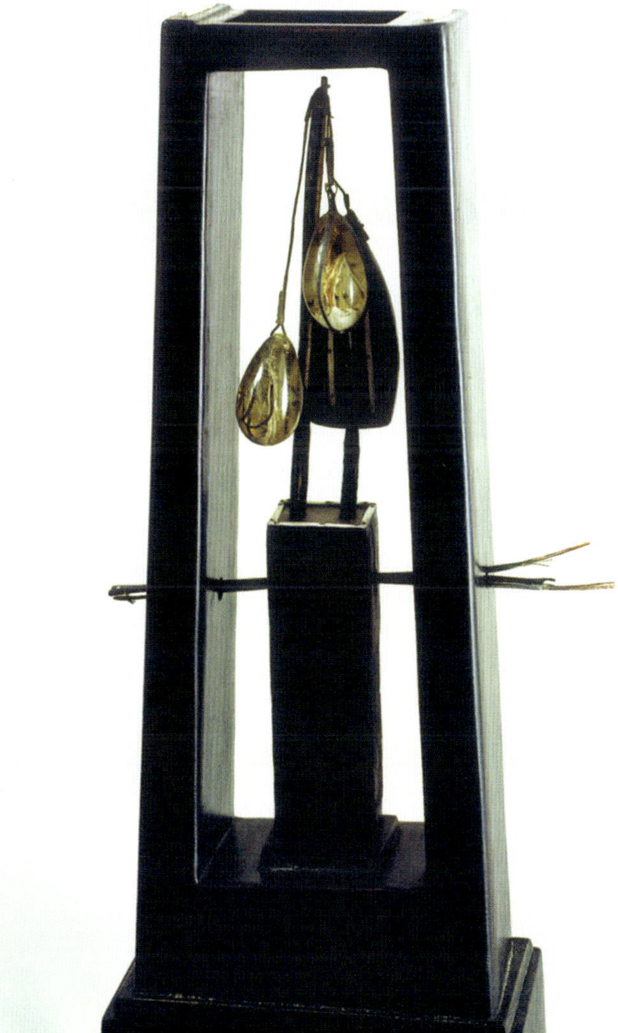

Atlantic Messengers/Hirta
1998, mixed-media sculpture, 104 x 30 x 15 cm
private collection

Artworks

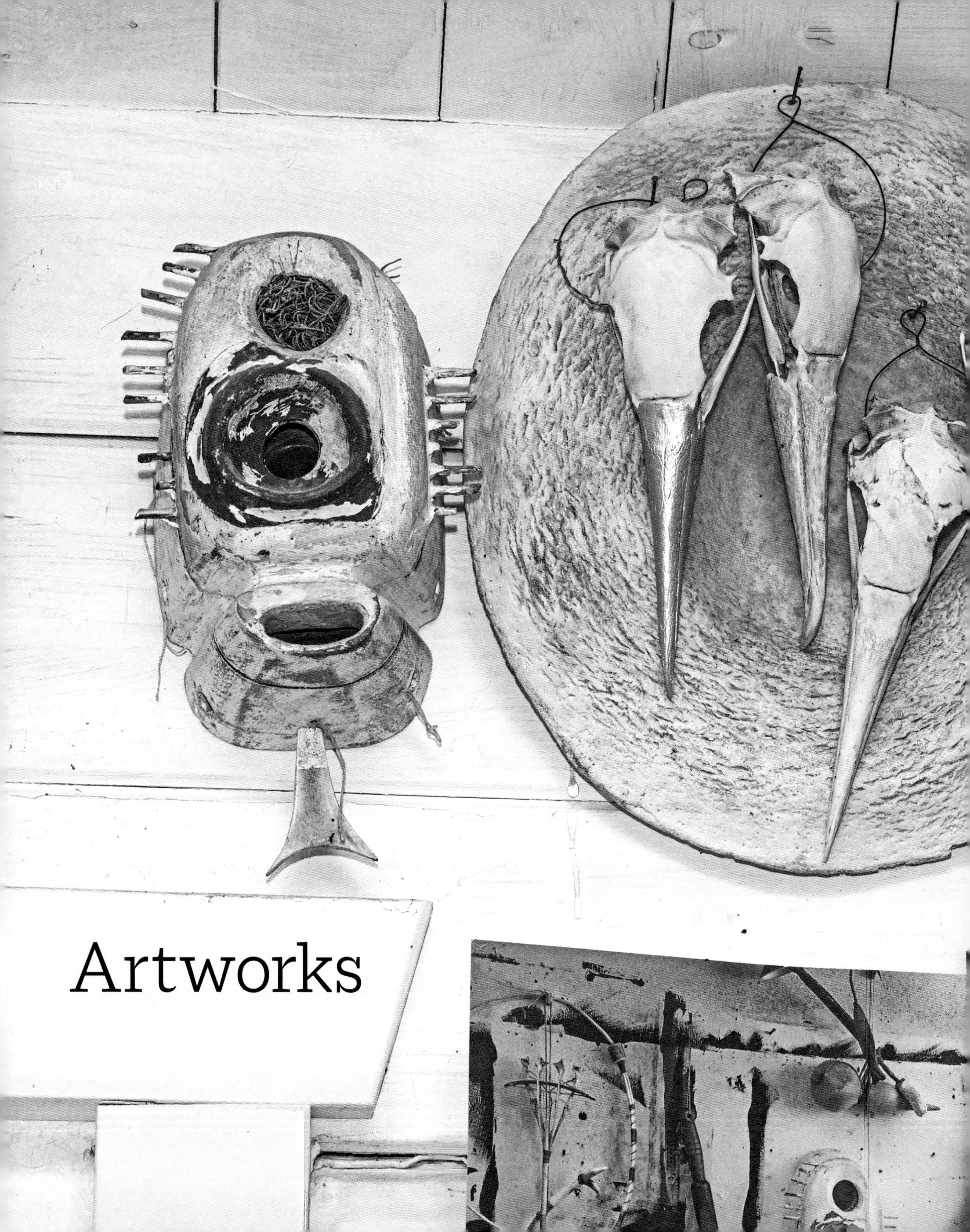

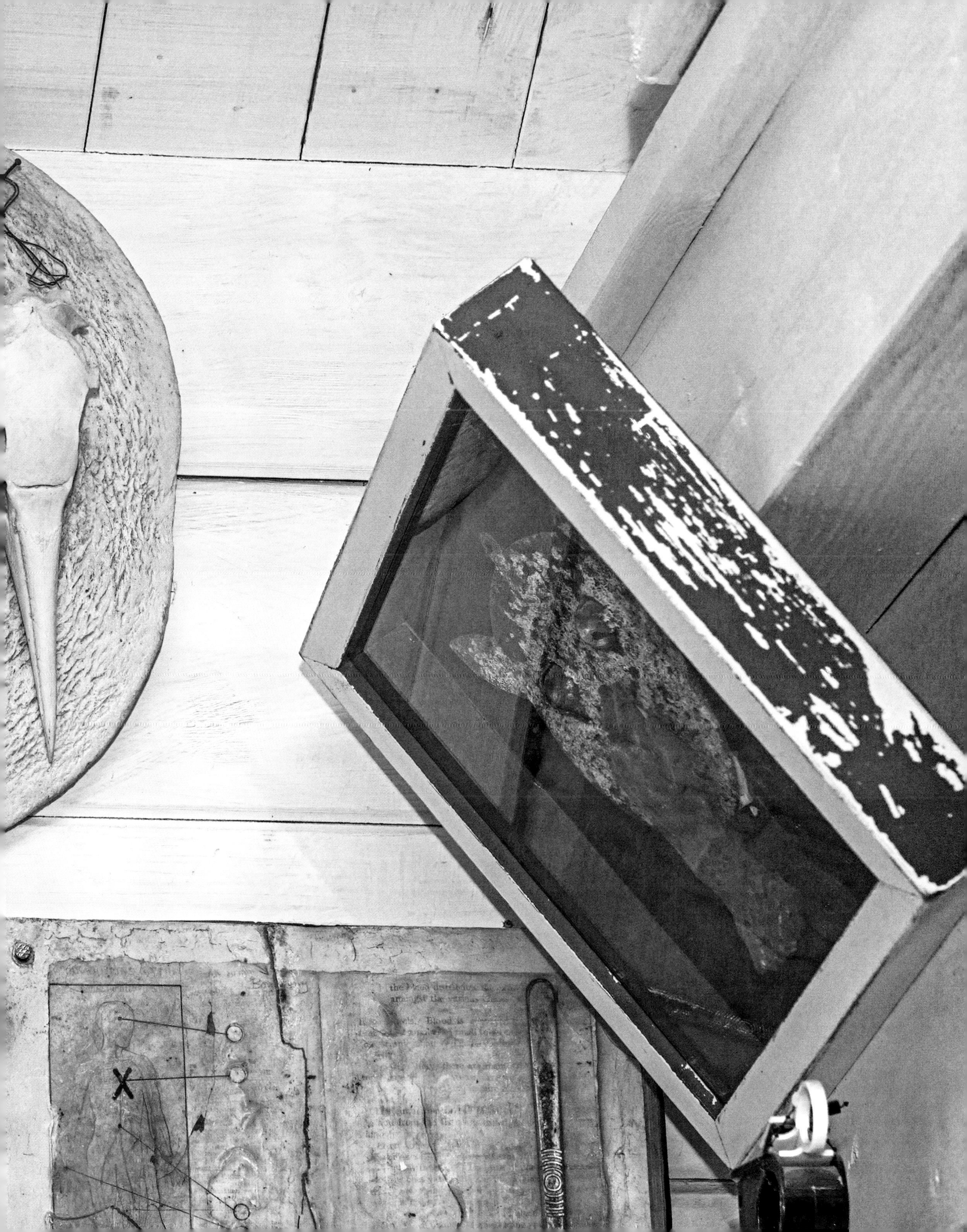

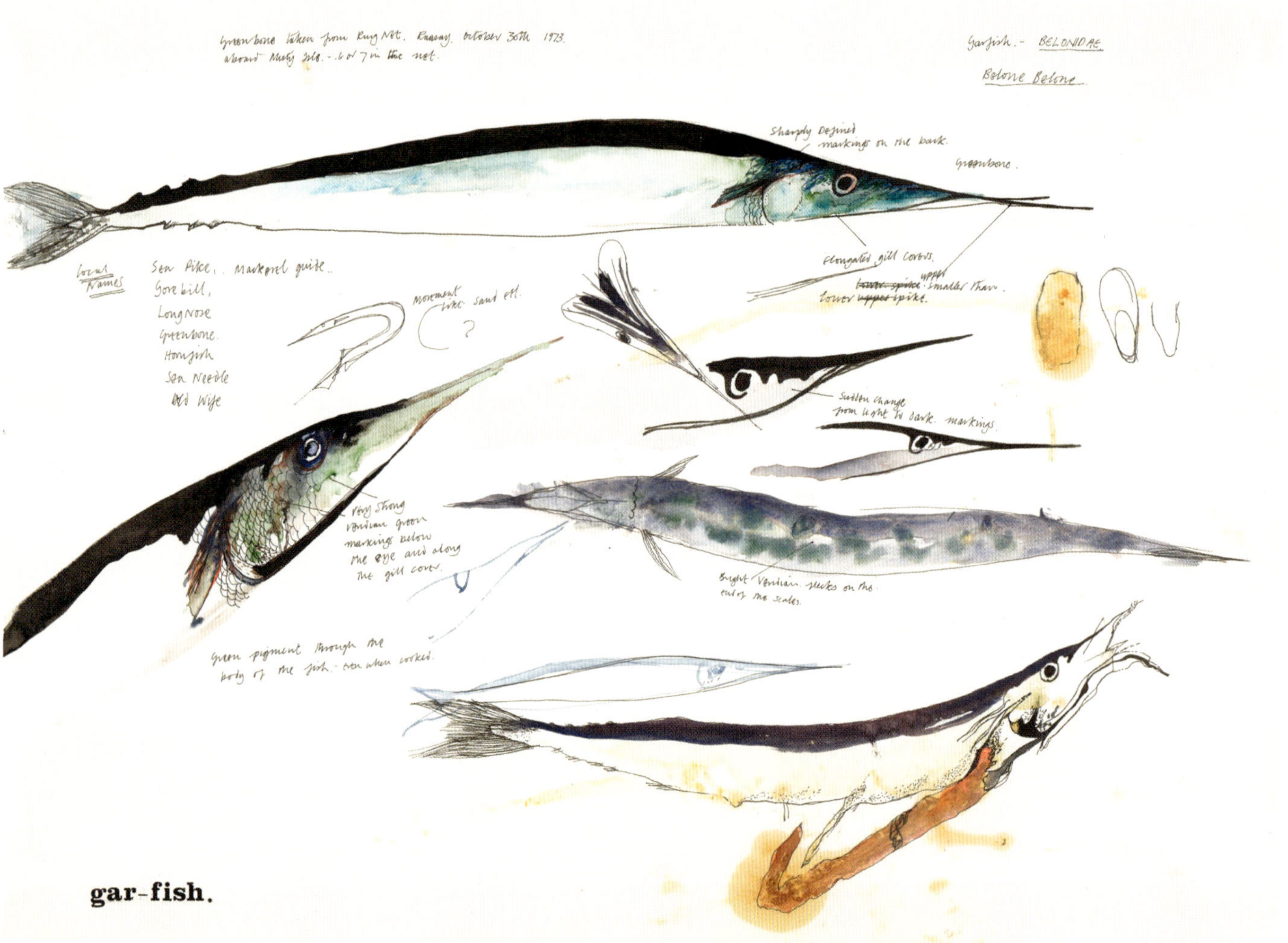

The Ring Net (gar-fish)

1973–8, pen and ink, watercolour and Letraset on paper, 35 x 48.5 cm · *National Galleries of Scotland, purchased 1978*

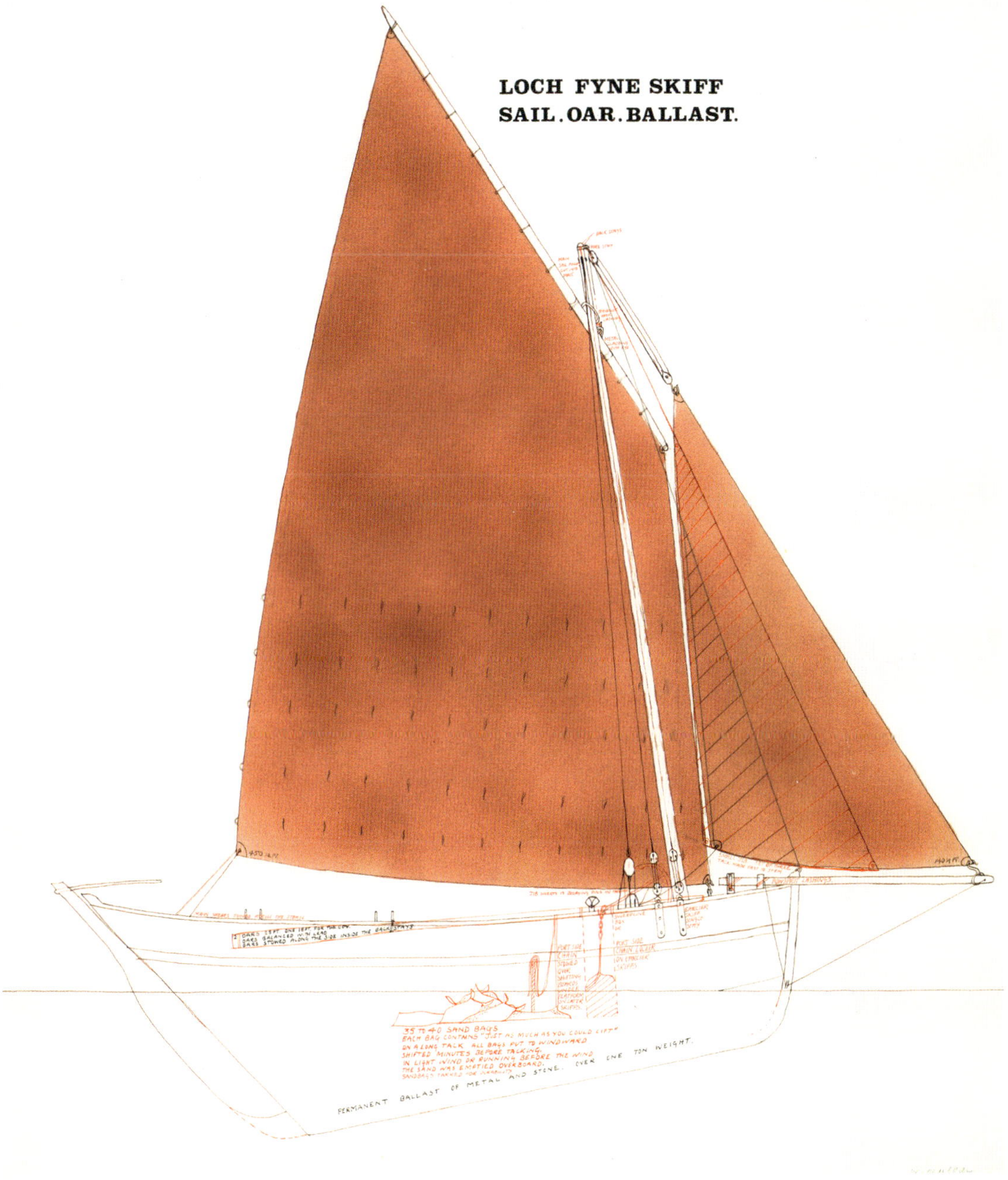

The Ring Net (Loch Fyne Skiff: Sail, Oar, Ballast)
1973–8, pen and coloured ink, Letraset and watercolour on paper, 61.5 x 49.5 cm · National Galleries of Scotland, purchased 1978

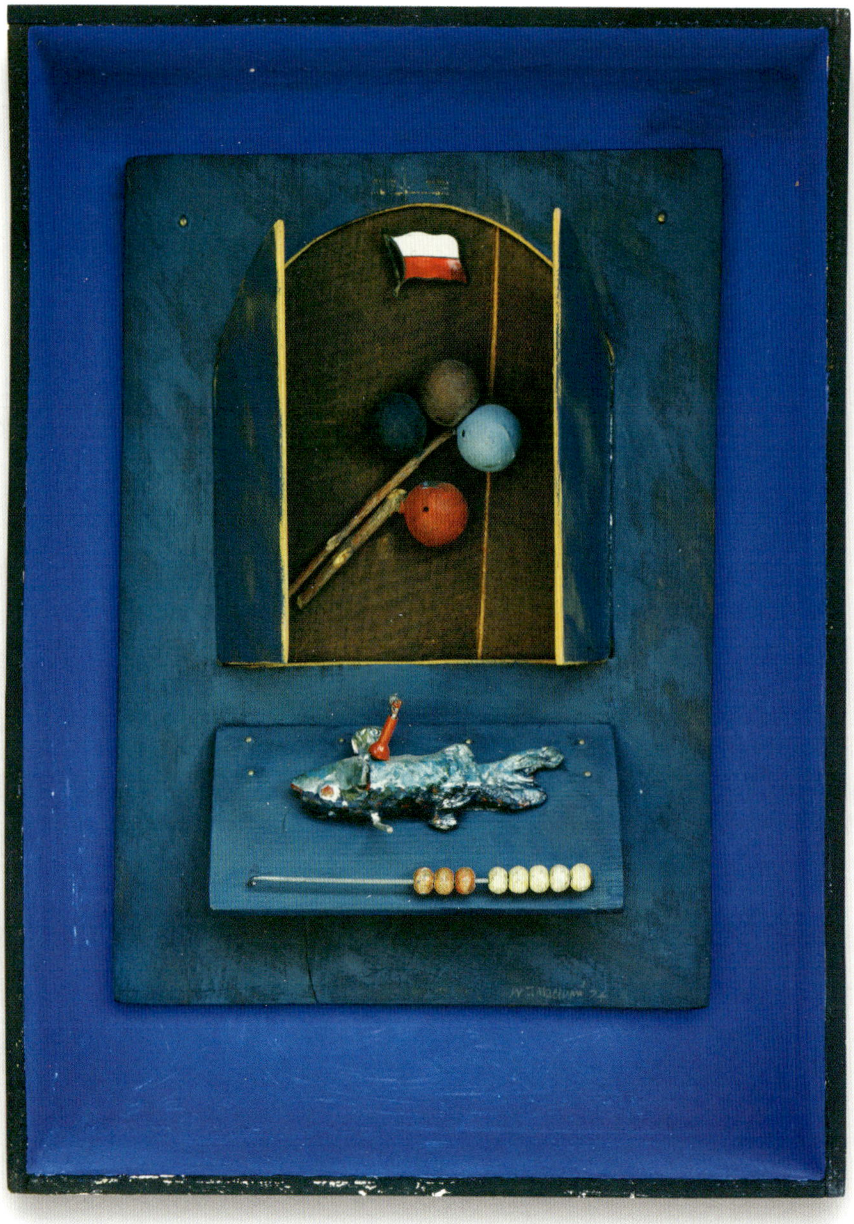

Requiem Construction (John Maclean)
1974, acrylic on box construction with found and painted objects, 34.5 x 26 cm · *Dundee Art Galleries and Museums Collection*

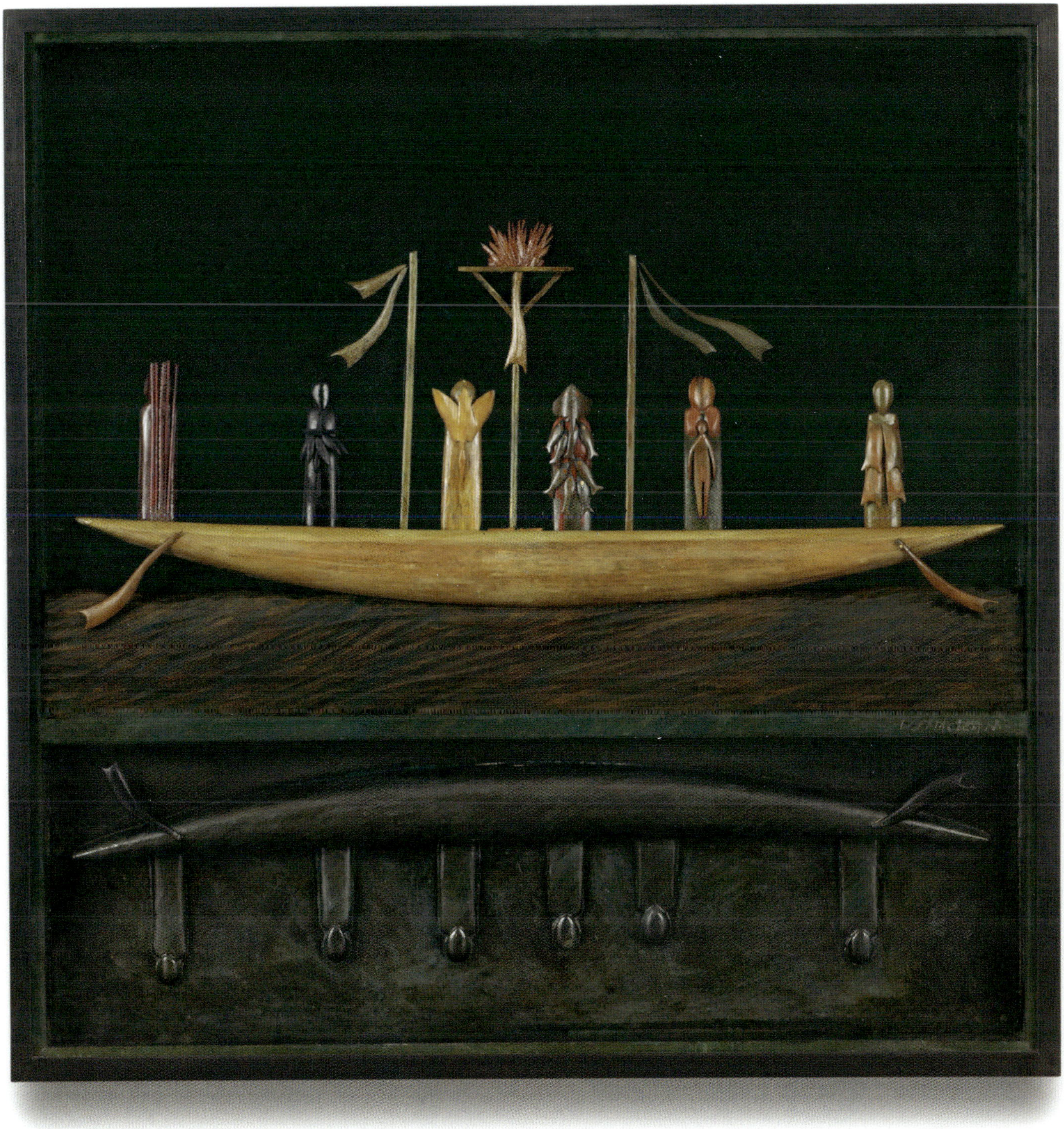

Spirit Boat · 1976, carved and painted wood, 59 x 71 x 8 cm · private collection

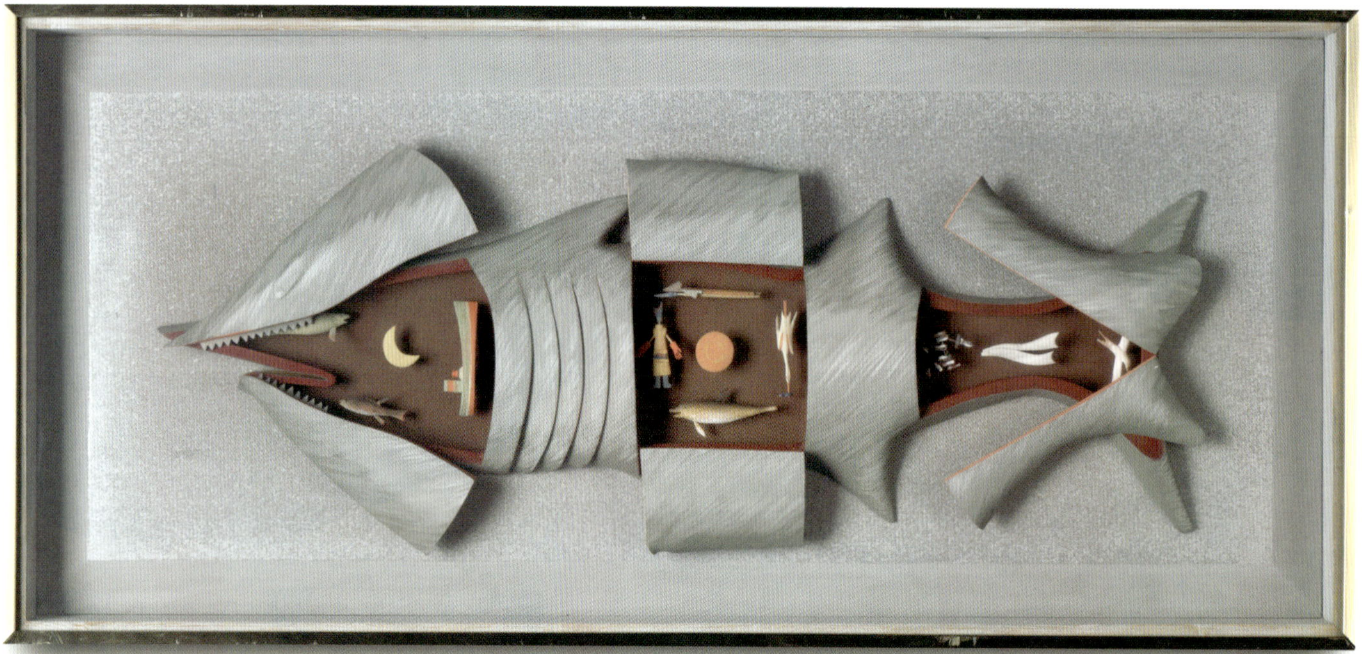

Legendary Predator · *1976, construction: oil on wood, 58 x 130 x 8 cm* · *Government Art Collection*

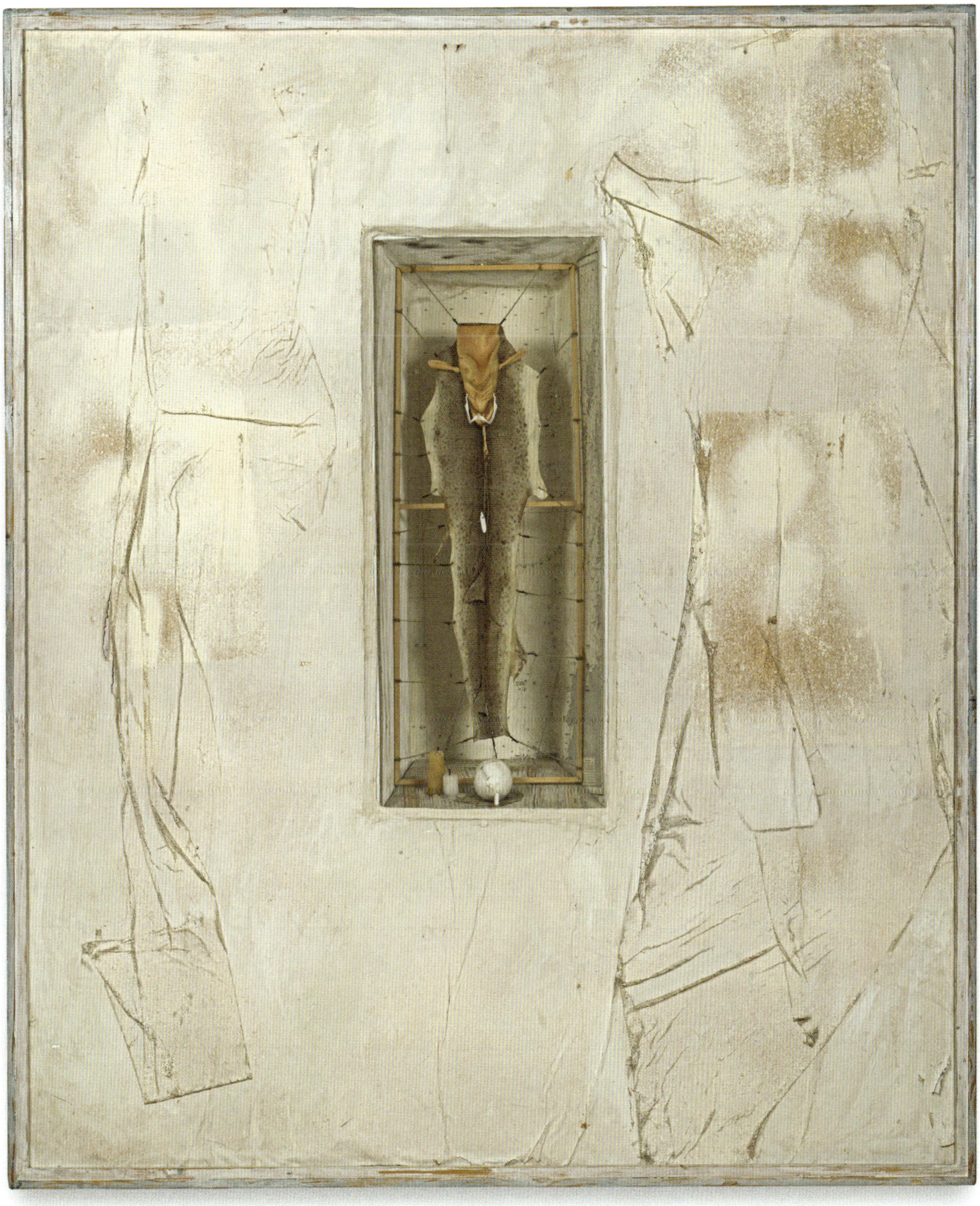

Homage to Hirta · *1977, mixed-media construction, 125 x 118 x 25 cm* · *Museum nan Eilean, photograph Antonia Reeve*

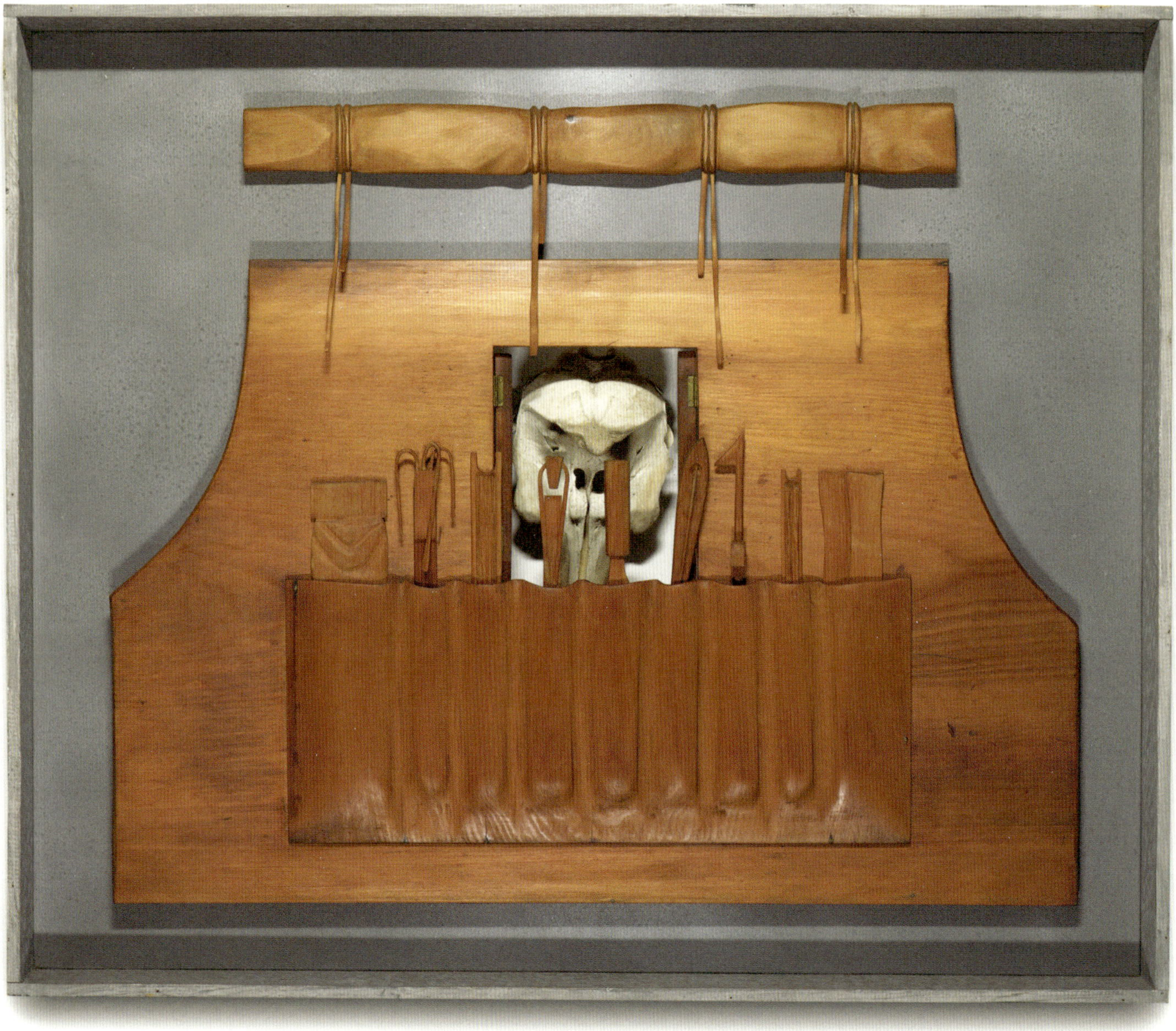

Symbols of Survival · 1976, mixed media, 88.5 x 106.2 x 22 cm · National Galleries Scotland, purchased 2013; photograph Antonia Reeve

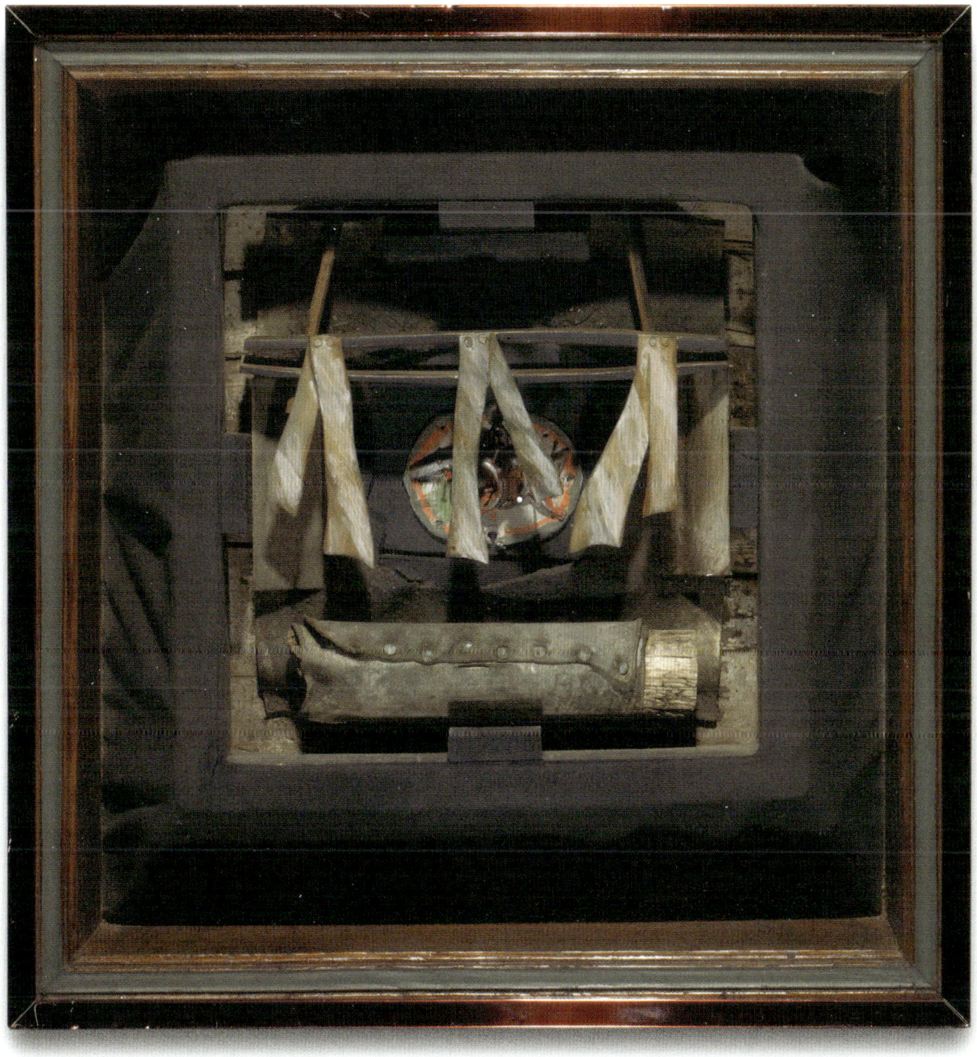

Dark Shore Box · *1978, mixed media and found objects, 46 x 52 x 15 cm*
City Art Centre, Edinburgh Museums and Galleries, photograph Antonia Reeve

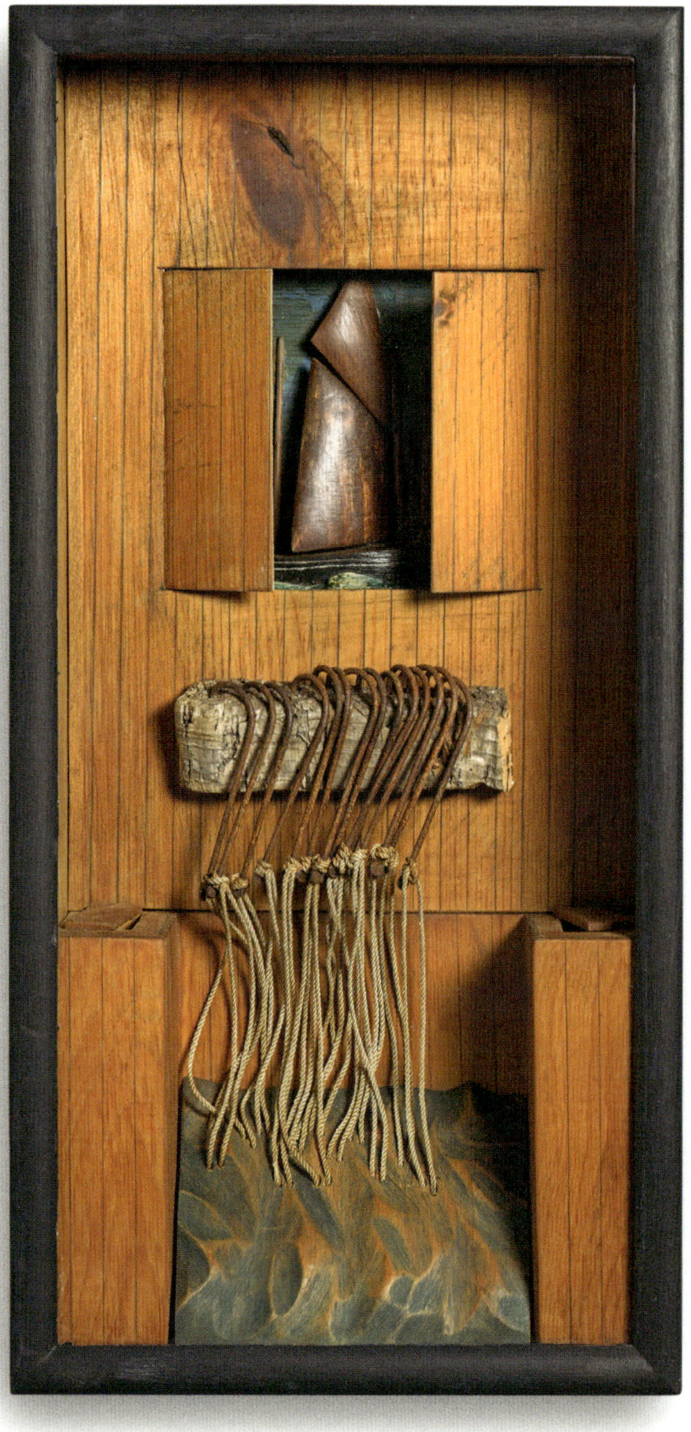

Nostalgic Locker · *1976, carved and painted wood, found objects, 56 x 30 x 15 cm* · *Ian Mayes QC; photograph Antonia Reeve*

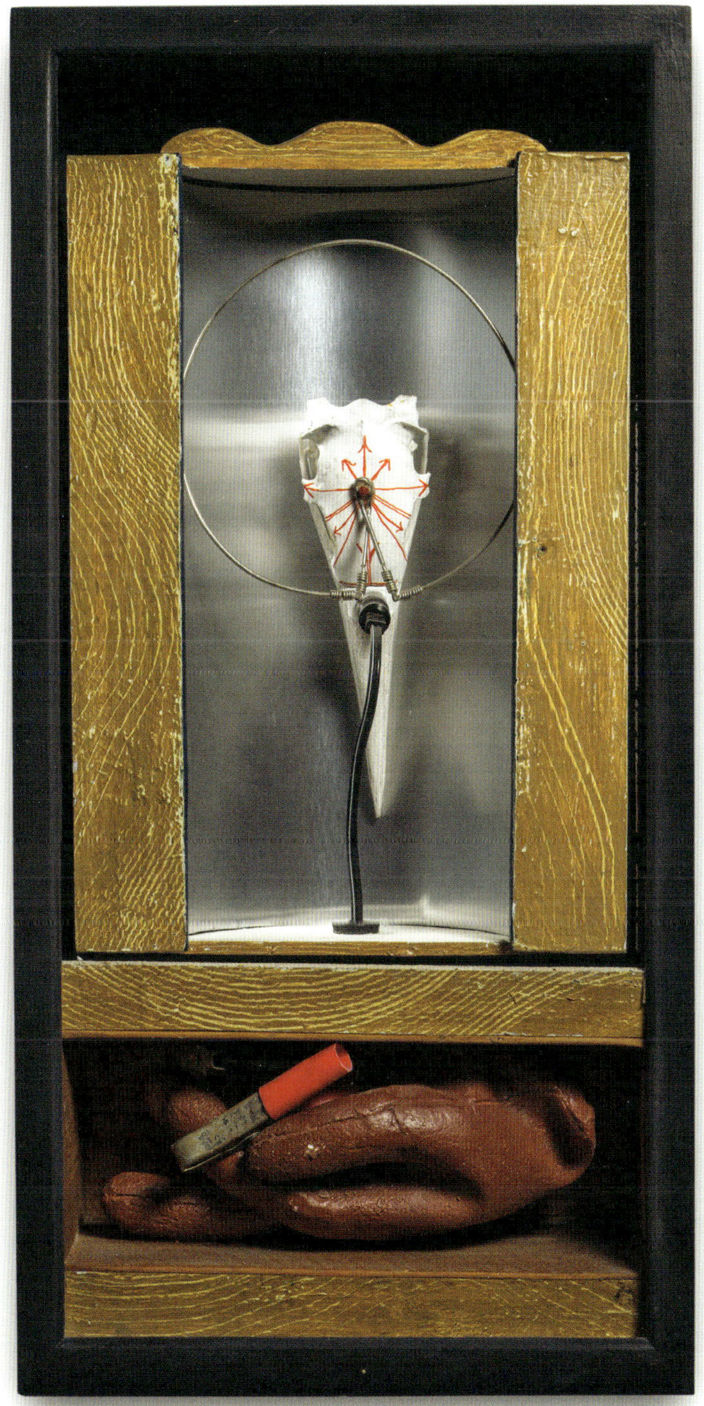

Song for the Solan · *1978, mixed-media construction and found objects, 56 x 30 x 15 cm* · *Ian Mayes QC, photograph Antonia Reeve*

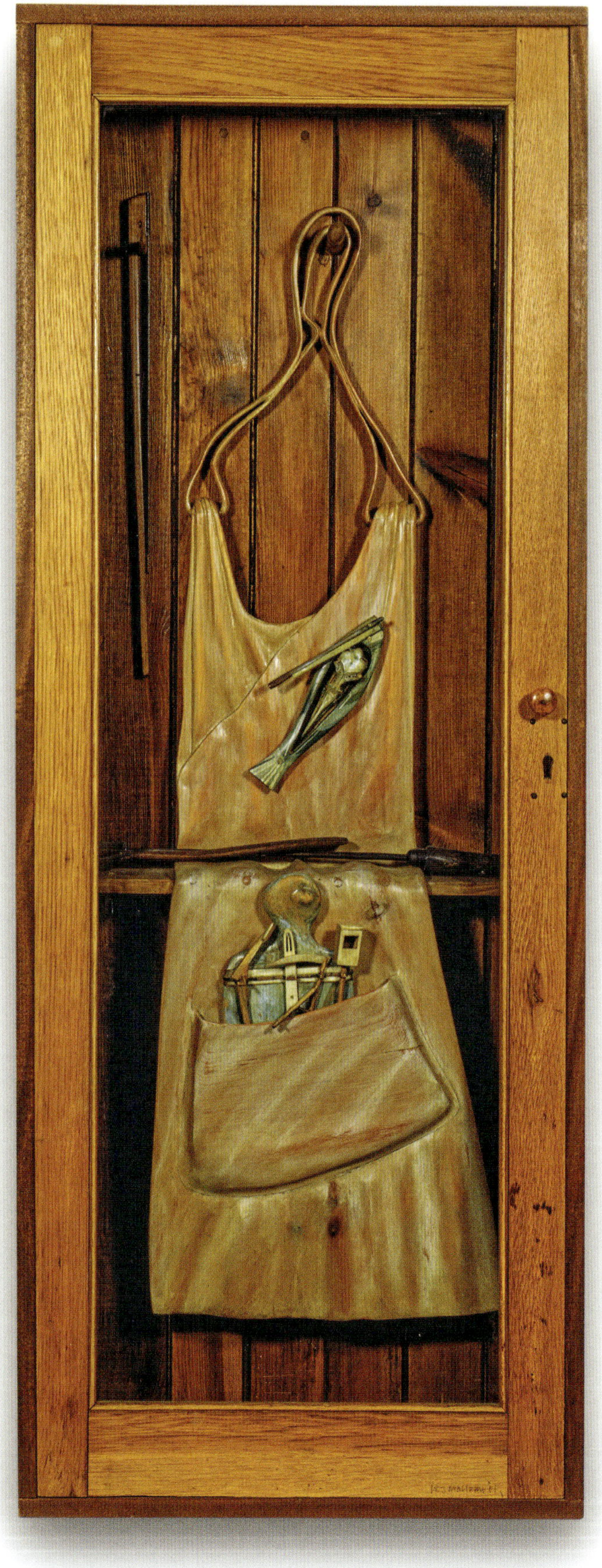

Abigail's Apron · *1980, painted wood, bone and metal, 214 x 50 x 15 cm* · *private collection, London*

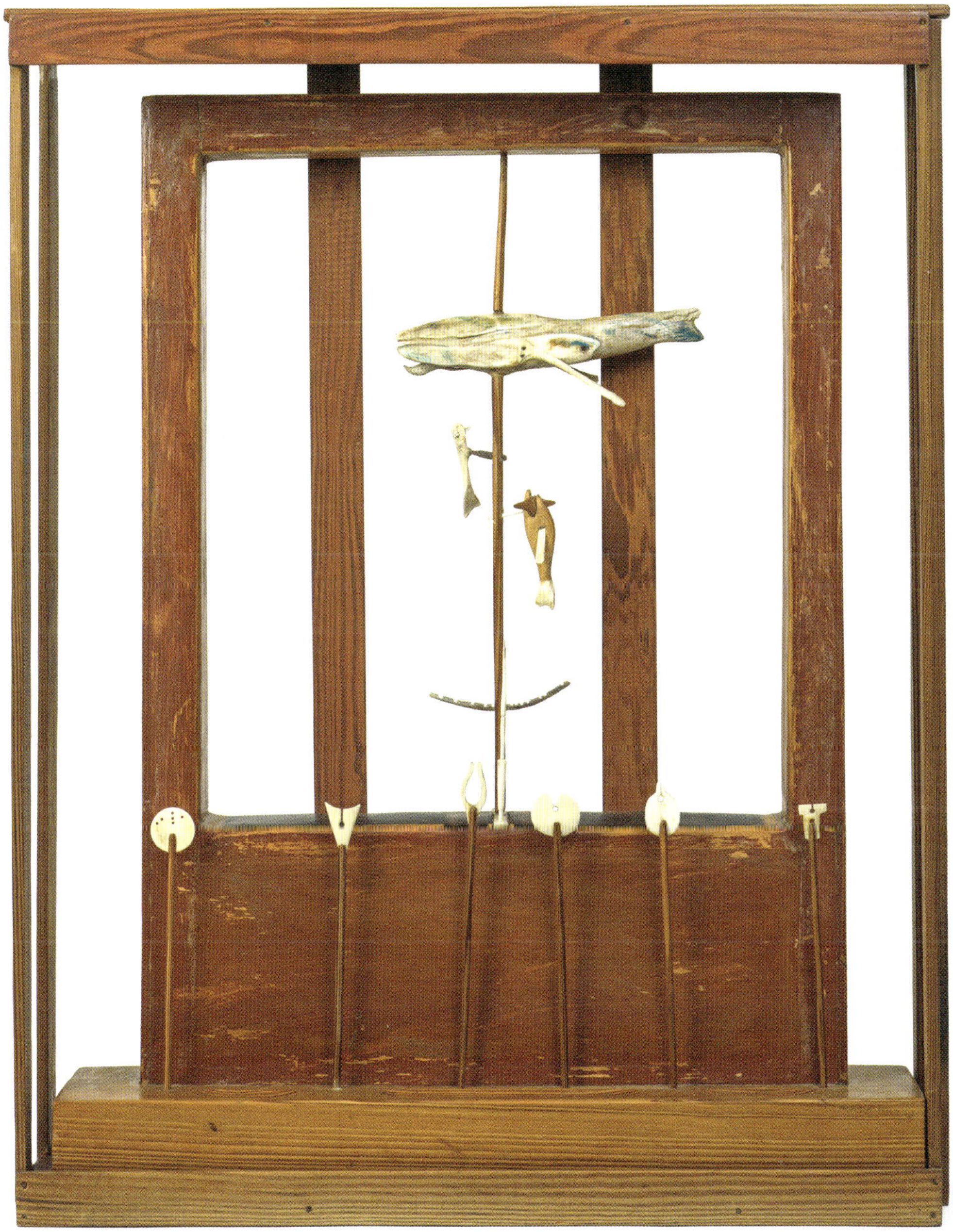

Alignment Frame Paradox · *1982, painted wood, bone and metal, 71 x 56 x 18 cm* · *private collection, London*

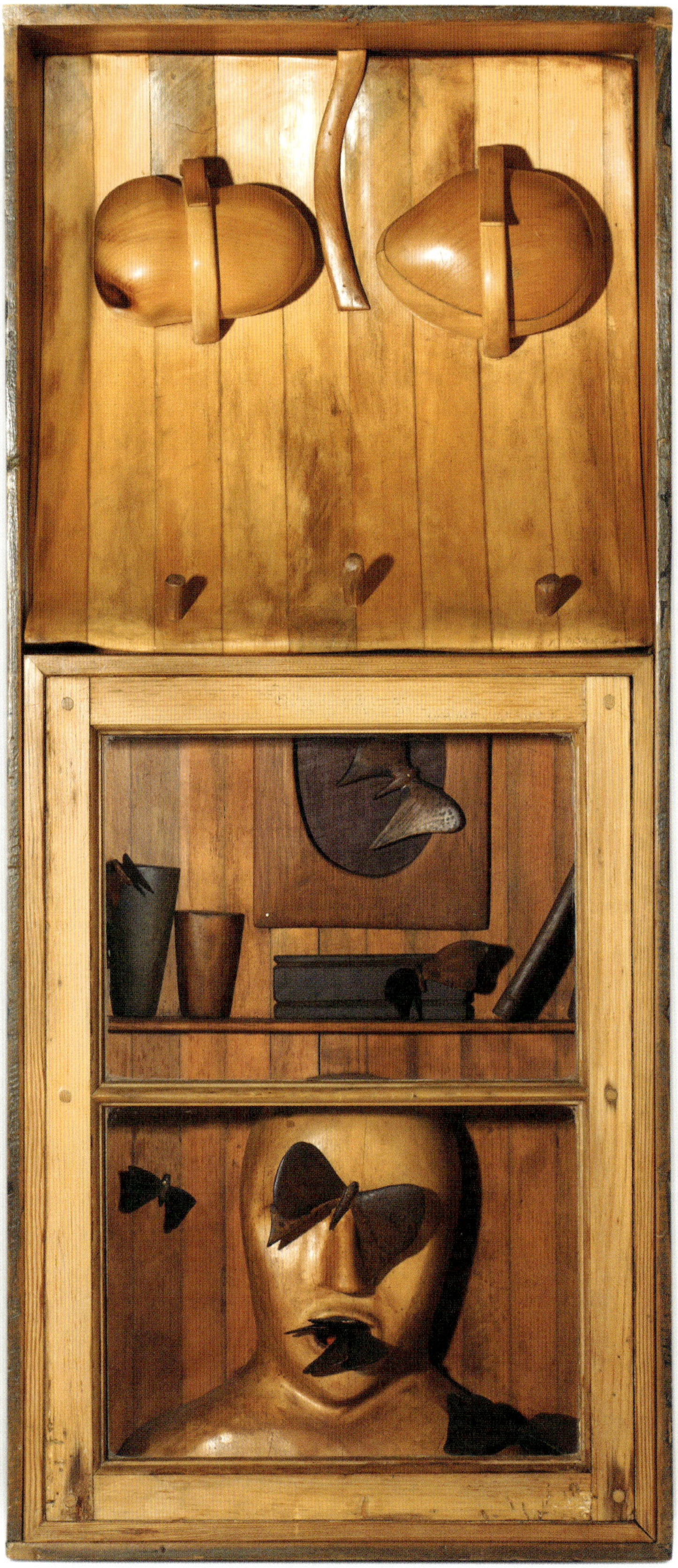

Window Visitation, North Uist · *1980, carved and painted wood, 104 x 46 x 18 cm*
Inverness Museum and Art Gallery (High Life Highland); photograph Highland Council

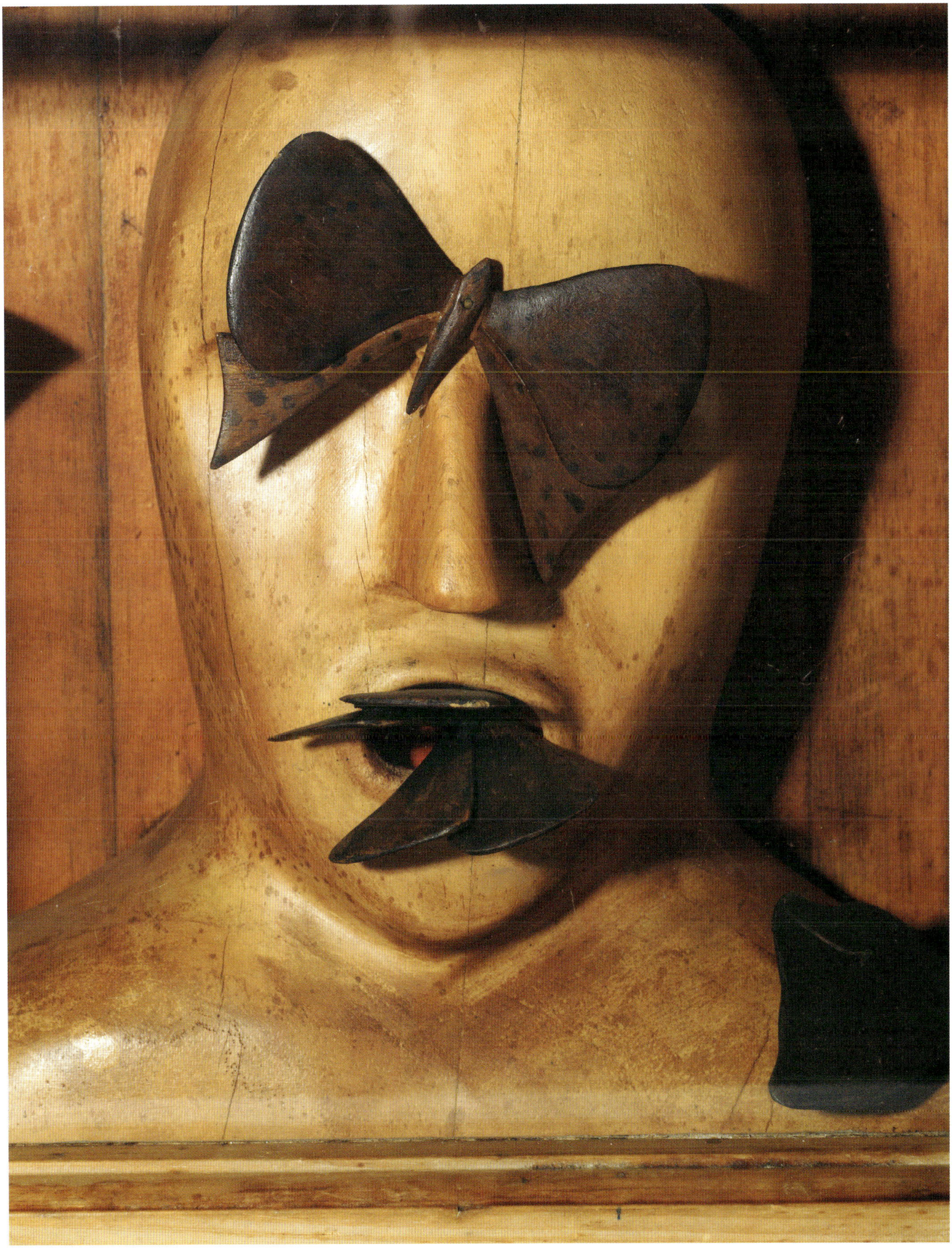

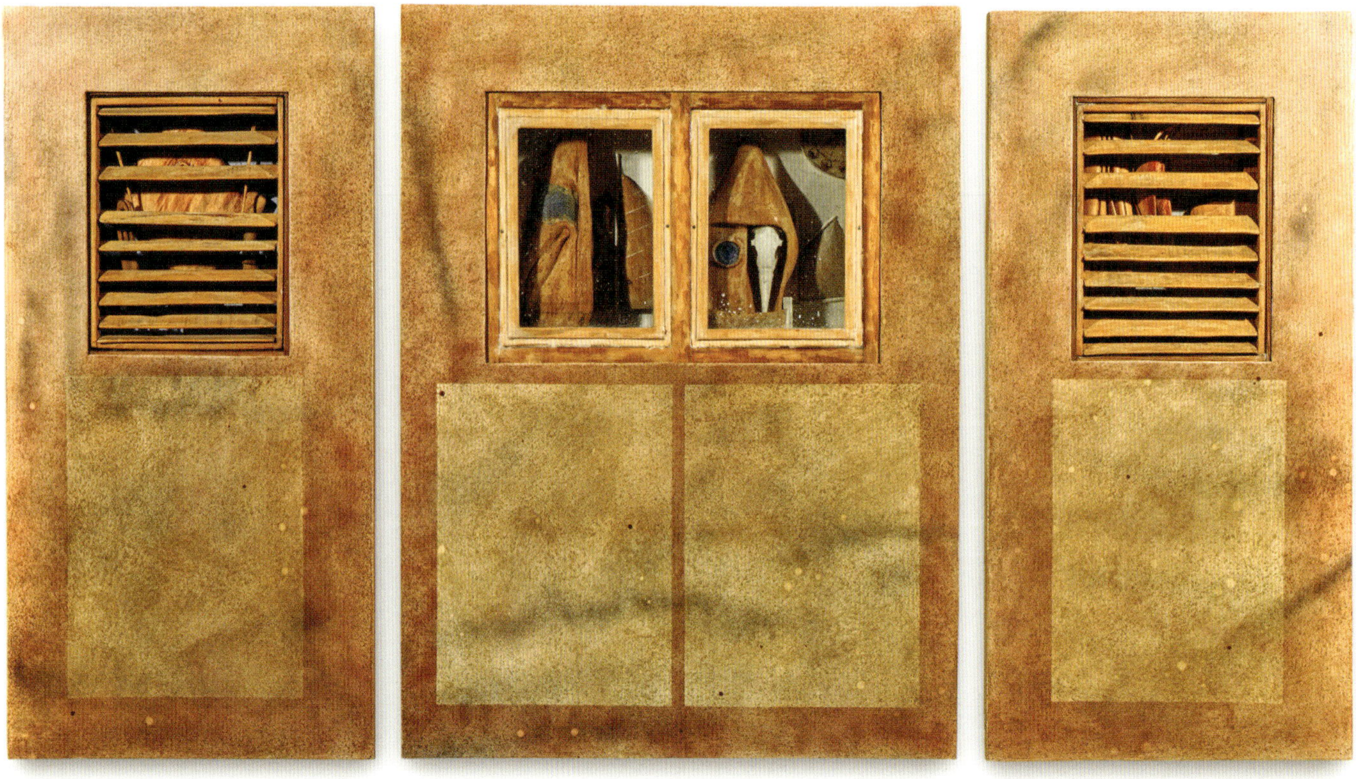

Wheelhouse Triptych
1981, carved and painted wood, bone and slate in three sections: 122 x 61 x 10, 122 x 91 x 16, 122 x 61 x 10 cm · *private collection, Cambridge.*

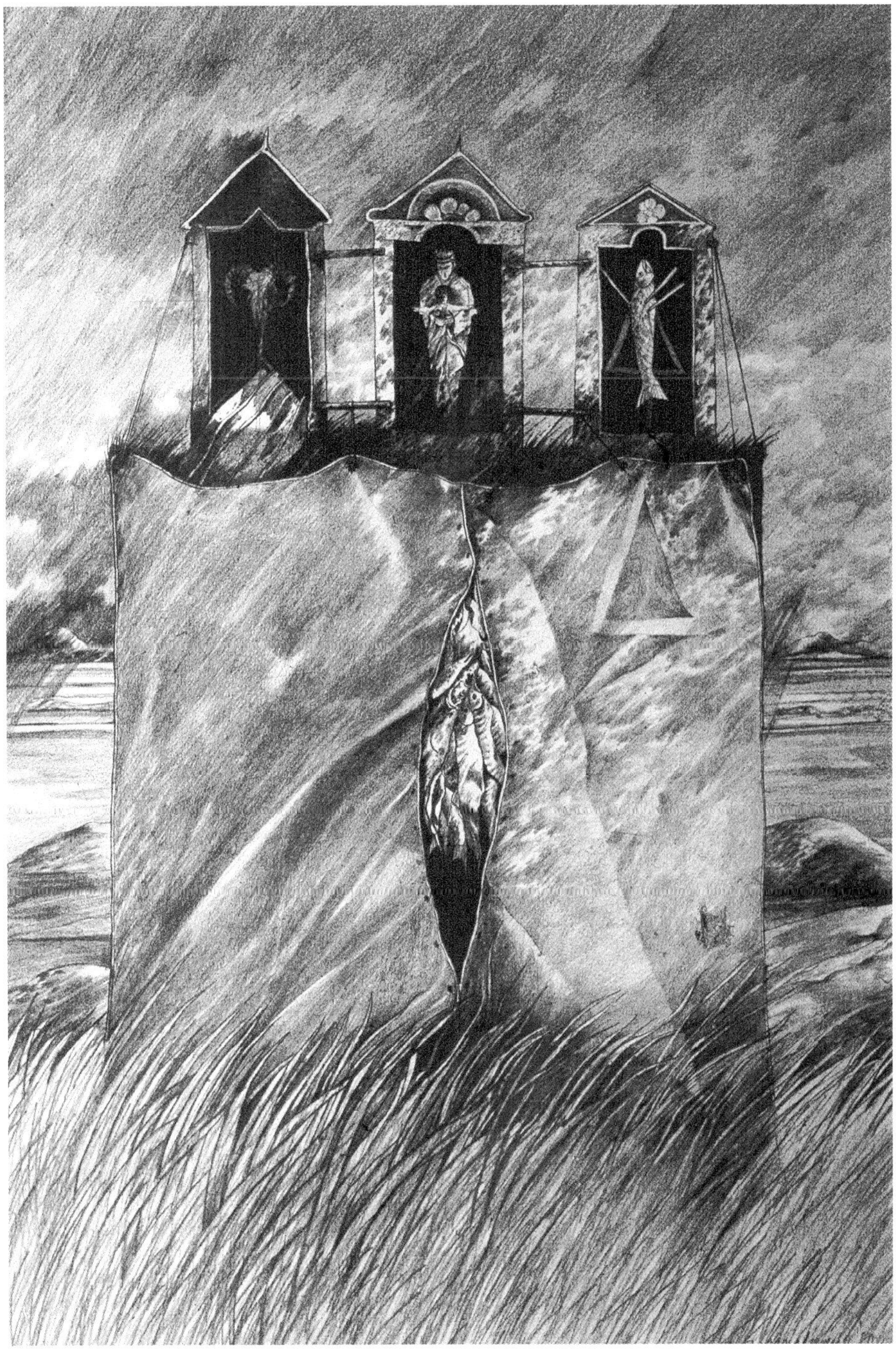

Welcome to South Uist · 1981, pencil on paper, 76 x 50 cm · private collection

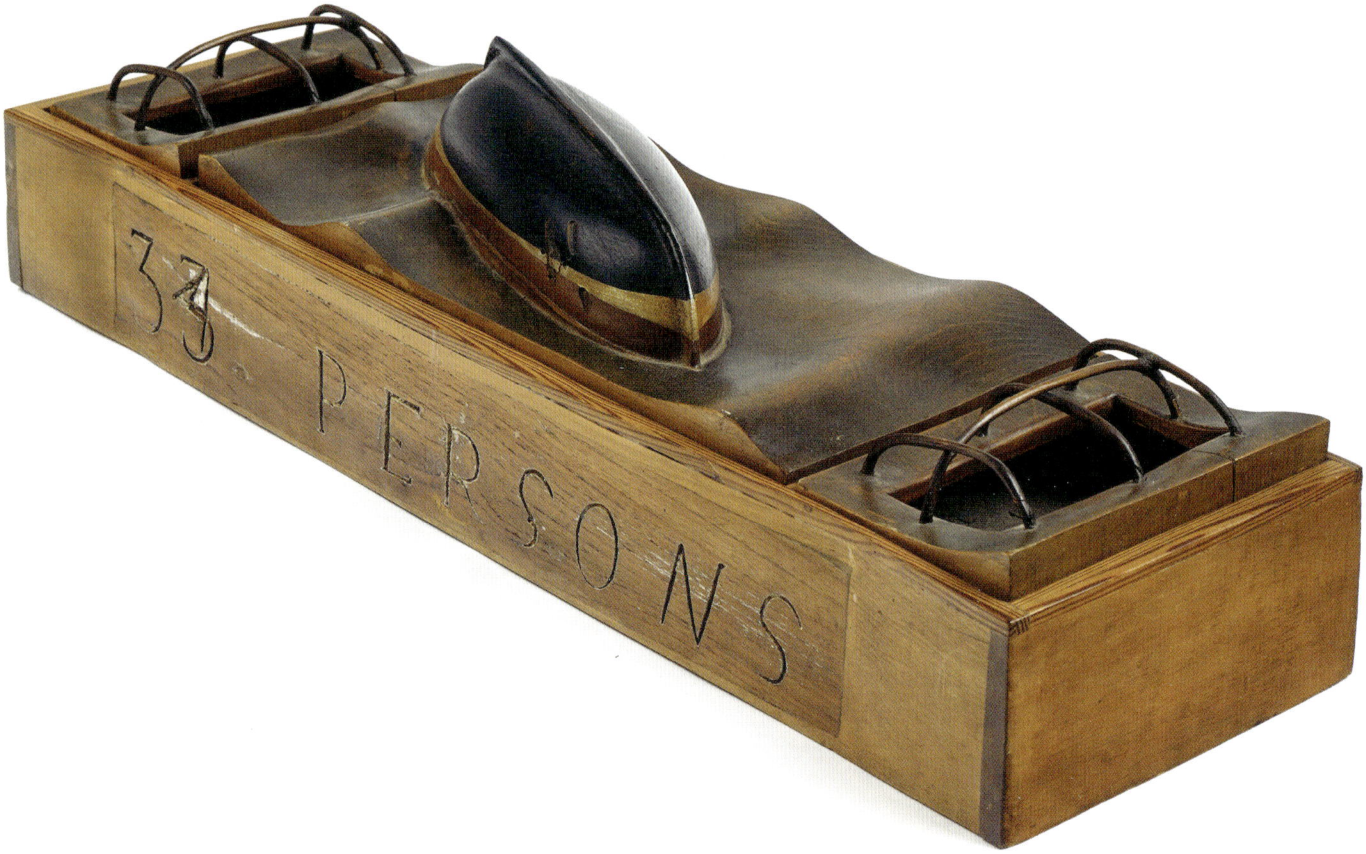

The Drowning *· 1983, wood construction, 71.1 x 21 x 20.5 cm · The Fine Art Society*

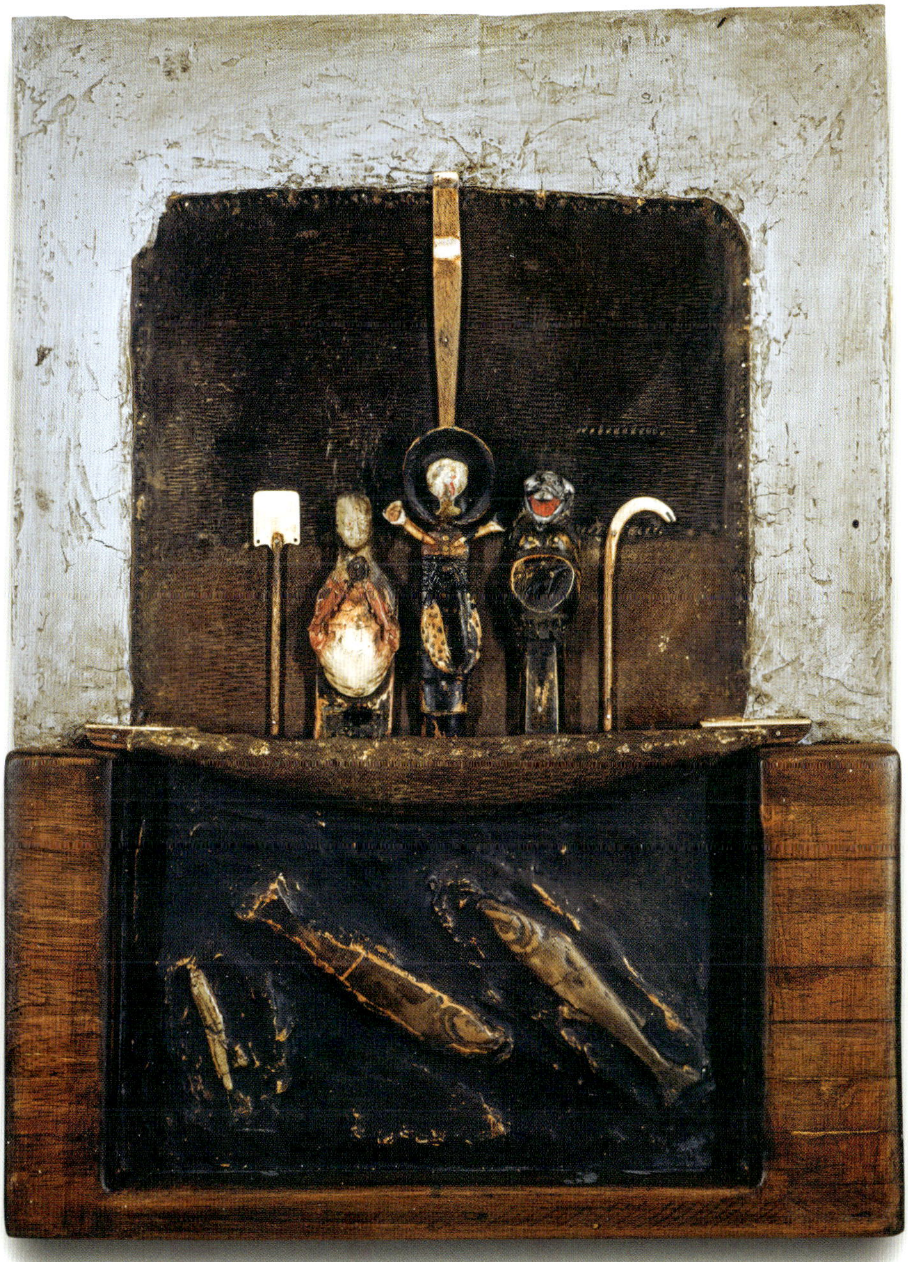

Bard Macintyre's Box · *1984, mixed-media assemblage, 66 x 46.5 x 7.5 cm* · *National Galleries Scotland, purchased 1986, photograph Antonia Reeve*

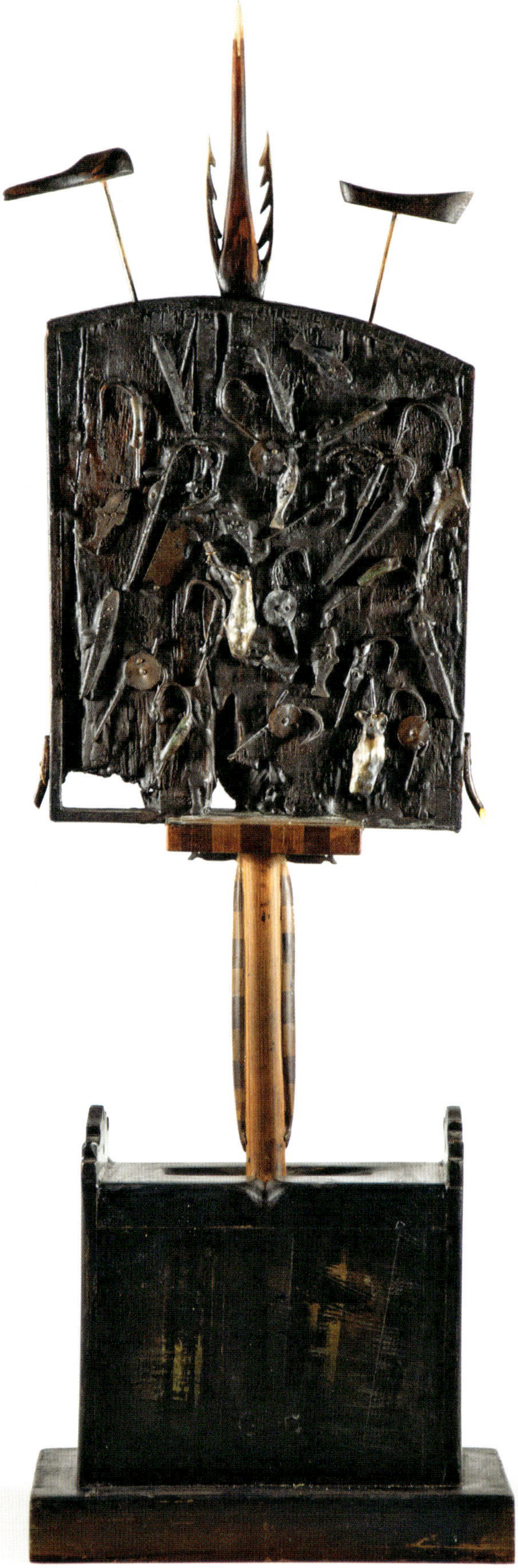

Sea Creed Banner · *1984, found objects, painted wood and metal, 86 x 40 x 25 cm* · *Maclaurin Trust, photograph Chris Delaney*

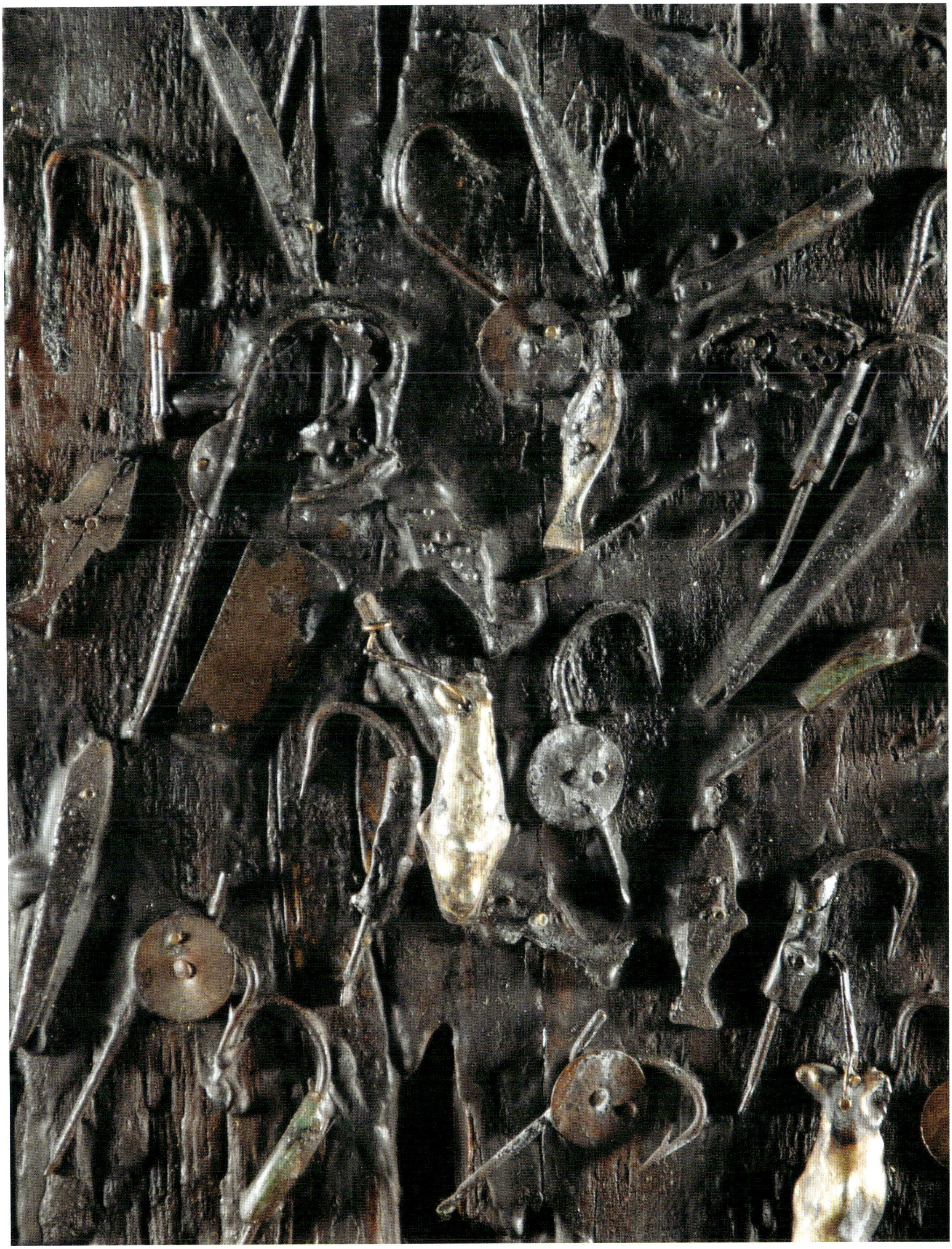

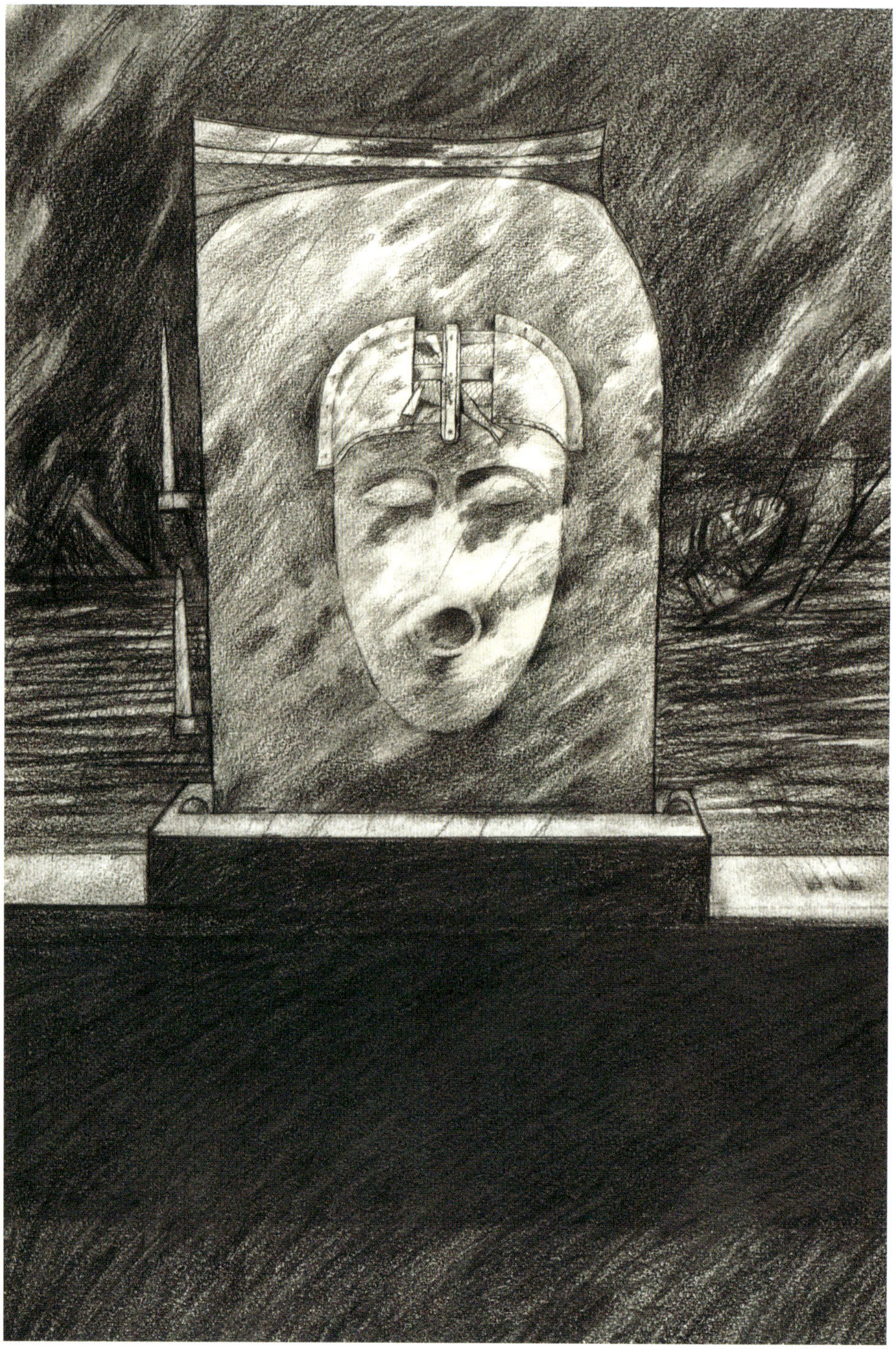

Study for Rudder Requiem · *1985, pencil on paper, 54 x 37 cm* · *private collection; photograph Antonia Reeve*

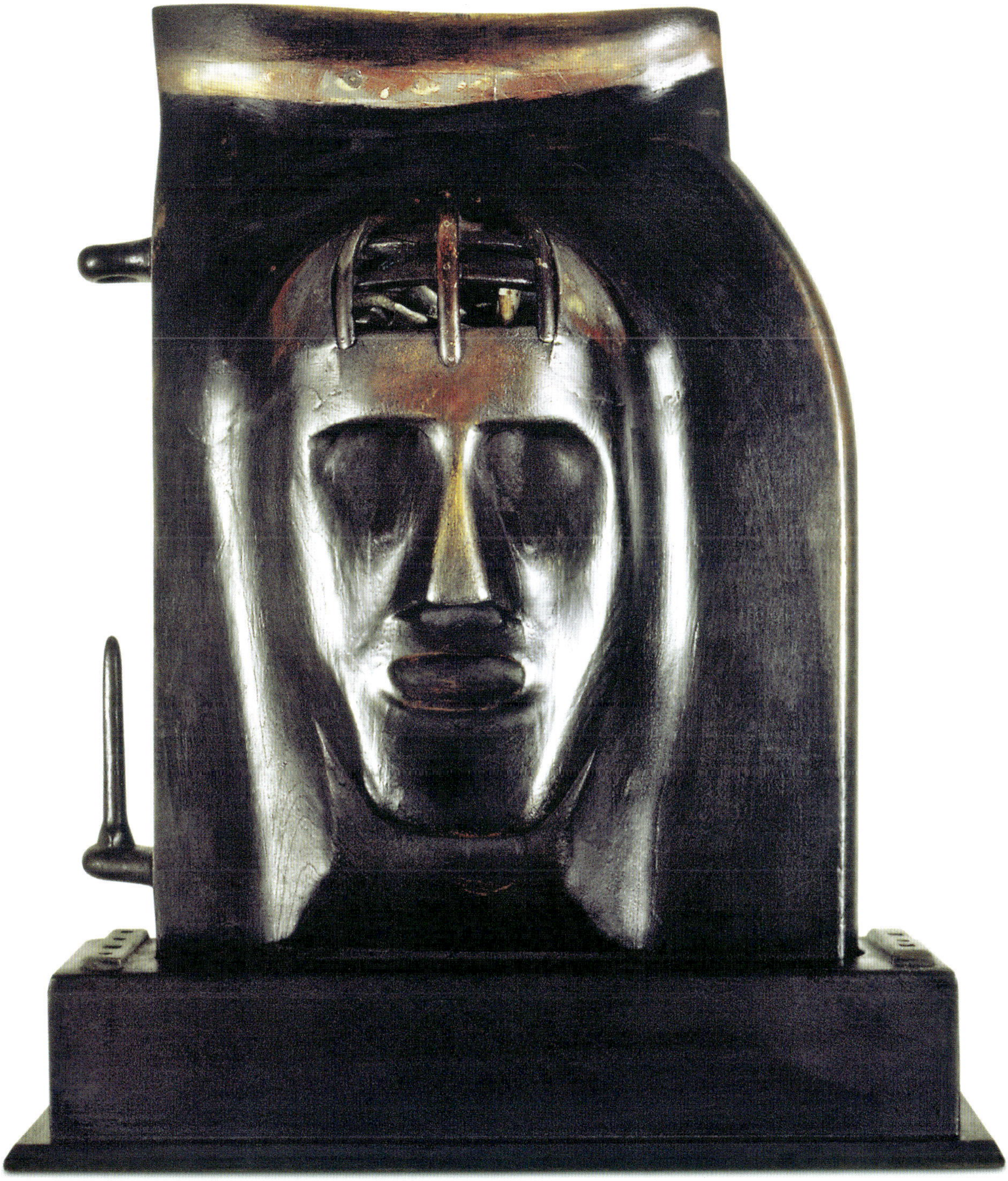

Rudder Requiem · *1985, painted wood and metal, 50 x 43 x 12 cm* · *private collection*

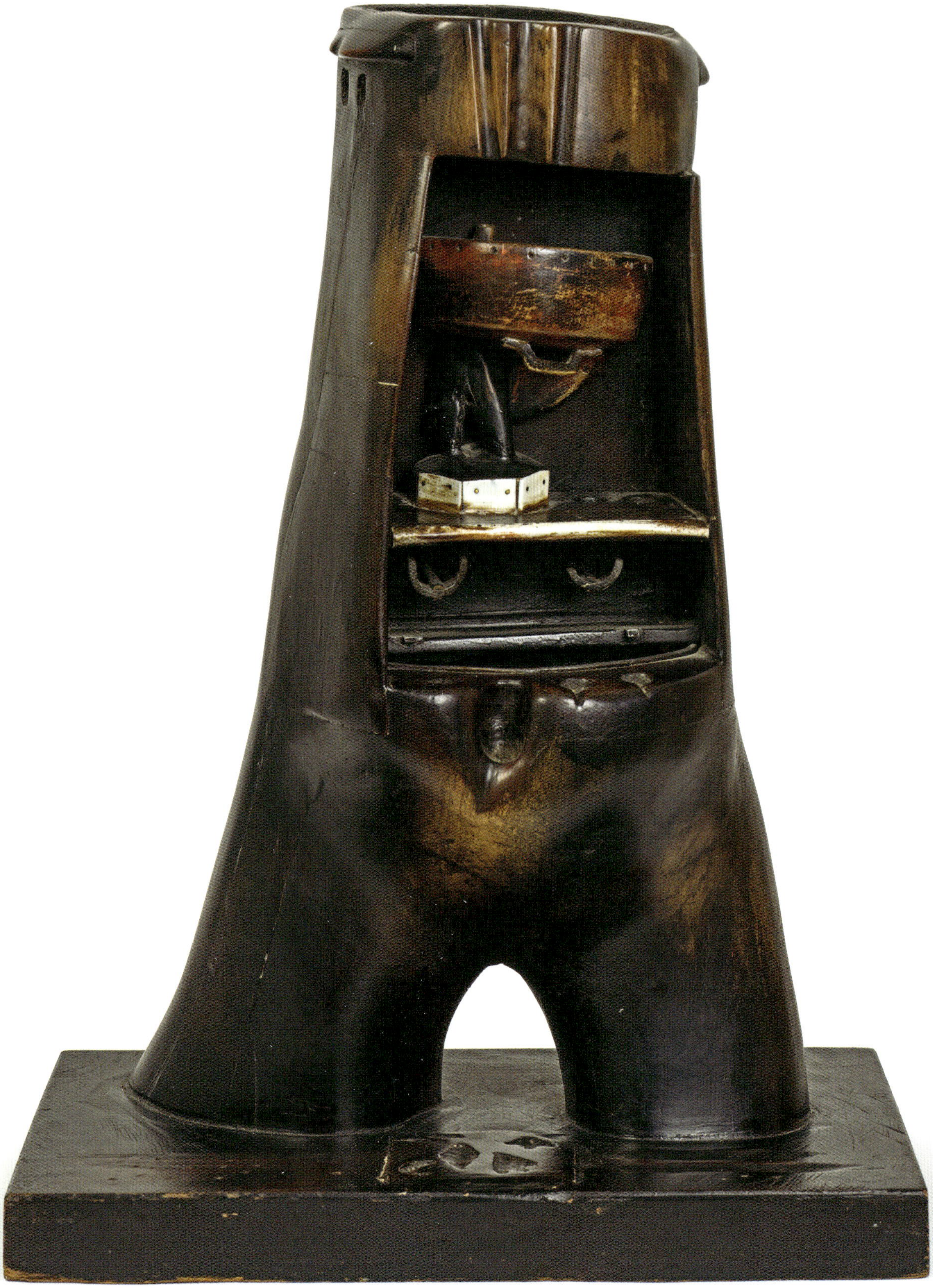

Fire Figure · *1985, laburnum wood and mixed media, 51 x 36 x 10 cm* · *Ian Mayes QC; photograph Antonia Reeve*

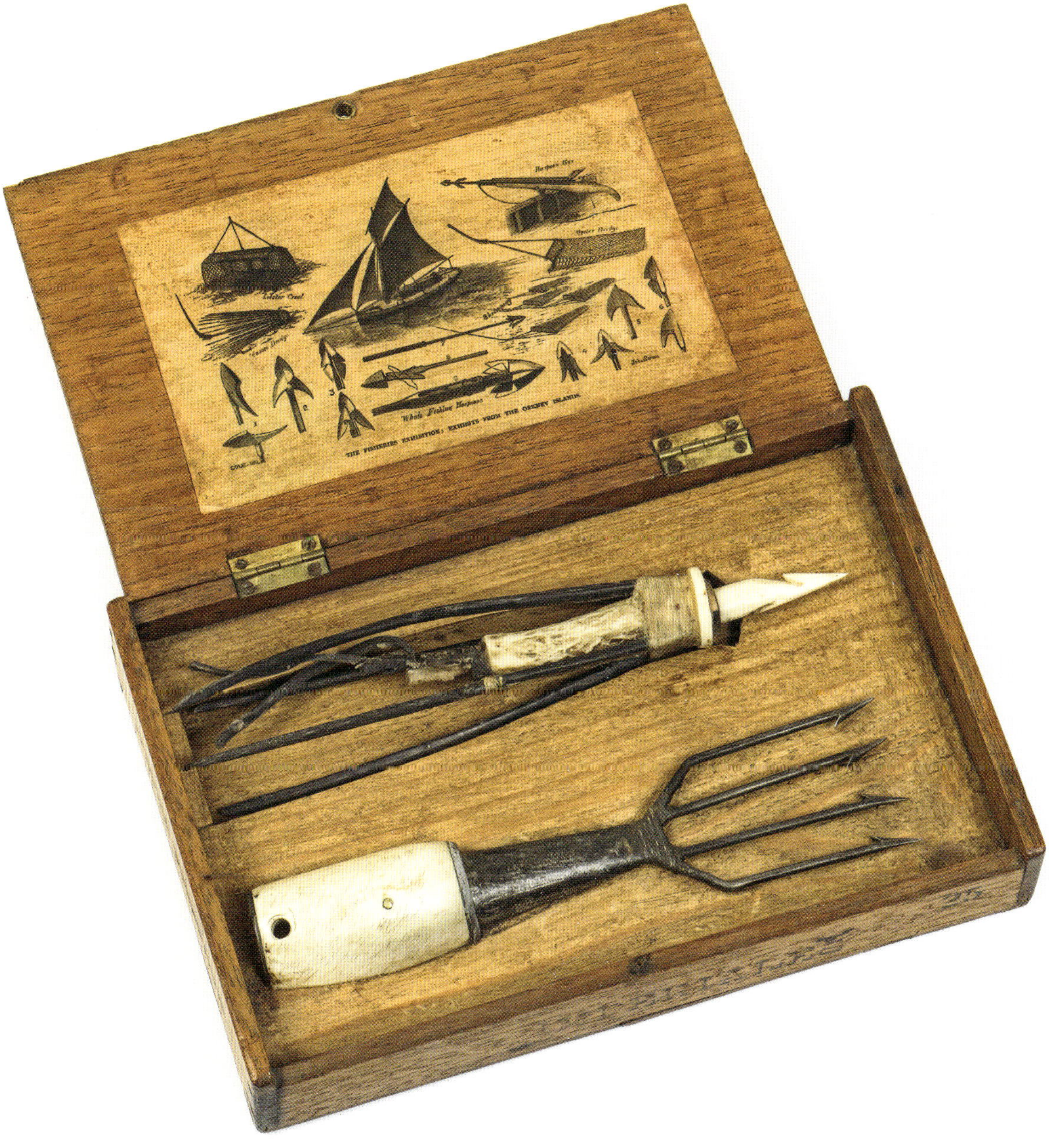

Harpoon Box *· 1987, mixed media and found objects, 14 x 22 cm ·* *Ian Mayes QC*

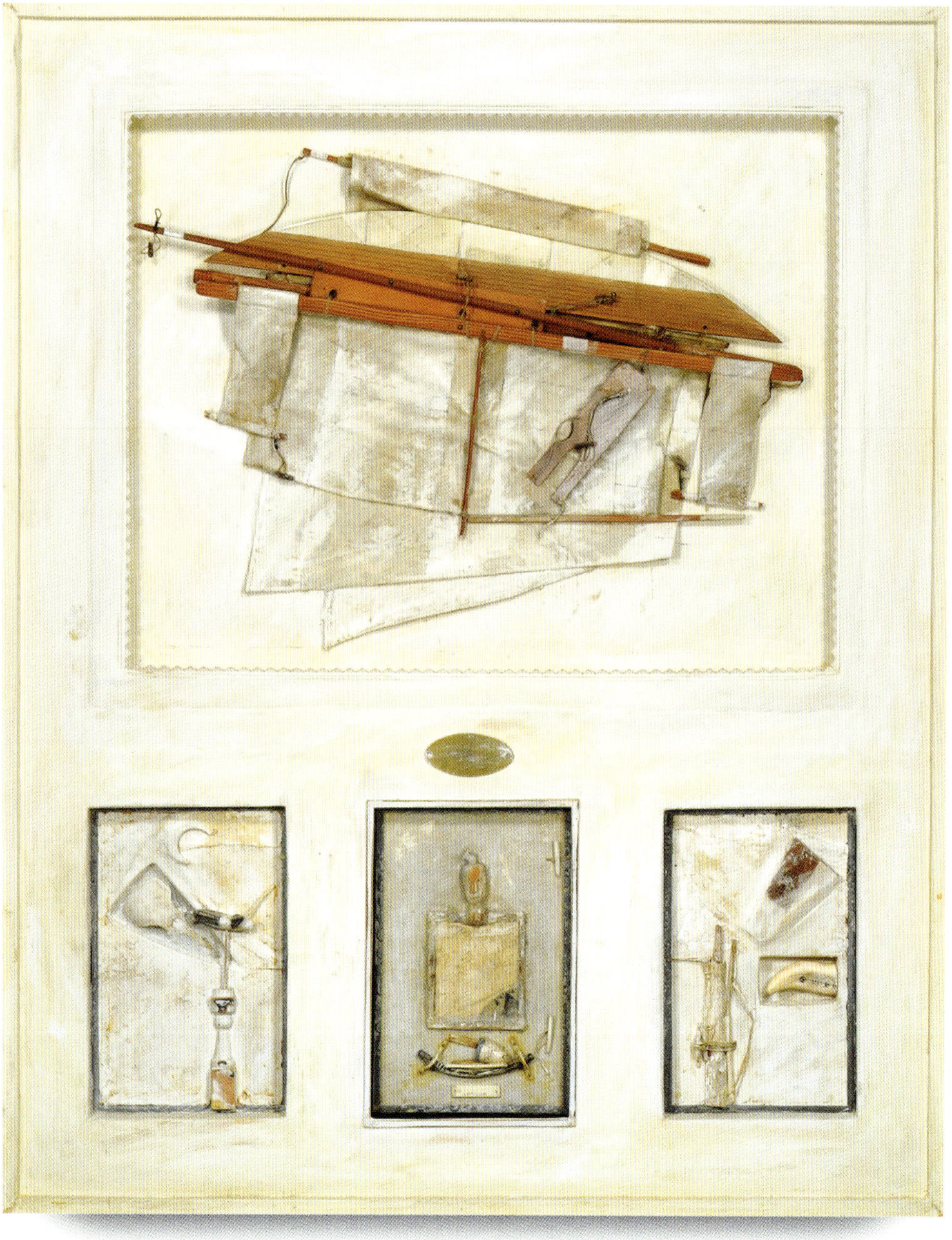

Log Book 1 — Polar Voyage
1986, painted wood, canvas and mixed media, 112 x 82 x 7 cm · McMaster Museum of Art, Hamilton, Ontario

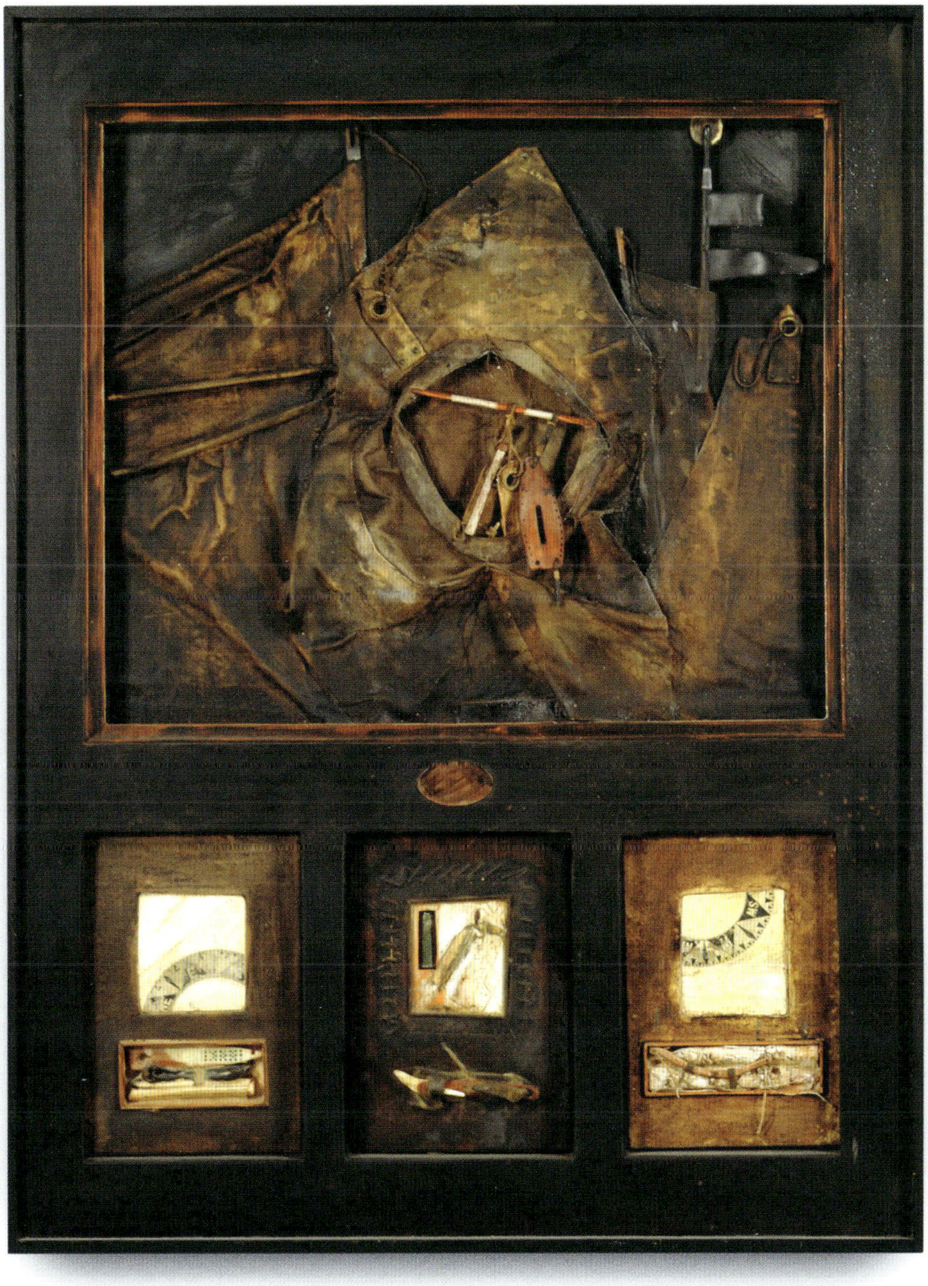

Log Book II — Winter Voyagee
1986, painted wood, canvas and mixed media, 112 x 82 x 7 cm · McMaster Museum of Art, Hamilton, Ontario

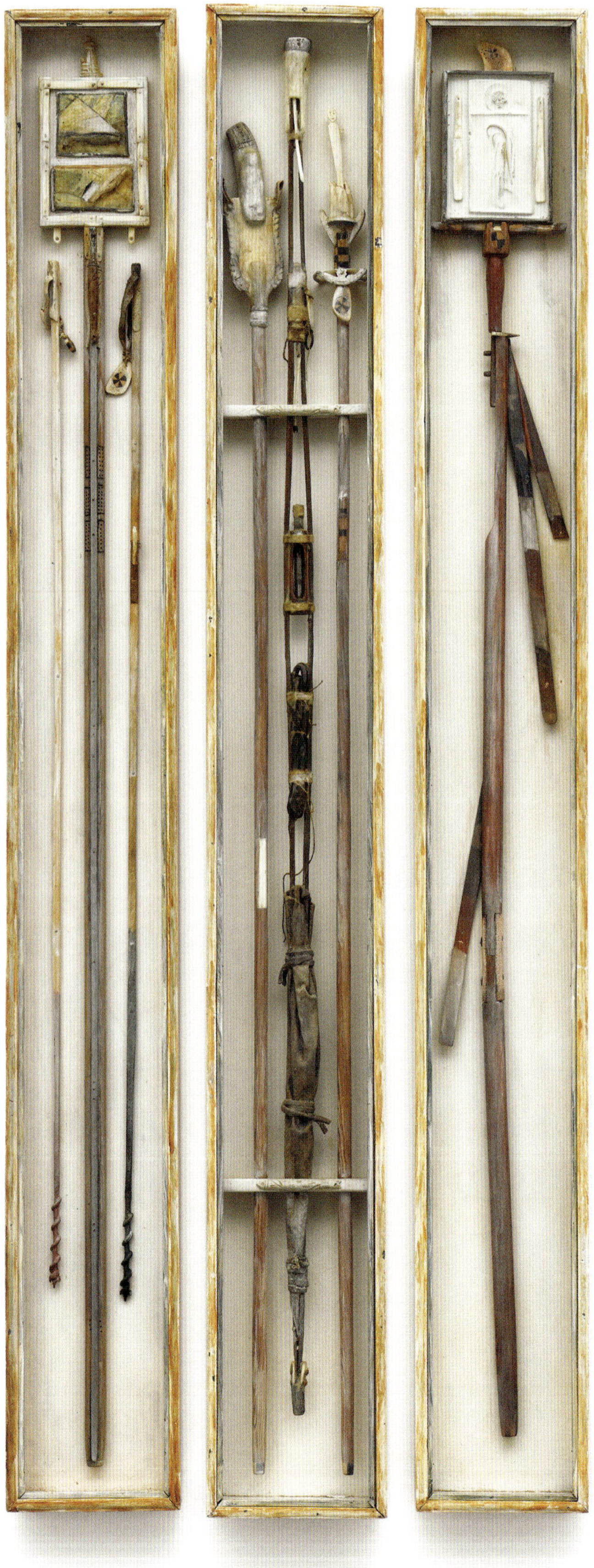

Pole Marker Triptych · *1987, mixed media, carved and found objects, 3 sections, each 180 x 18 x 7 cm*

private collection, London; photograph White Cube/Theo Cristelis

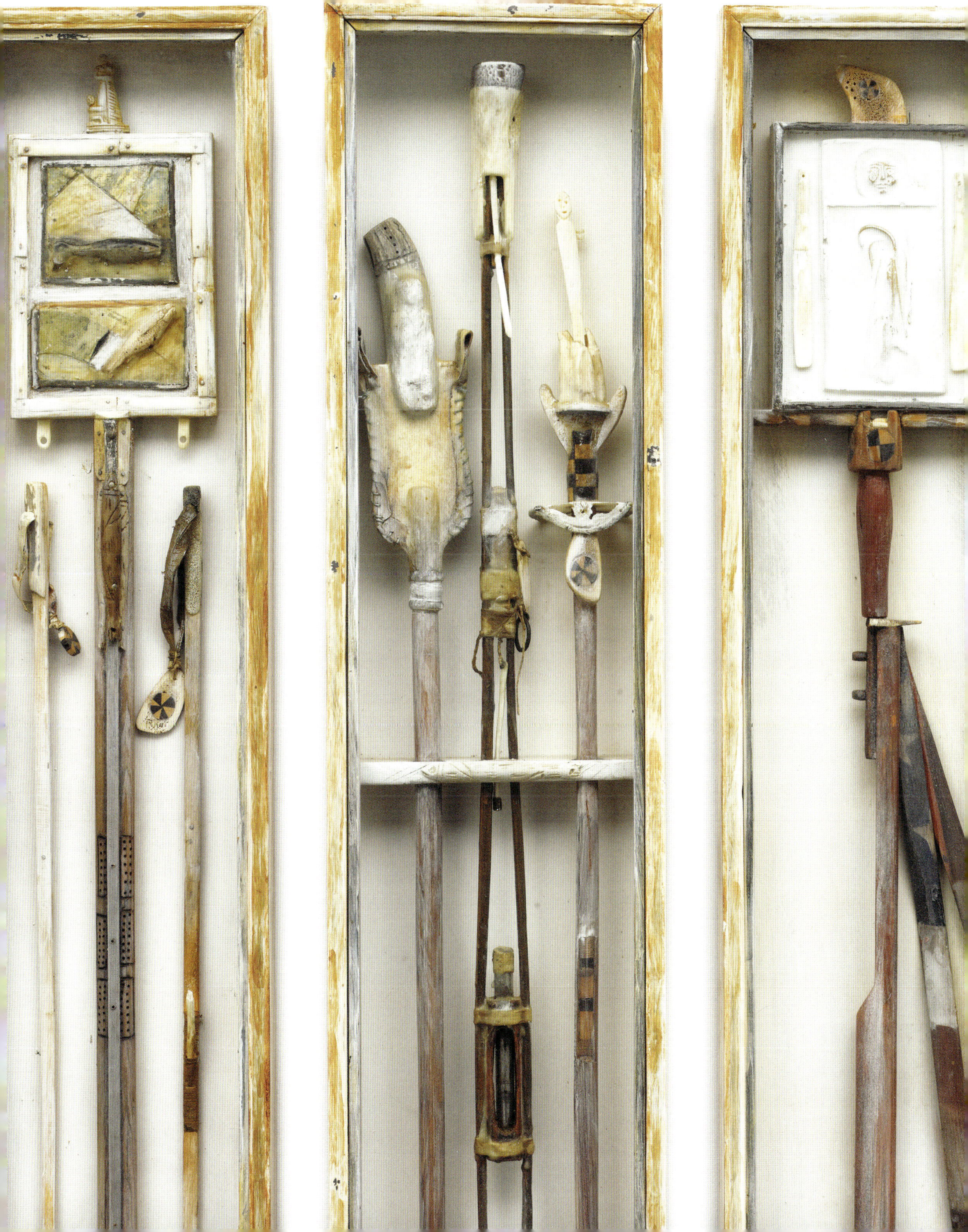

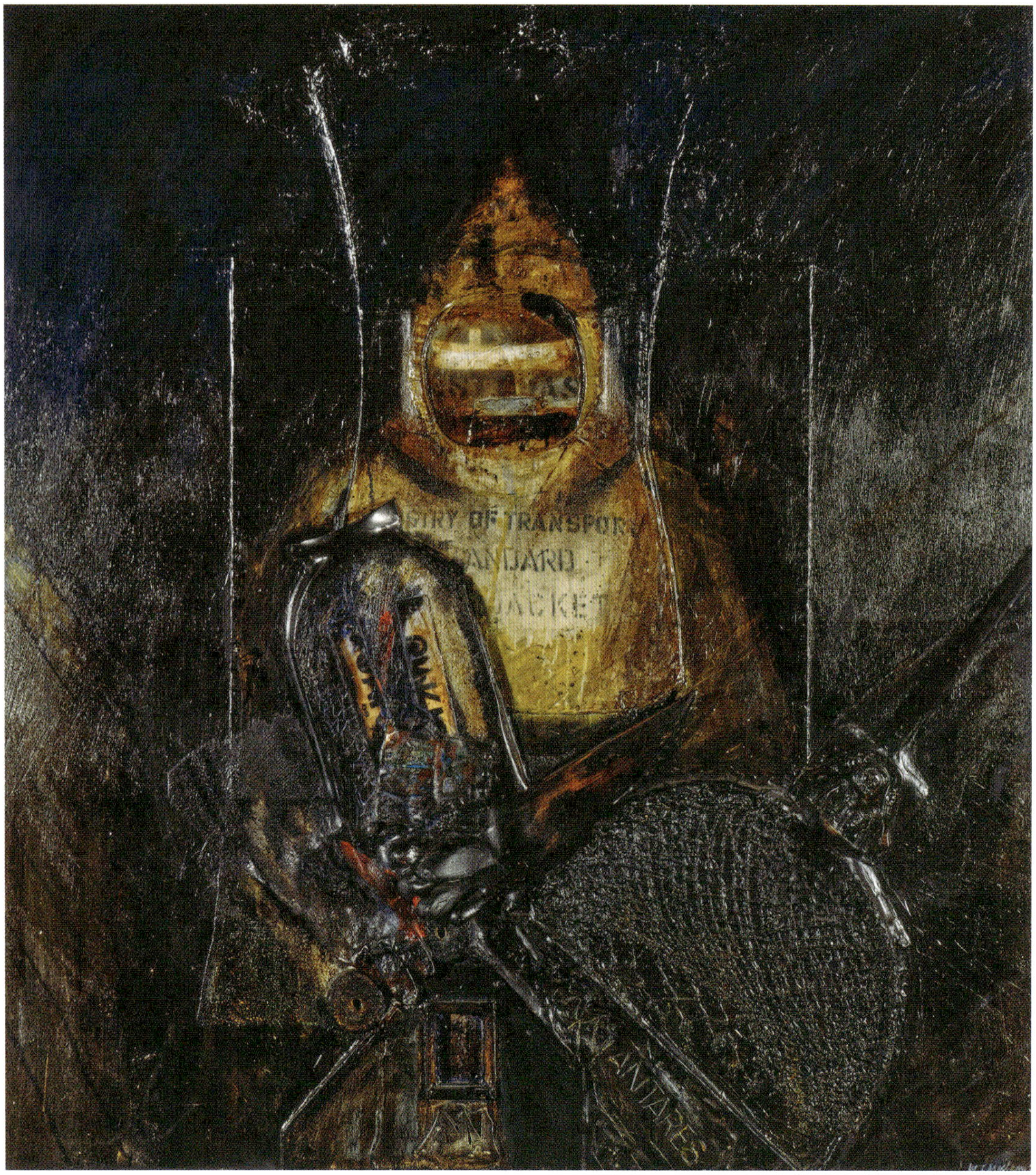

Skye Fisherman, in Memoriam · *1989, collage, found objects and acrylic on board, 129.5 x 119.5 x 6 cm* · *Dundee Art Galleries and Museums Collection*

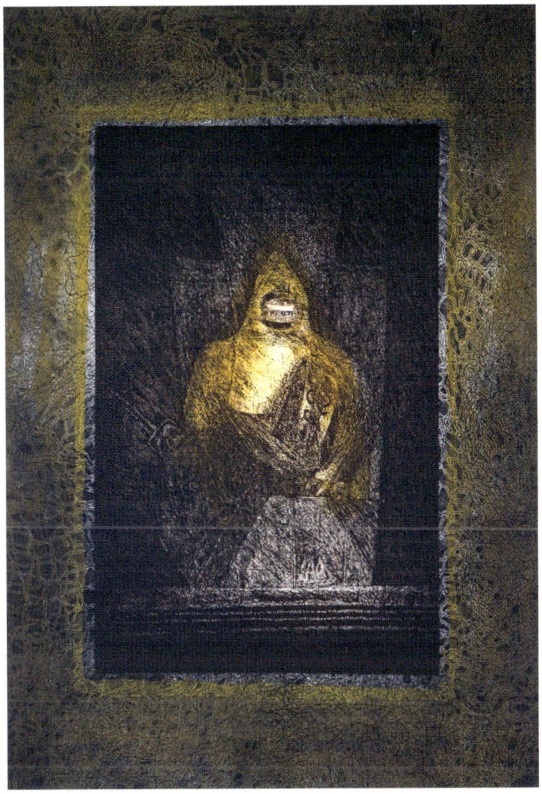

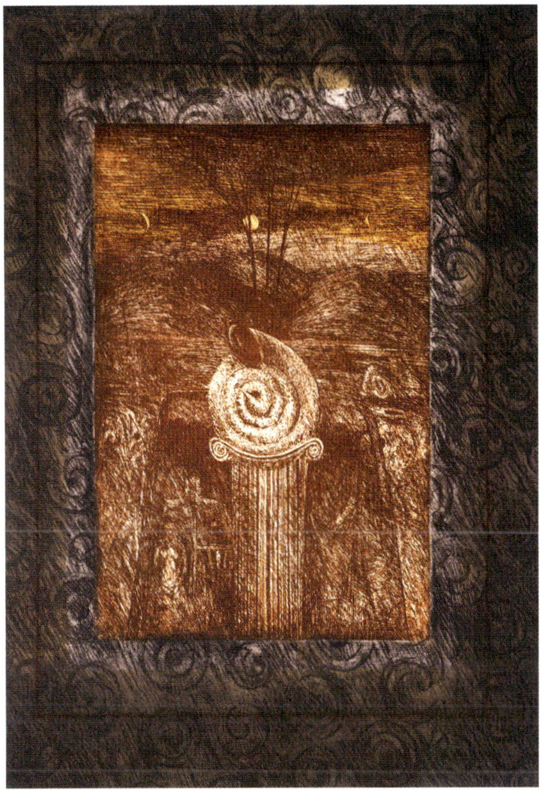

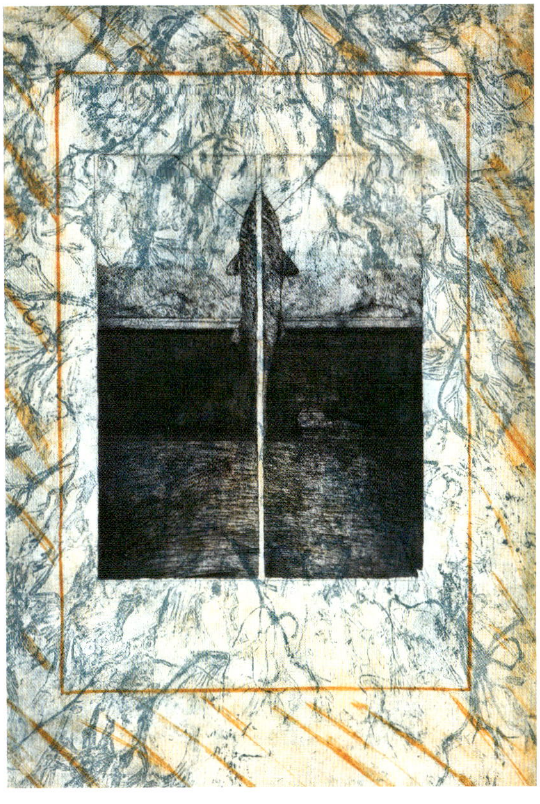

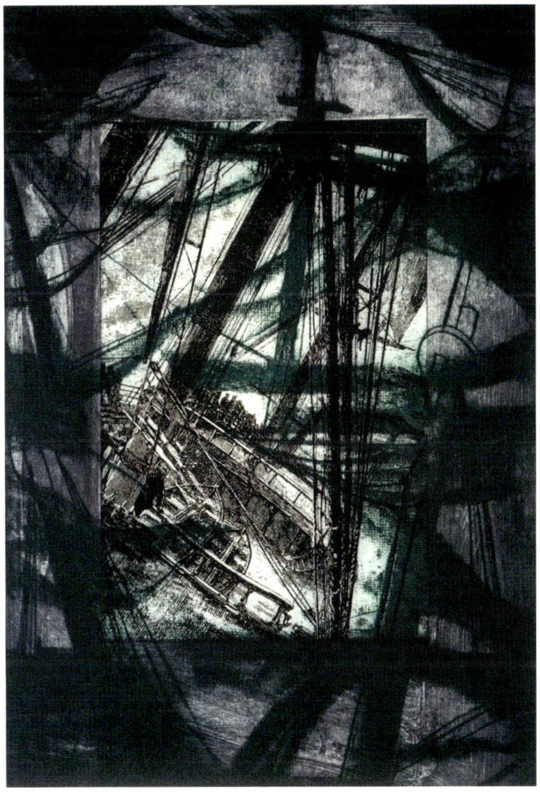

clockwise from top left · *Dancers* · *Trio* · *King's Fish* · *Adam's Clan*
1991, coloured etchings on paper, 80 x 55 cm; from ***A Night of Islands****, suite of 10* · *Royal Scottish Academy of Art and Architecture*

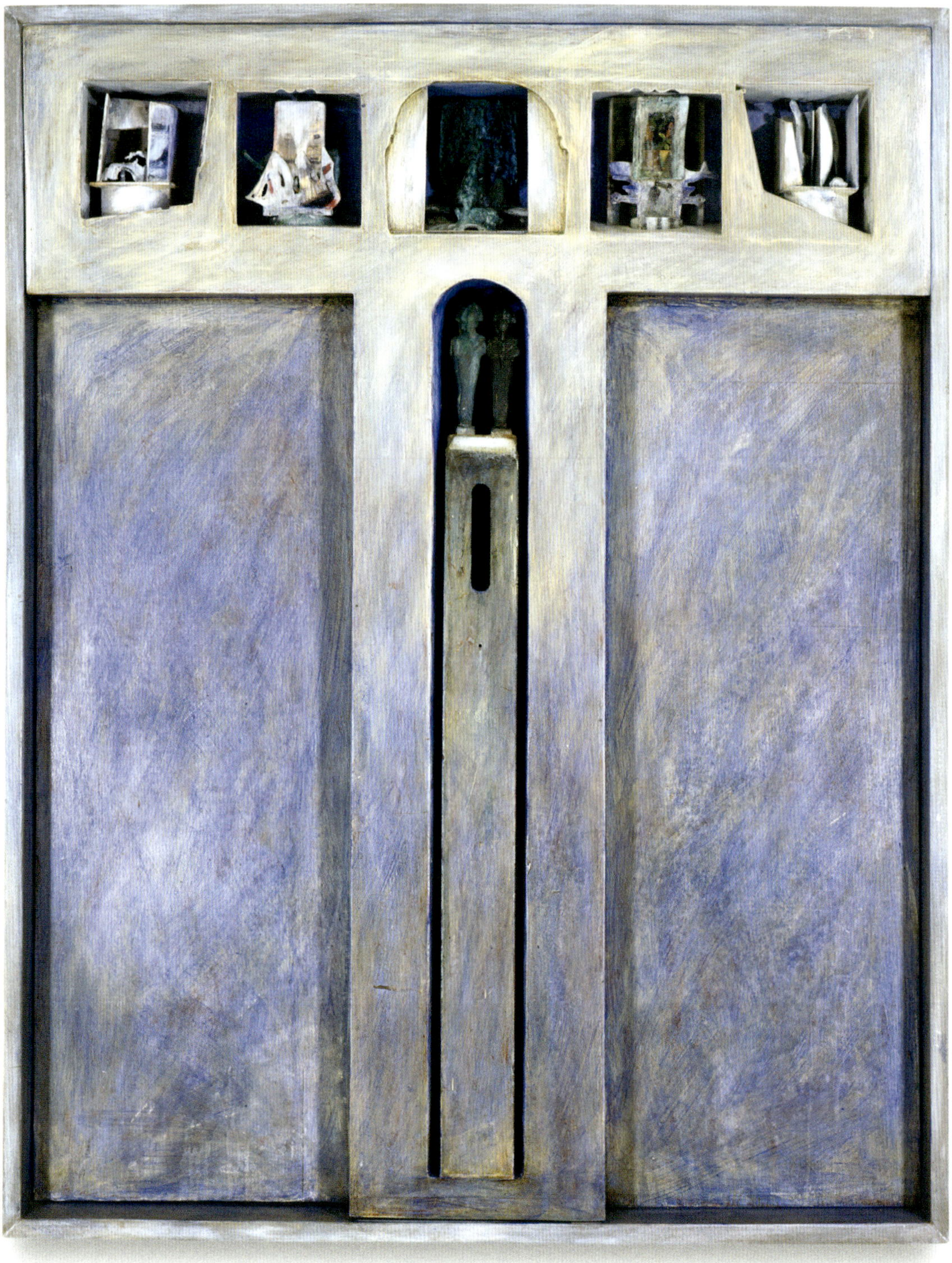

Boston T *· 1989, mixed-media construction, 115 x 93 x 10 cm · Royal Scottish Academy of Art and Architecture*

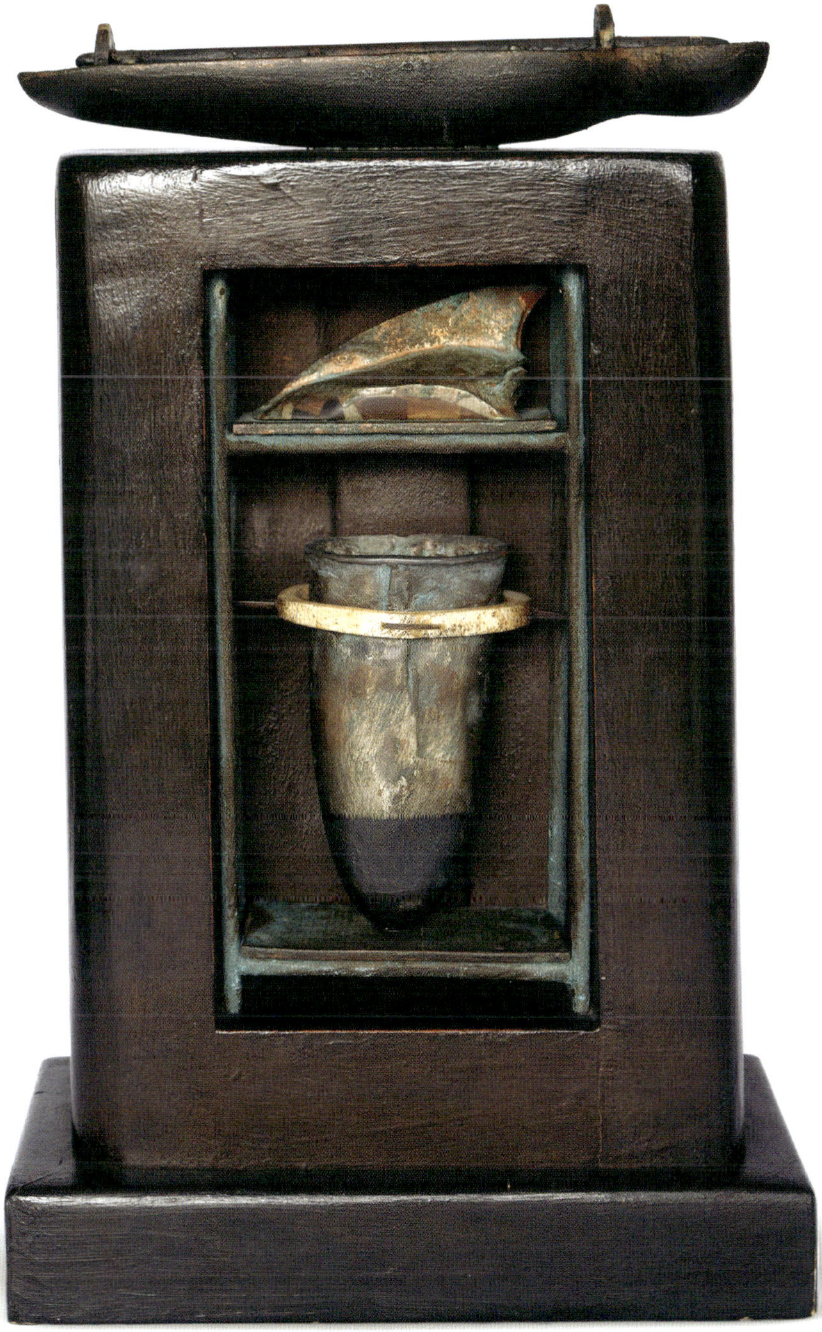

Museum Casket · *1989, painted wood, bone and lead, 44 x 28 x 14 cm* · *private collection; photograph Jim Mackie*

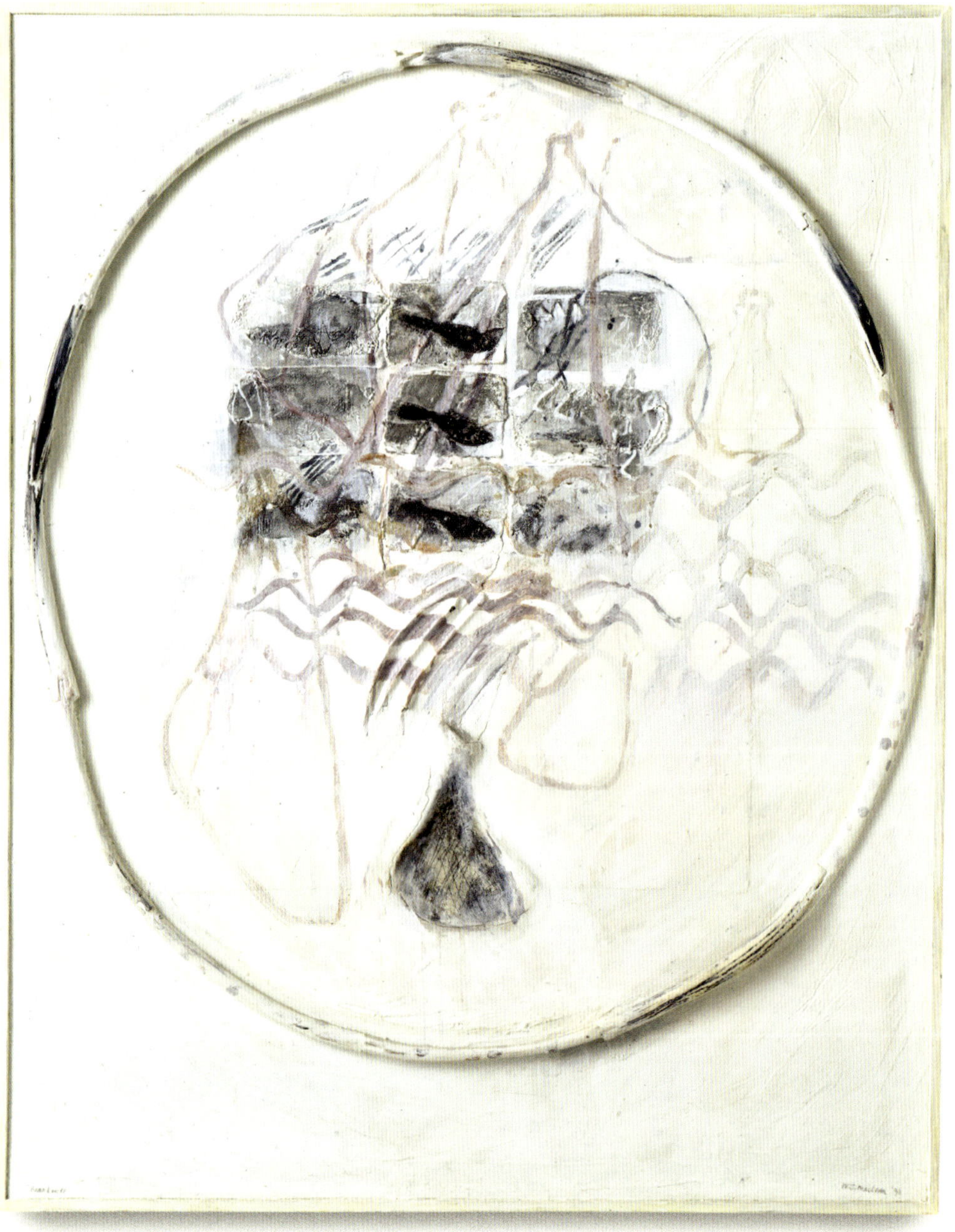

Bone Circle · *1990, mixed-media construction, 42 x 36 x 4 cm* · *Galerie Herold, Hamburg*

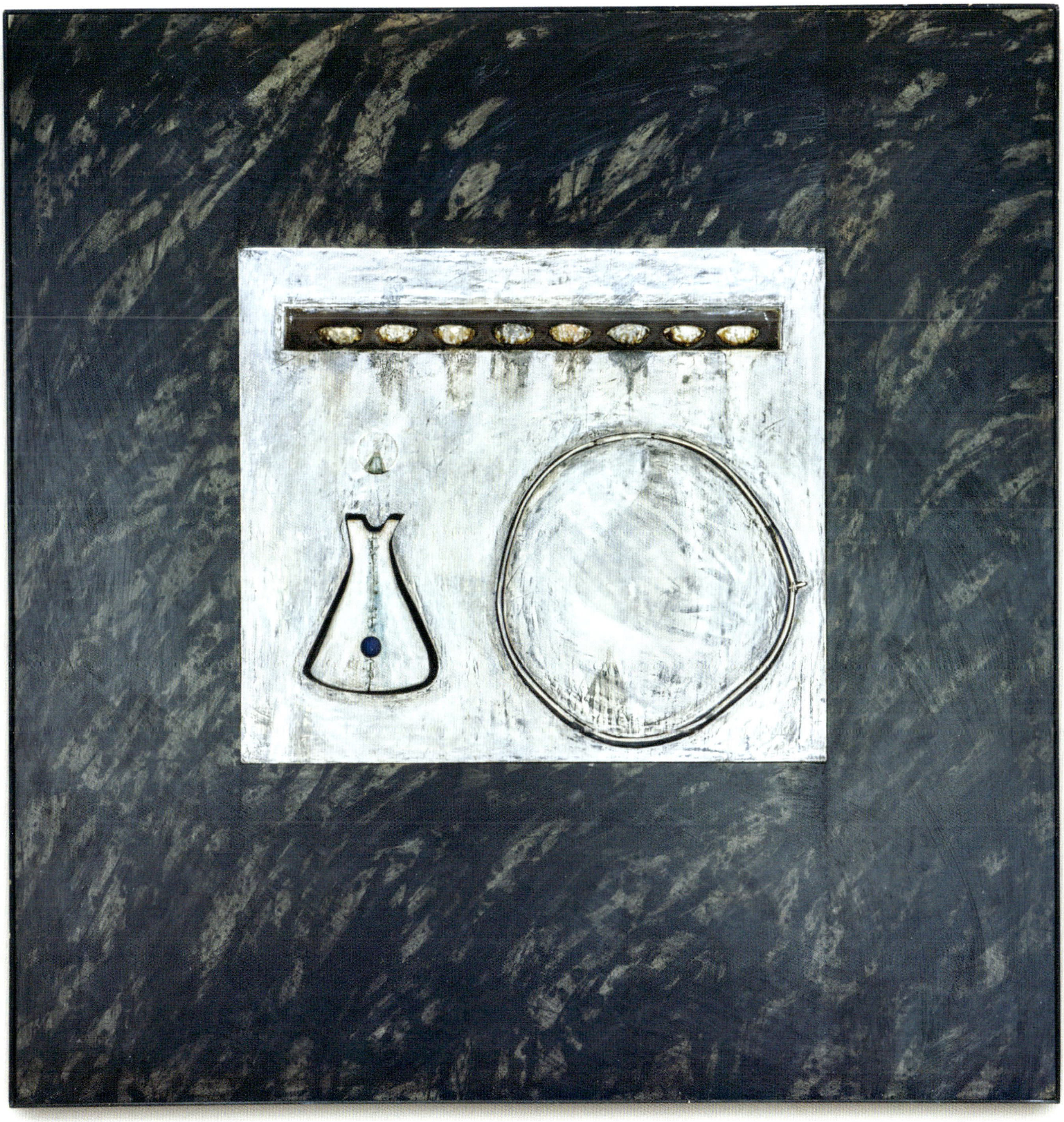

Diviner's Wall · *1992, mixed-media construction, 162 x 162 x 8 cm* · *private collection*

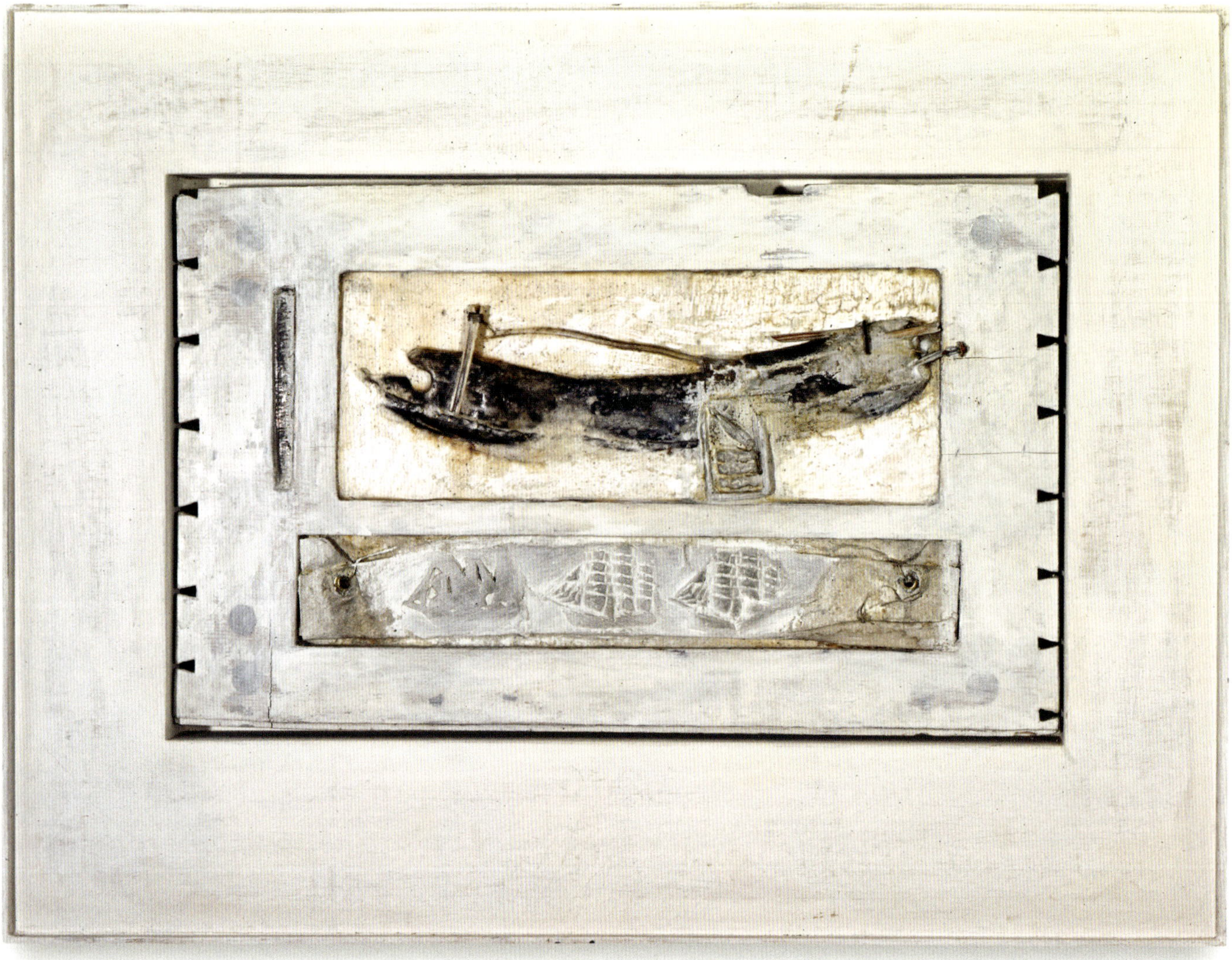

North West Passage, Arctic Route · *1994, mixed-media construction, 73 x 101 cm* · *The Fleming Collection*

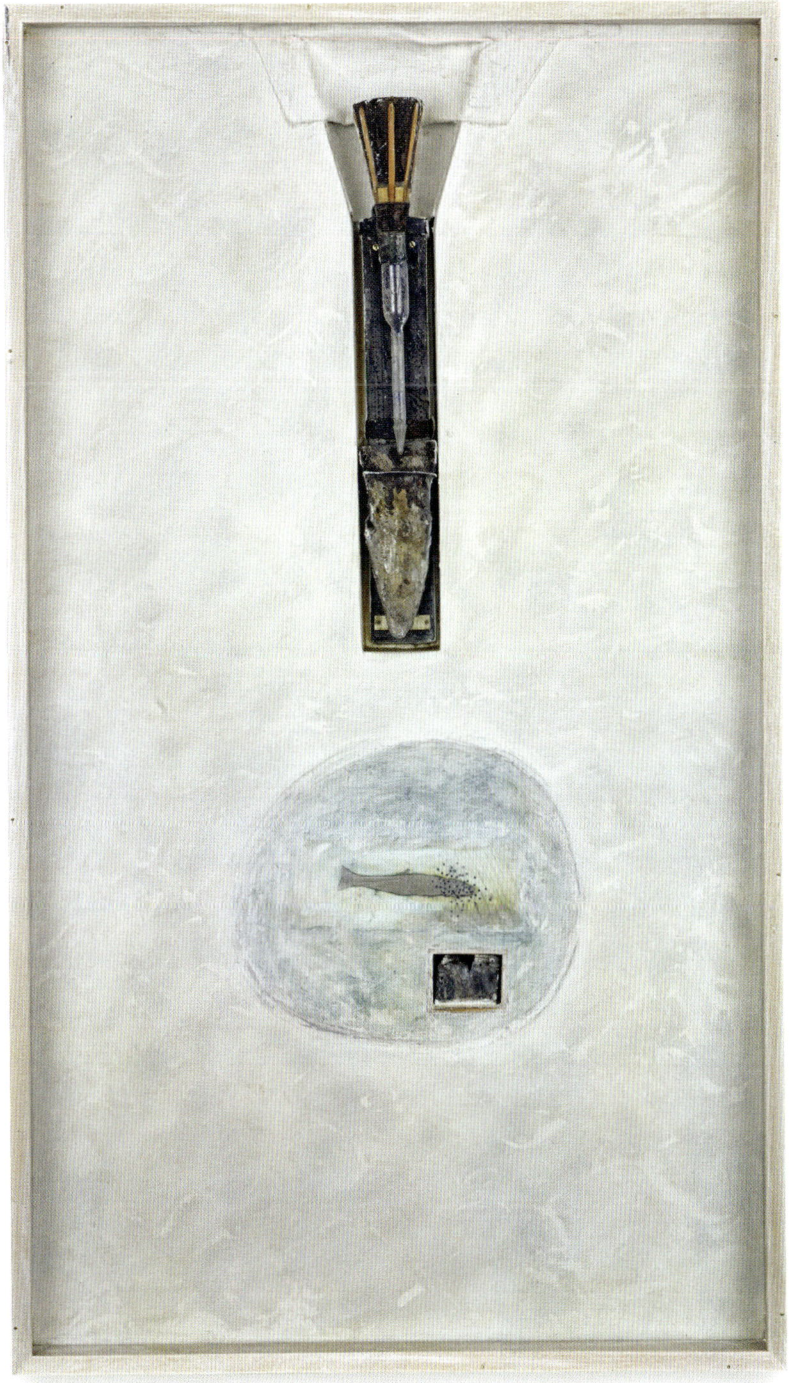

Ice Log · *1998, mixed media and found objects, 121 x 71 x 10 cm* · *private collection*

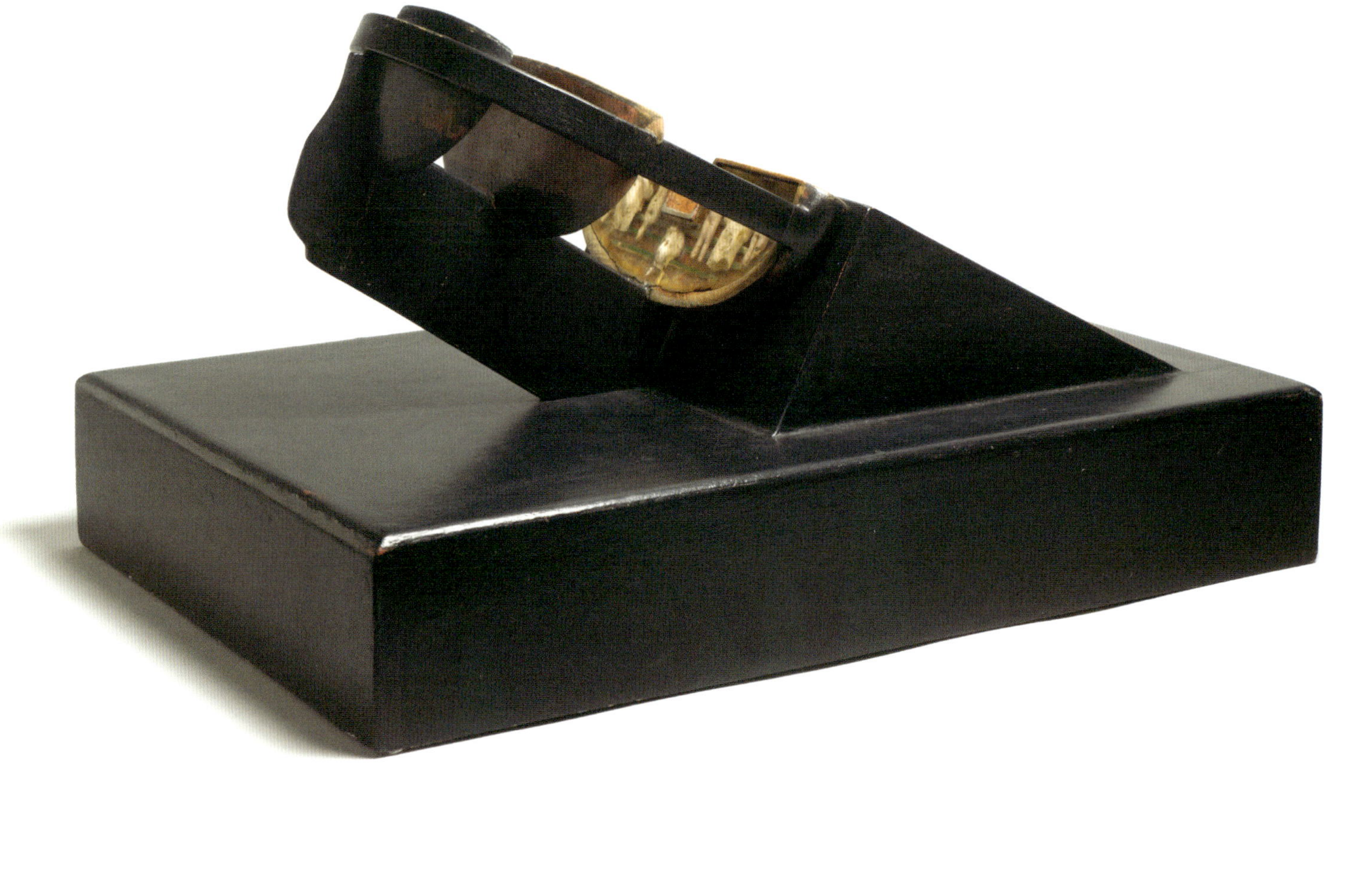

Black Vessel Foundering · *1994, painted wood, acrylic and found objects, 30 x 39 x 58 cm* · *Scottish Maritime Museum*

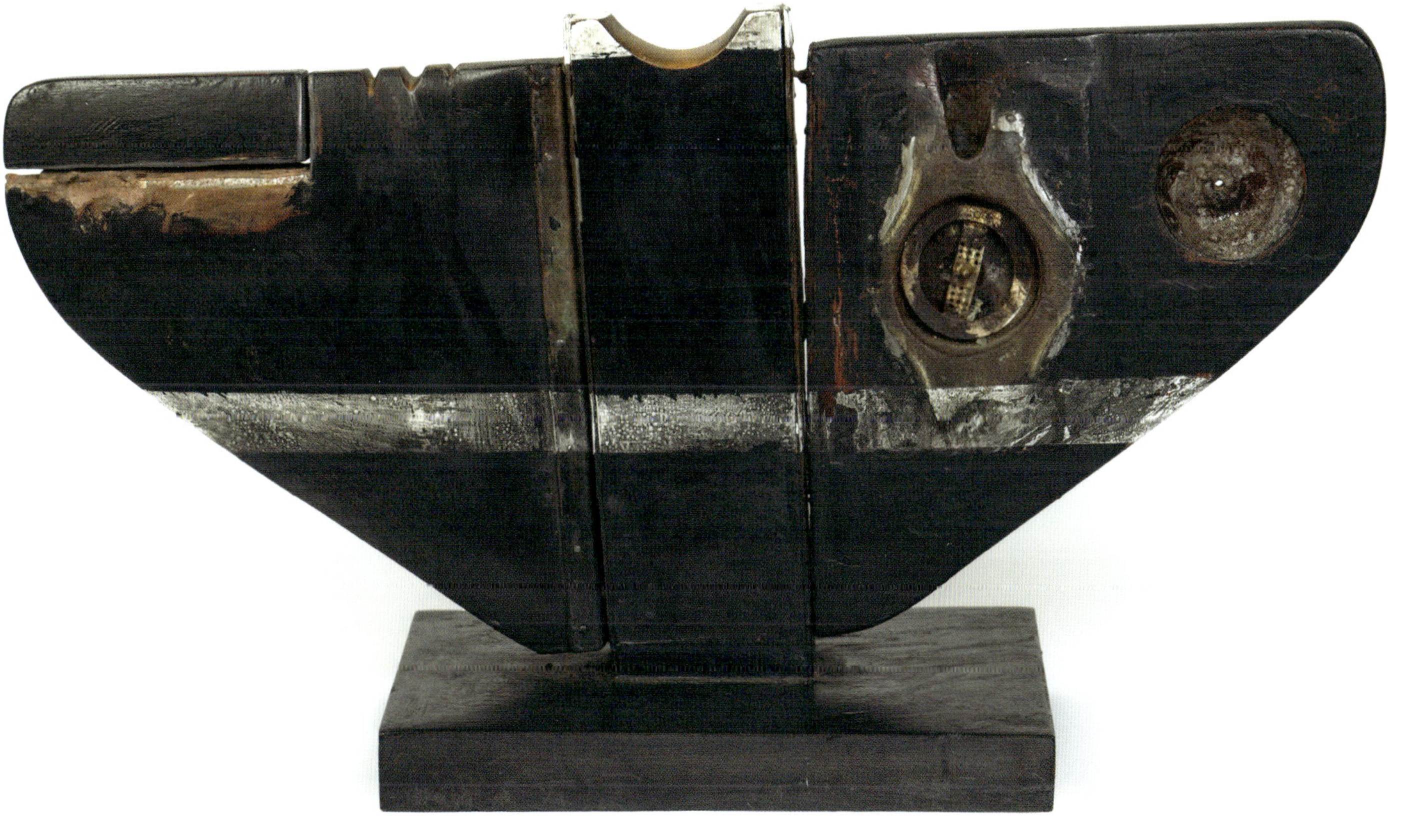

Transom *· 1993, painted wood, metal and bone, 30 x 58 x 39 cm · private collection; photograph Antonia Reeve*

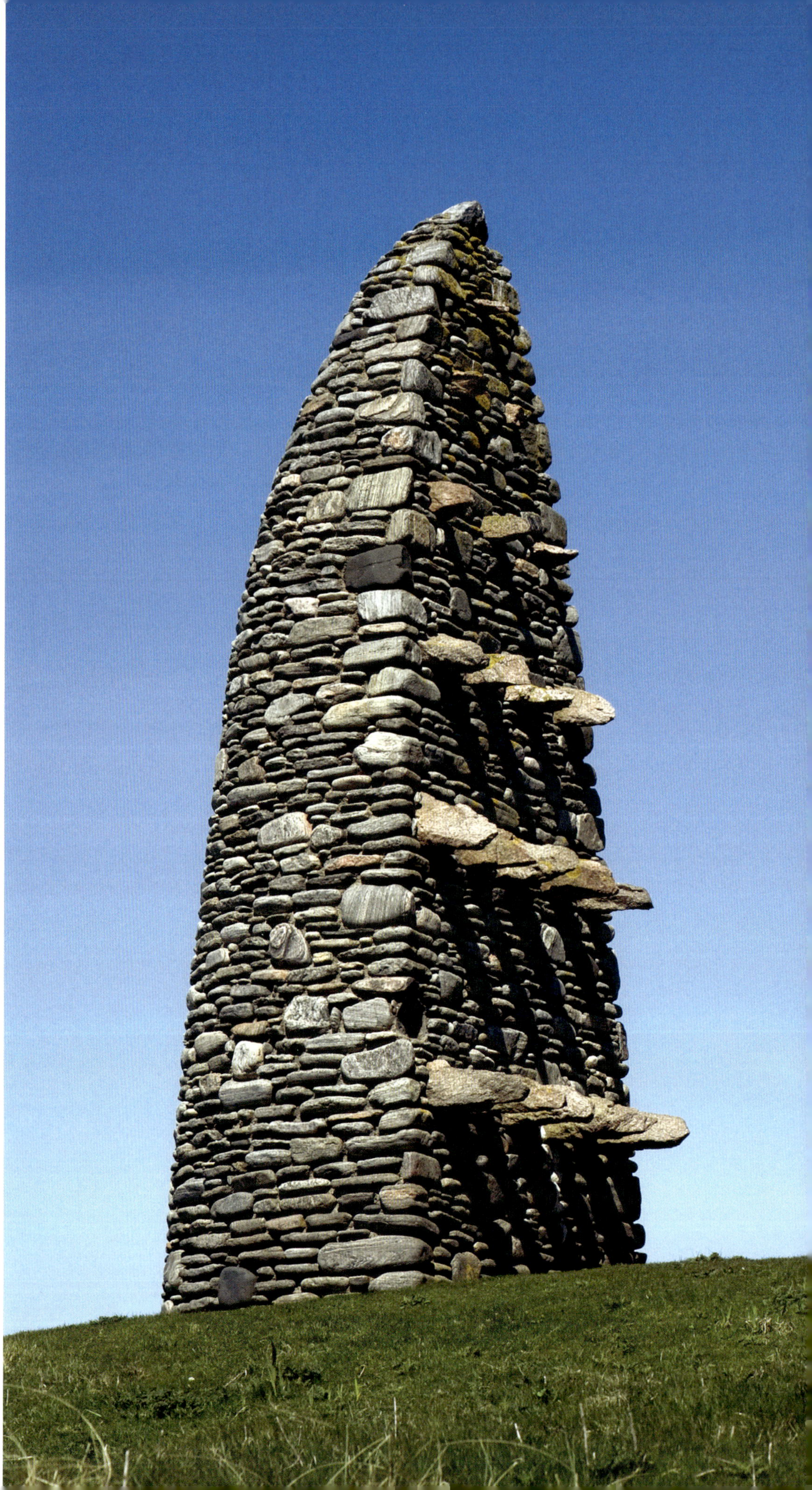

Aignish Memorial
Isle of Lewis; in collaboration with stonemason James Crawford, 1996
photograph Robin Gillanders

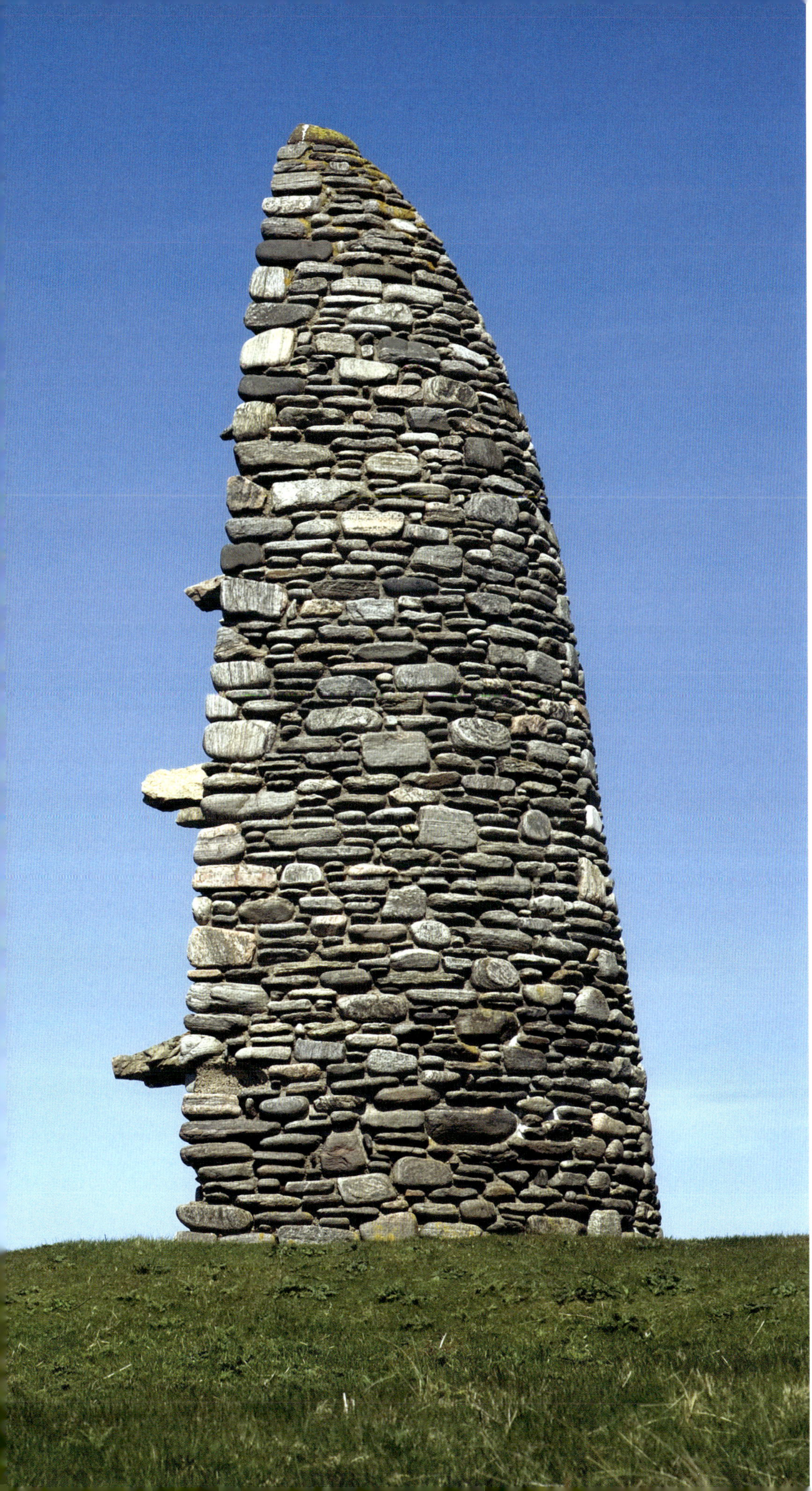

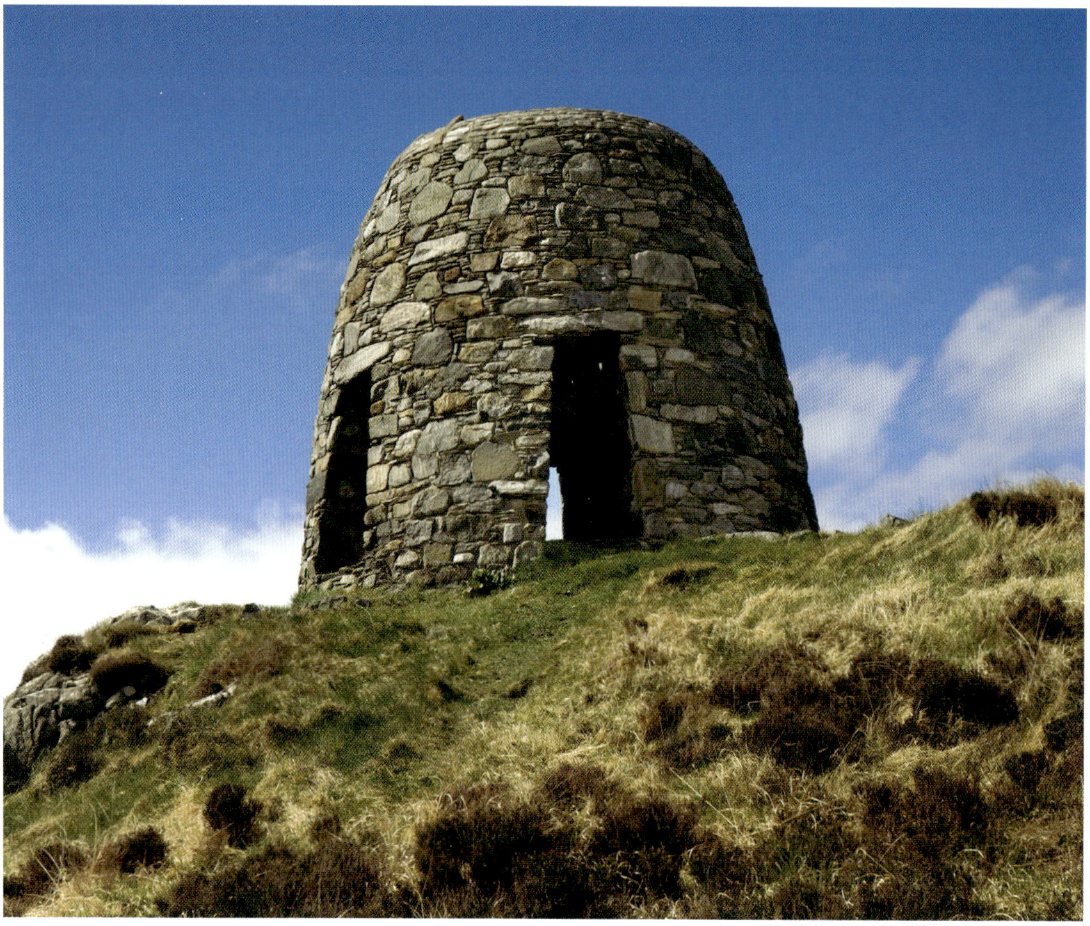

Balallan Memorial · *Isle of Lewis; in collaboration with stonemason James Crawford, 1994* · *photograph Robin Gillanders*

Gress Memorial · *Isle of Lewis; in collaboration with stonemason James Crawford, 1996* · *photograph Robin Gillanders*

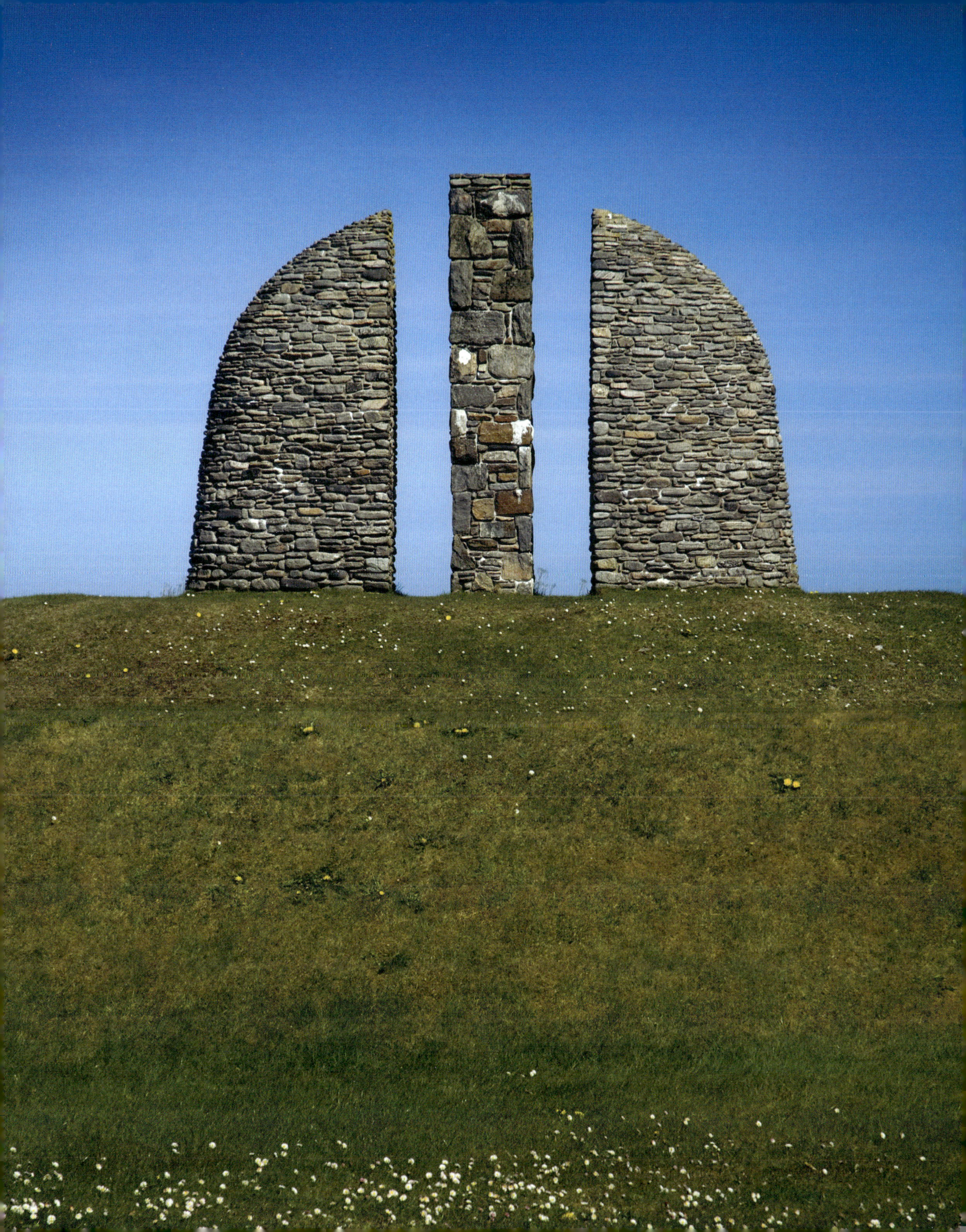

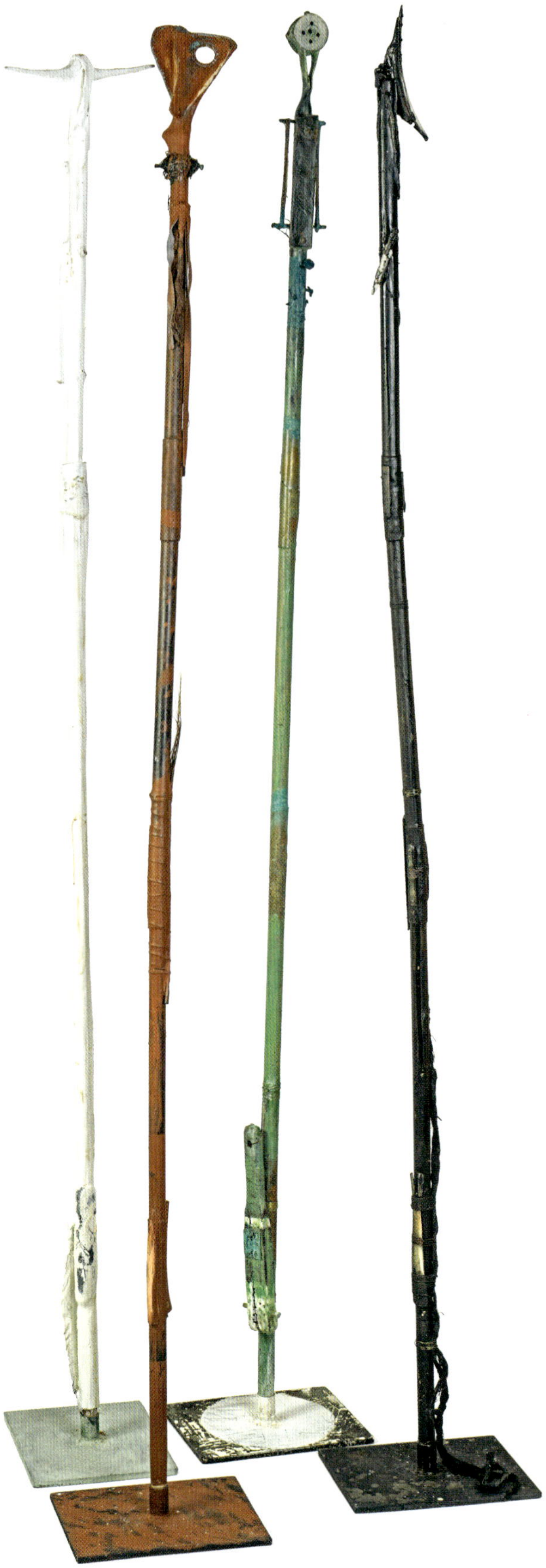

Rudder Guardians · *1999, mixed media, 4 pieces each 169 cm high* · *private collection, photograph Antonia Reeve*

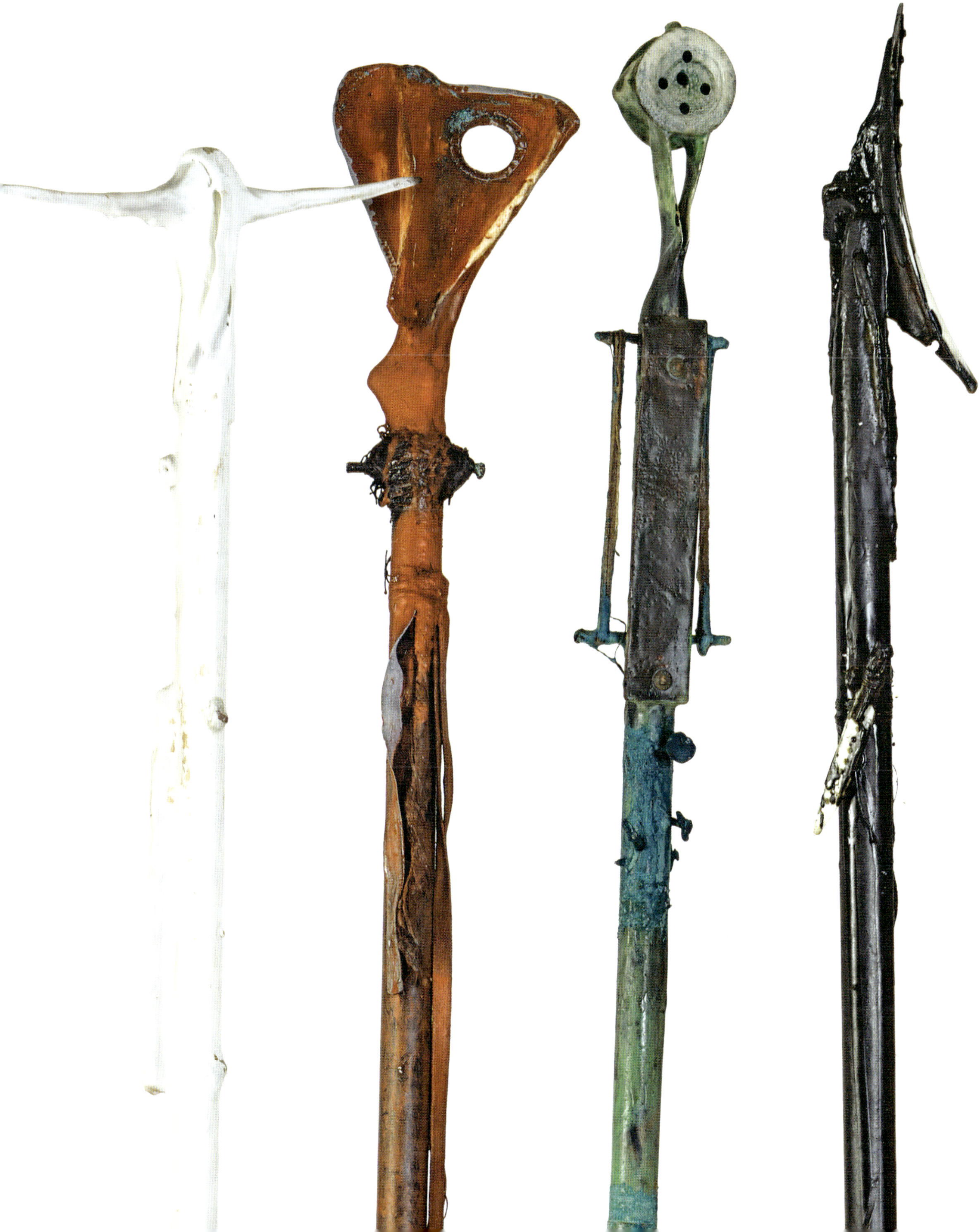

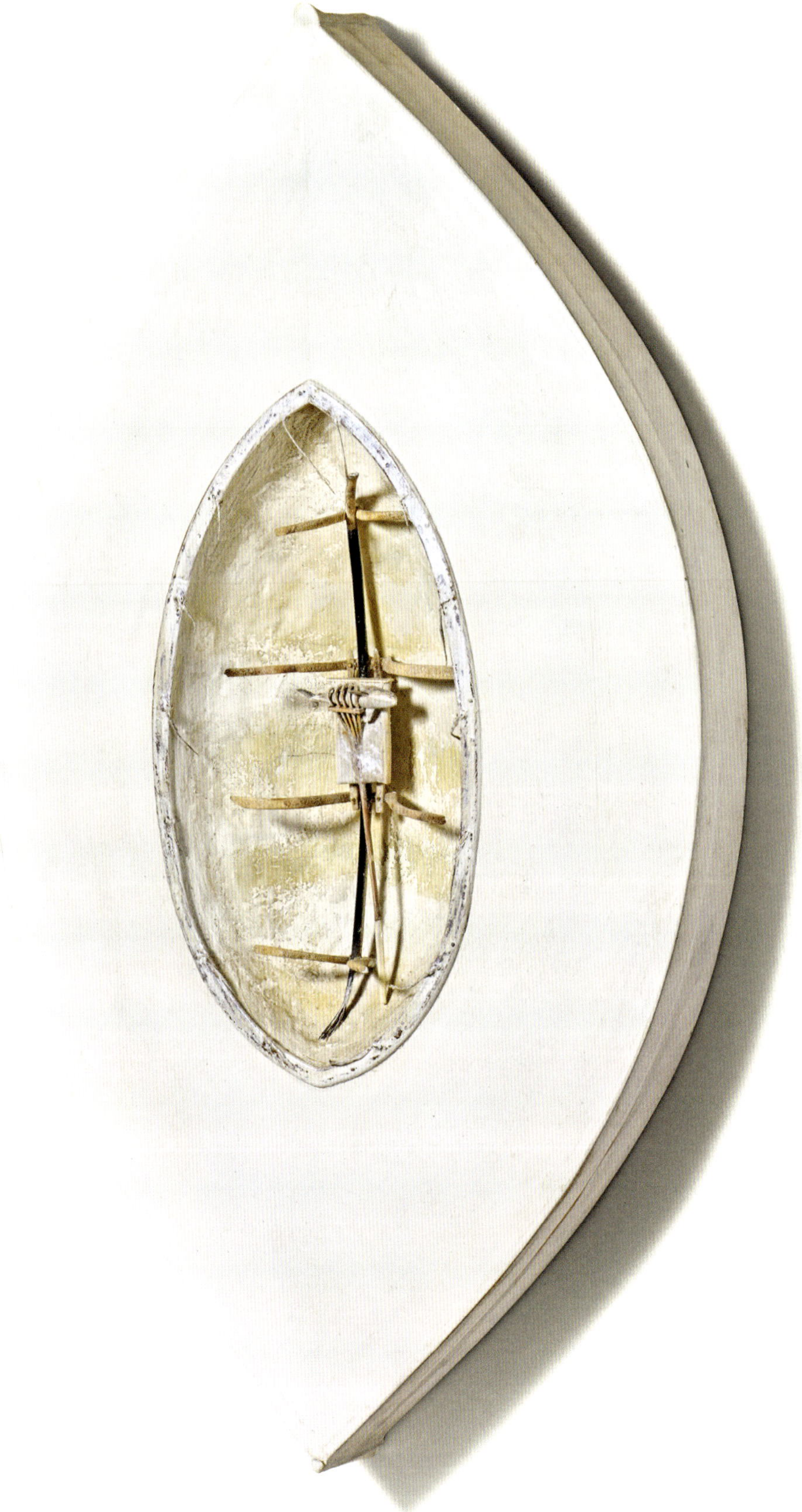

Nautilus Aground · *1998, found objects and mixed media, 99 x 58 x 10 cm* · *private collection, London*

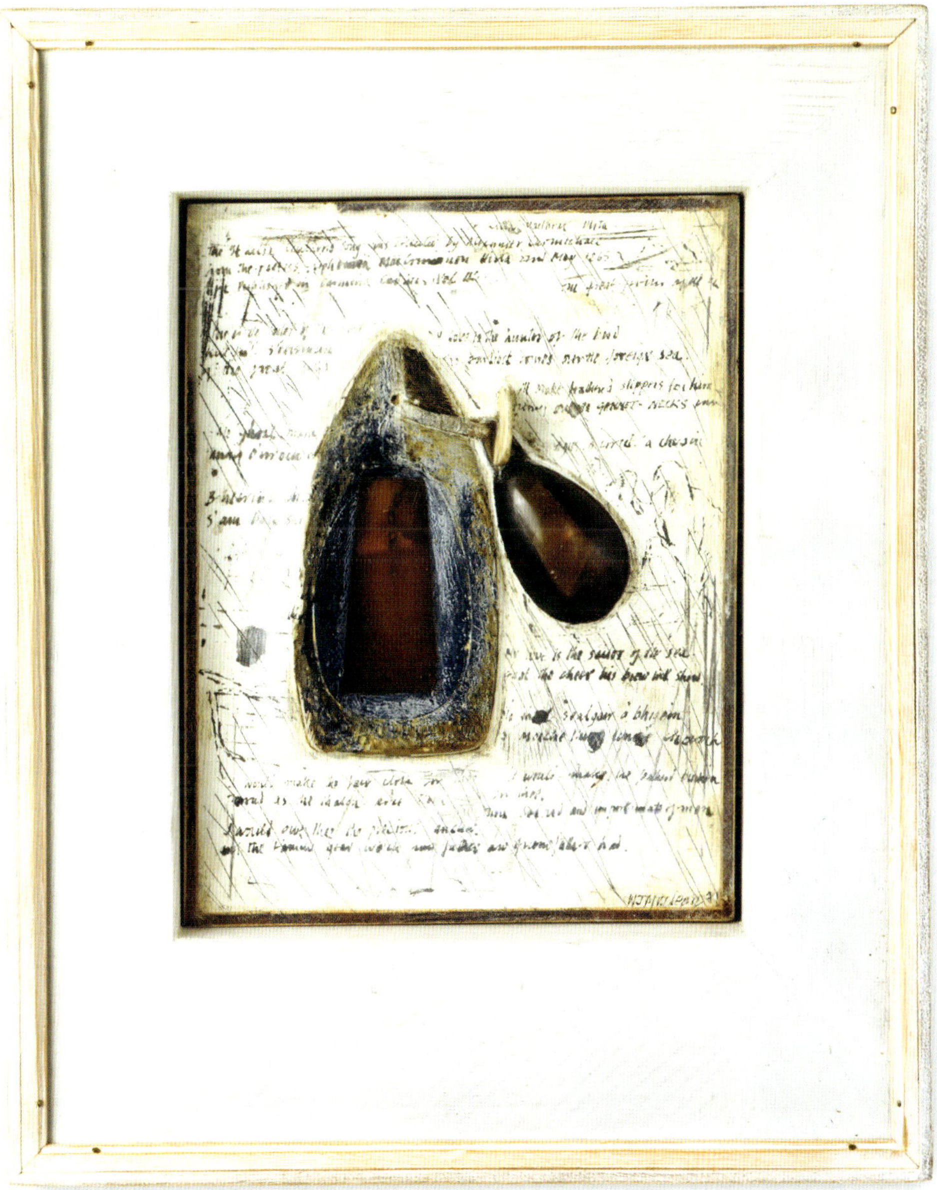

Ocean Letter · *1999, mixed-media construction, 43 x 35 x 6 cm* · *private collection, London*

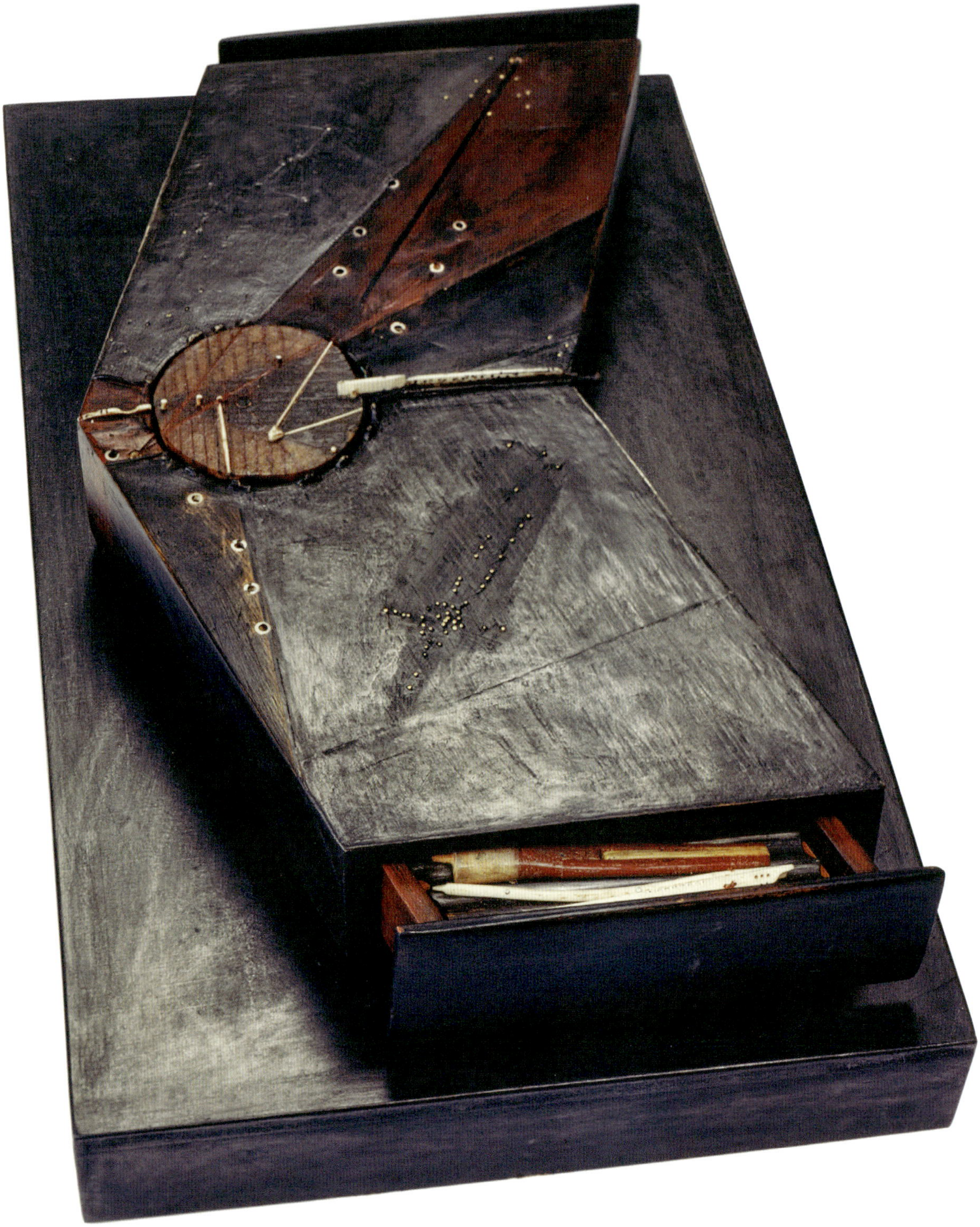

Alignment Receiver/Calanais · *1994–2008, mixed-media sculpture, 45 x 77 x 11 cm* · *private collection*

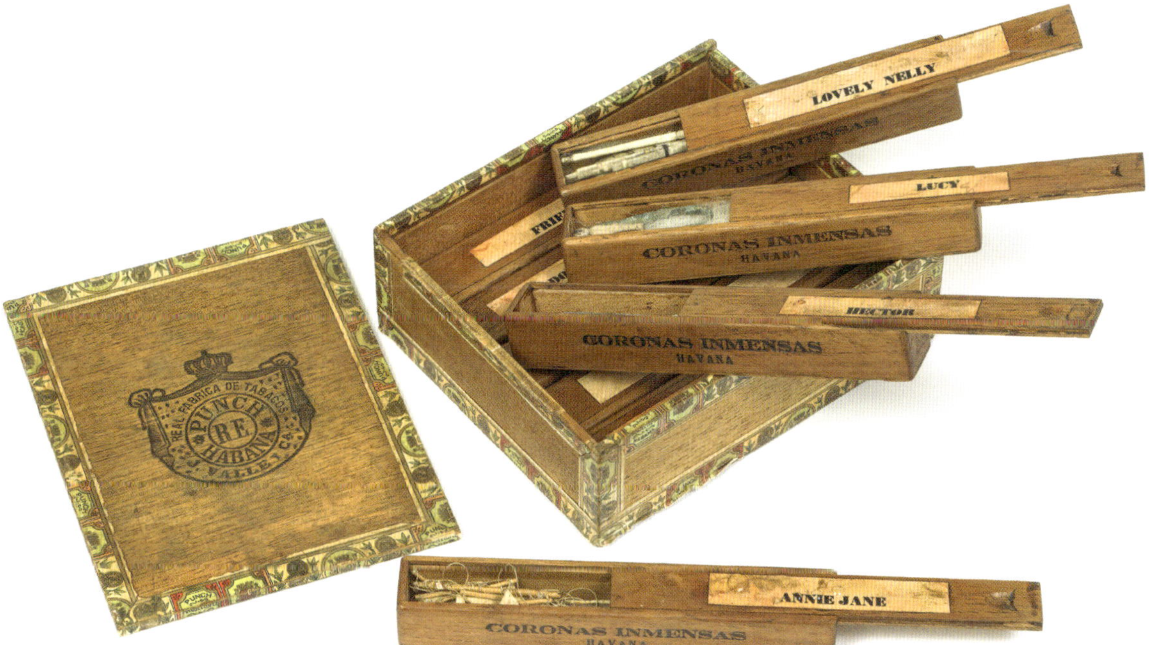

Manifest Box · *2002, found objects and acrylic, 6 x 15 x 18 cm* · *private collection*

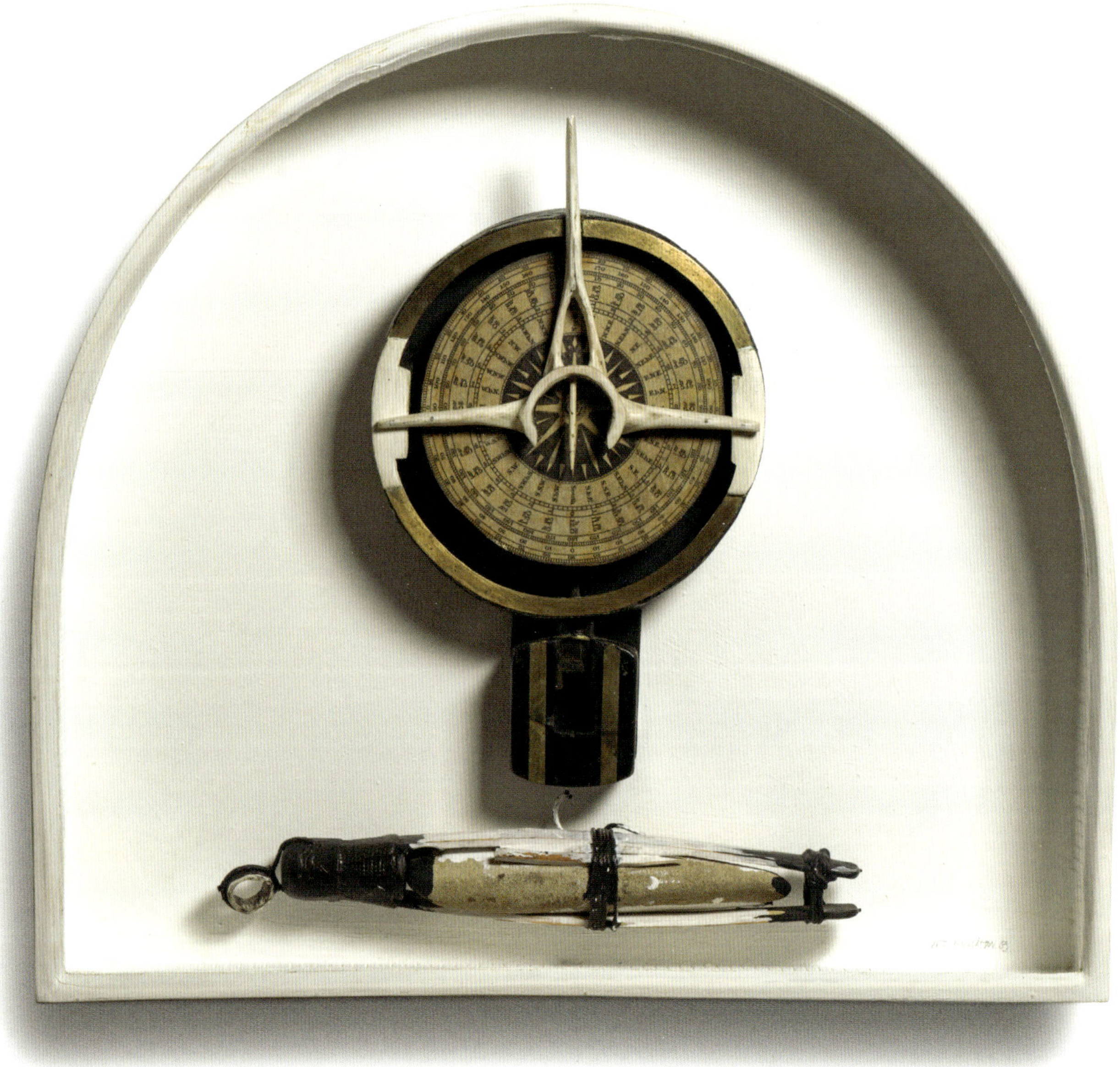

The Navigator's Museum — Stone Log · *2003, mixed media and found objects, 46 x 52 x 9 cm* · *Ian Mayes QC; photograph Antonia Reeve*

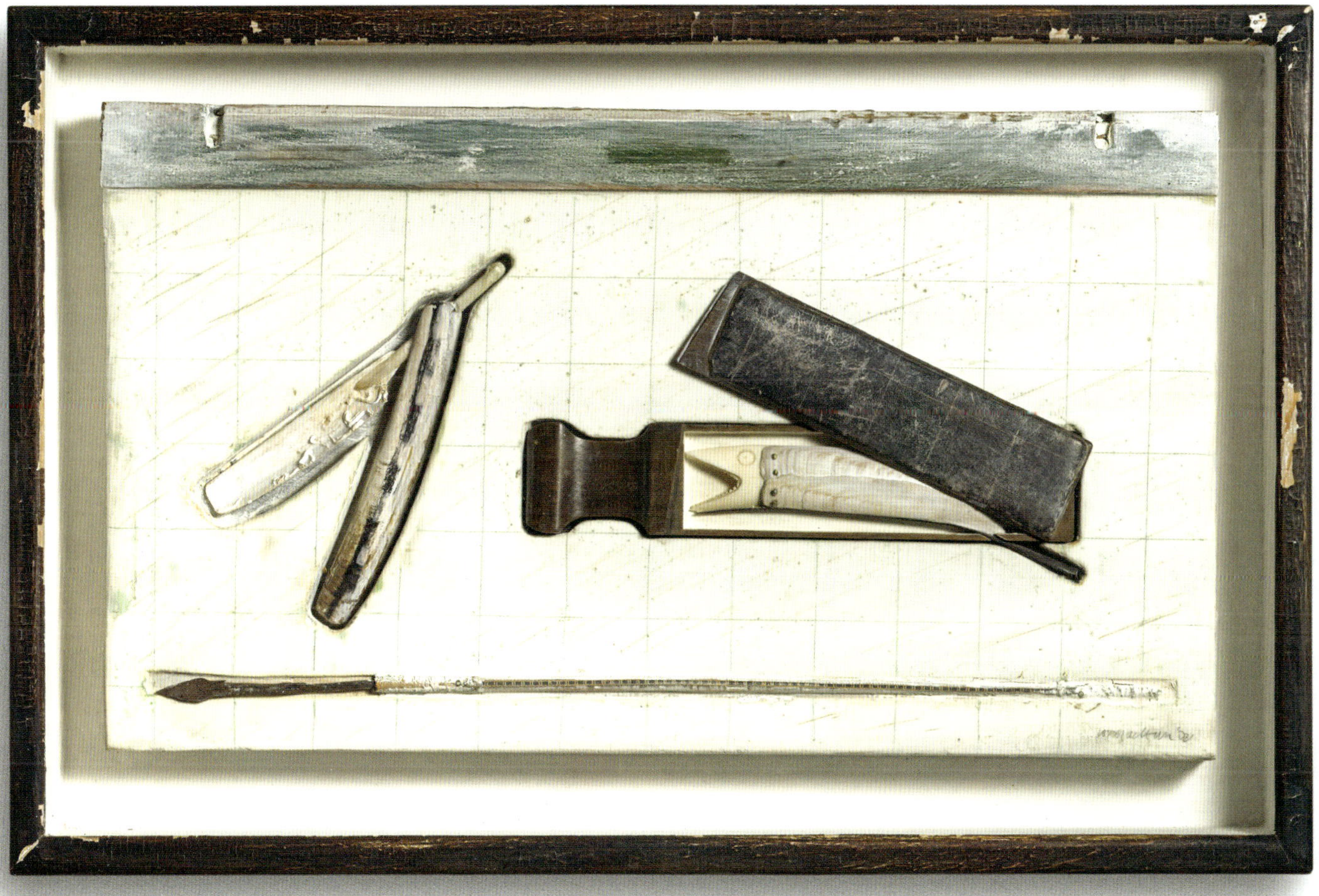

First Contact · *2003, mixed media and found objects, 38 x 60 x 7 cm* · *Ian Mayes QC; photograph Antonia Reeve*

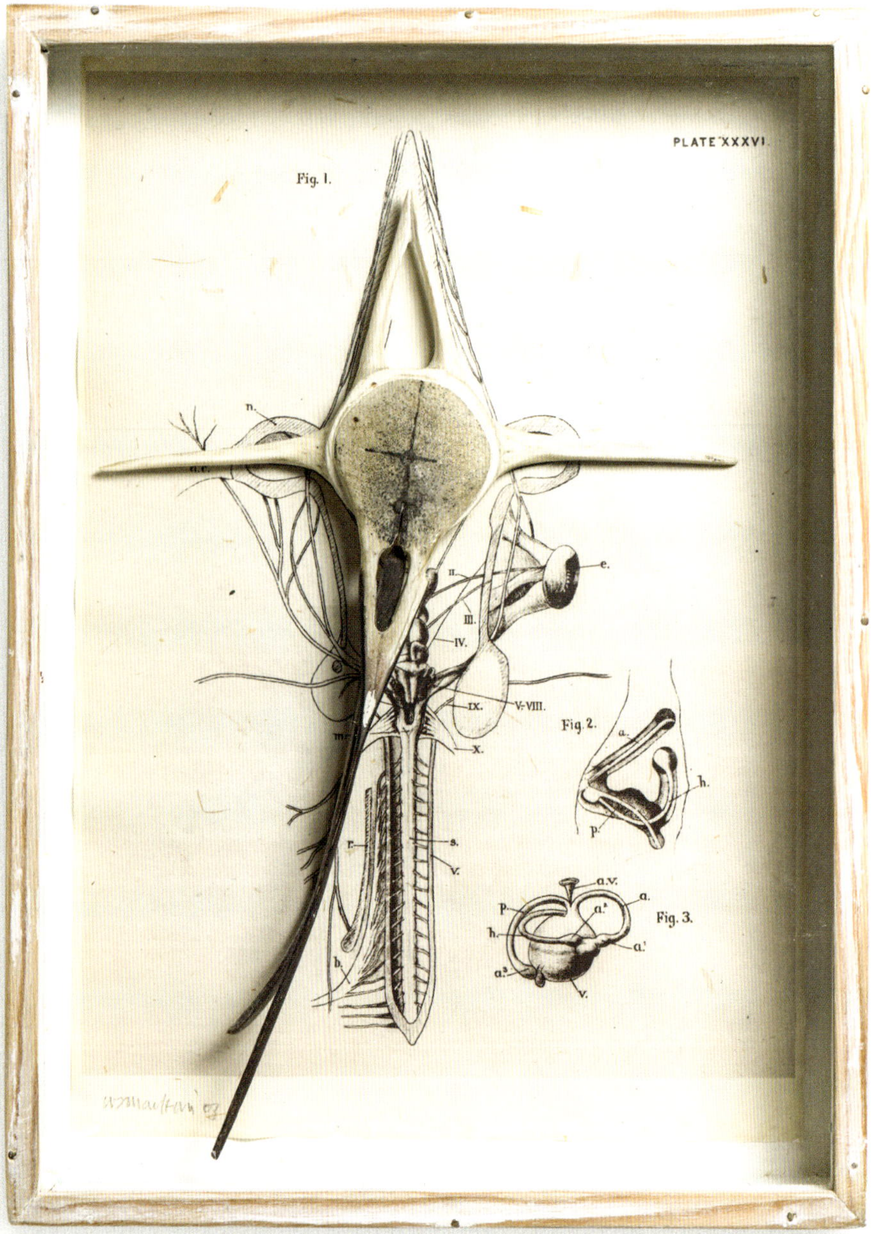

Natural History of the Skate Fig 2 · *2004, found objects and mixed media, 32 x 24 x 5 cm* · *private collection; photograph Antonia Reeve*

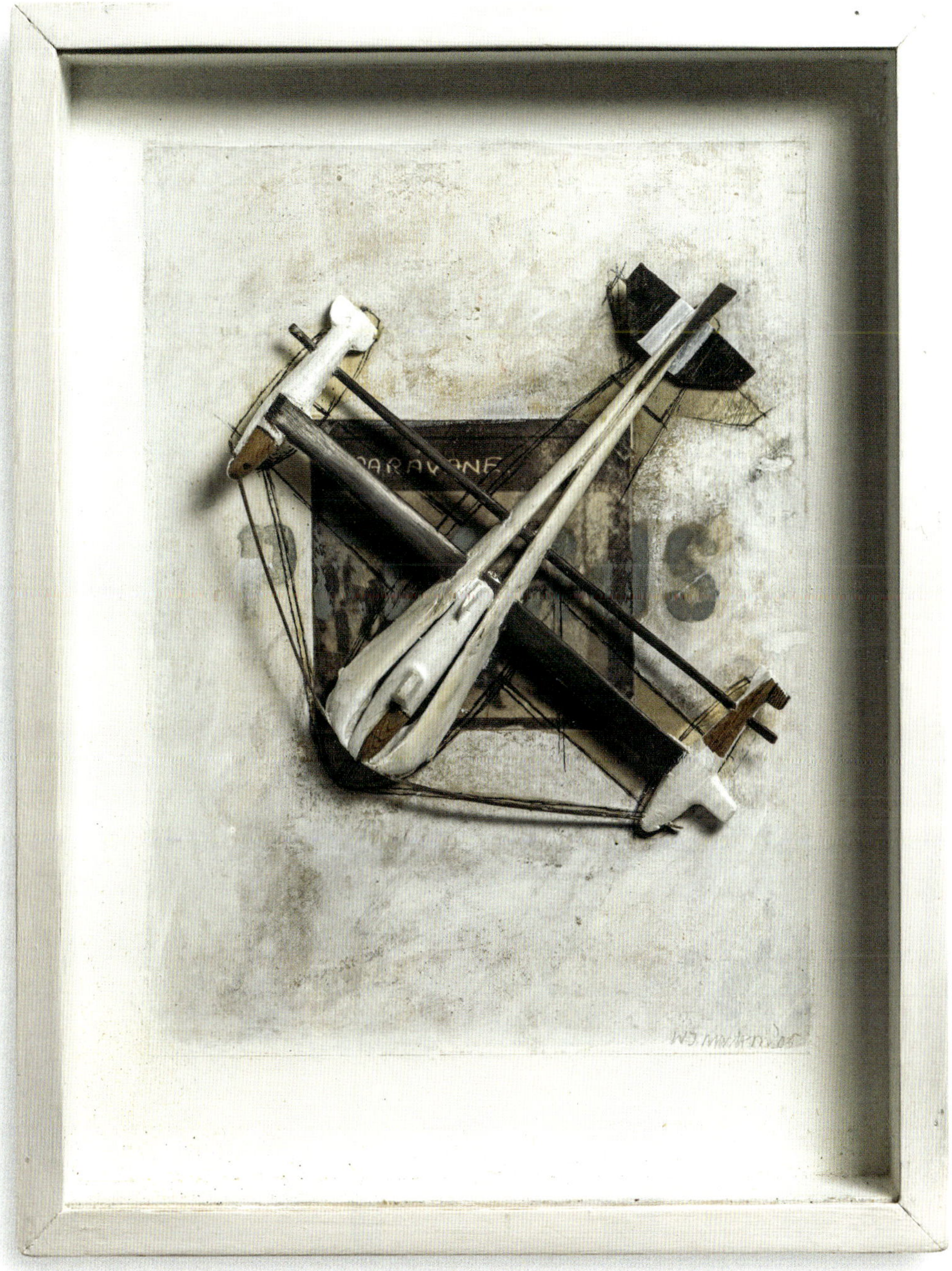

Sulidae Torpedo · *2005, mixed-media and found objects, 35 x 28 x 6 cm* · *private collection; photograph Antonia Reeve*

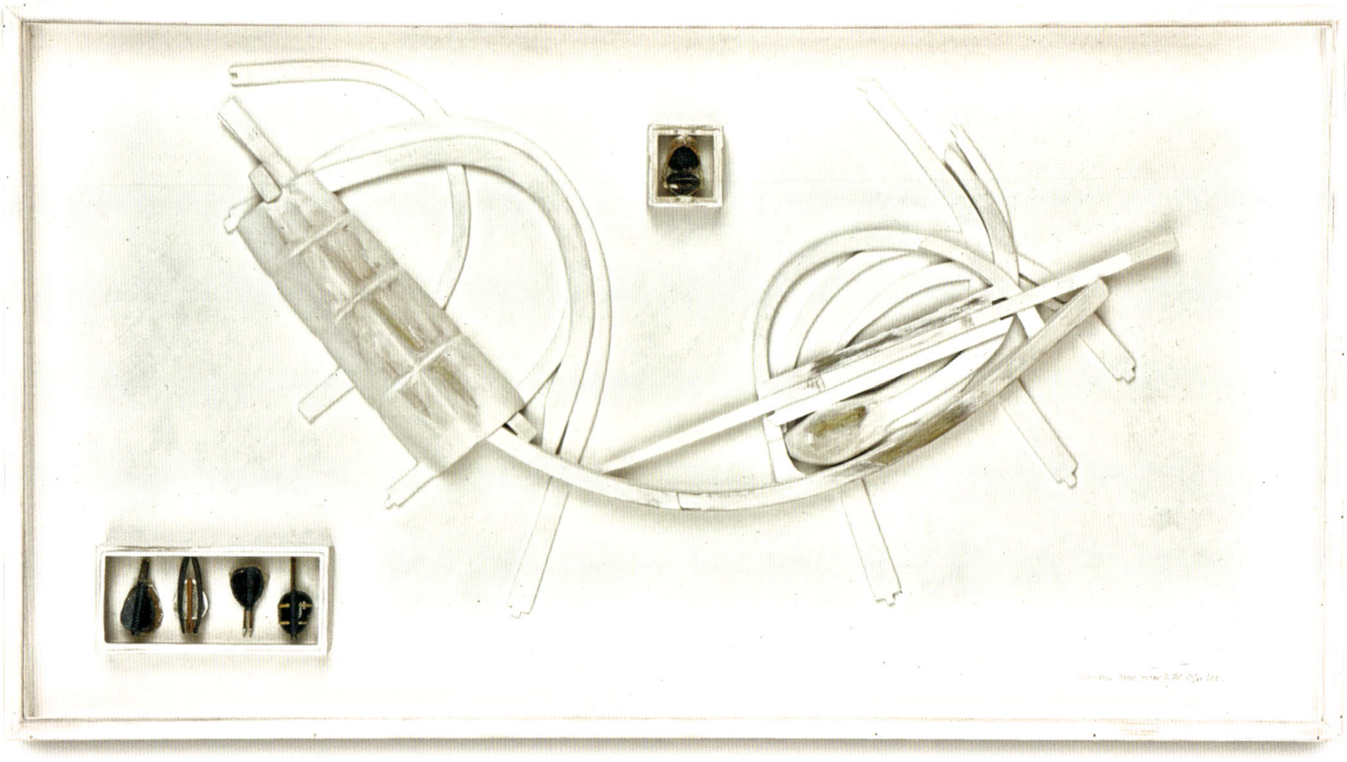

Franklin's Second Journey to the Polar Sea · 2003, mixed-media construction, 62 x 118 x 8 cm · private collection

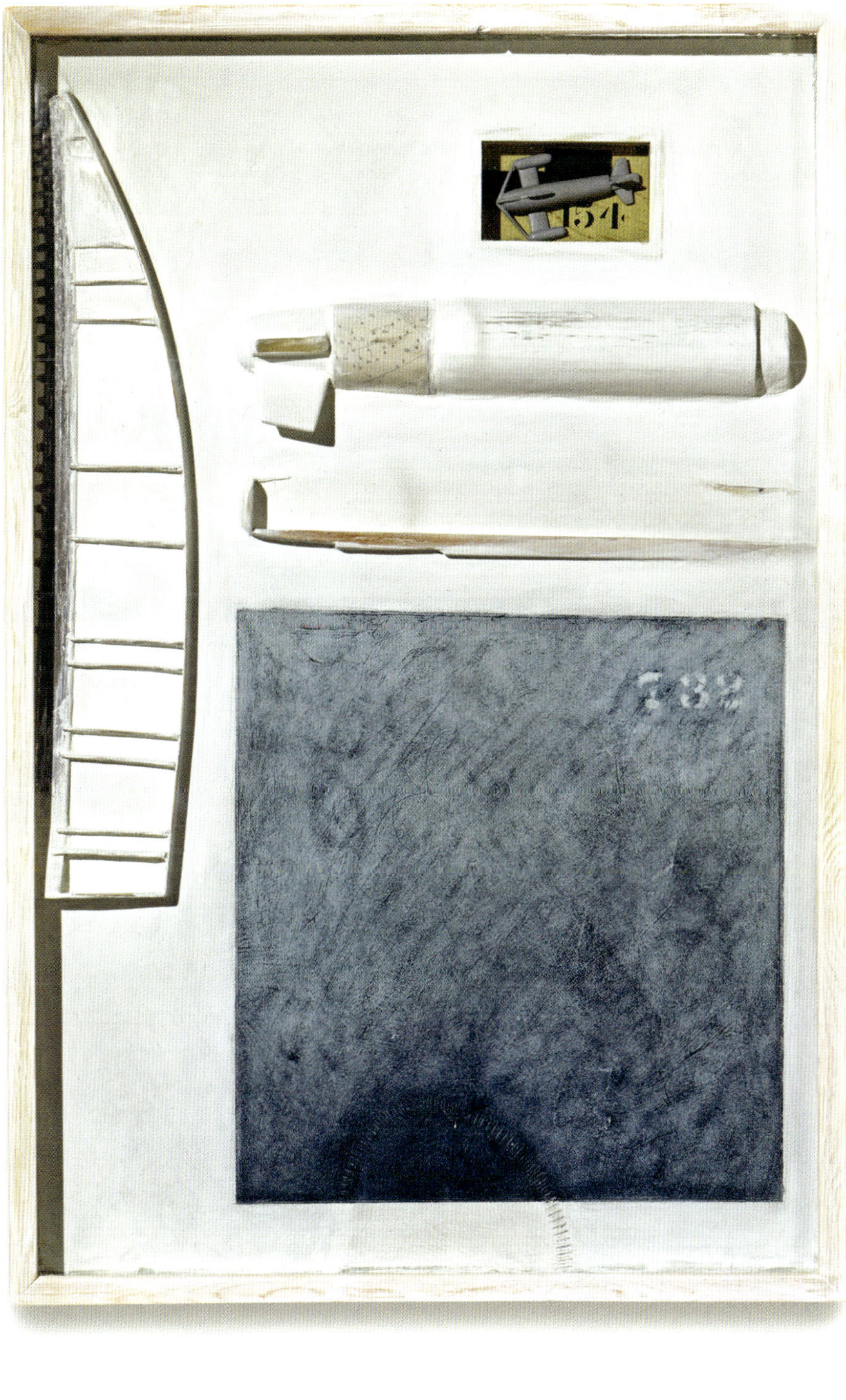

Navigator's Museum: Instructions for Coastwatchers 1 · *2004, mixed-media construction, 94 x 63 x 10 cm* · *private collection*

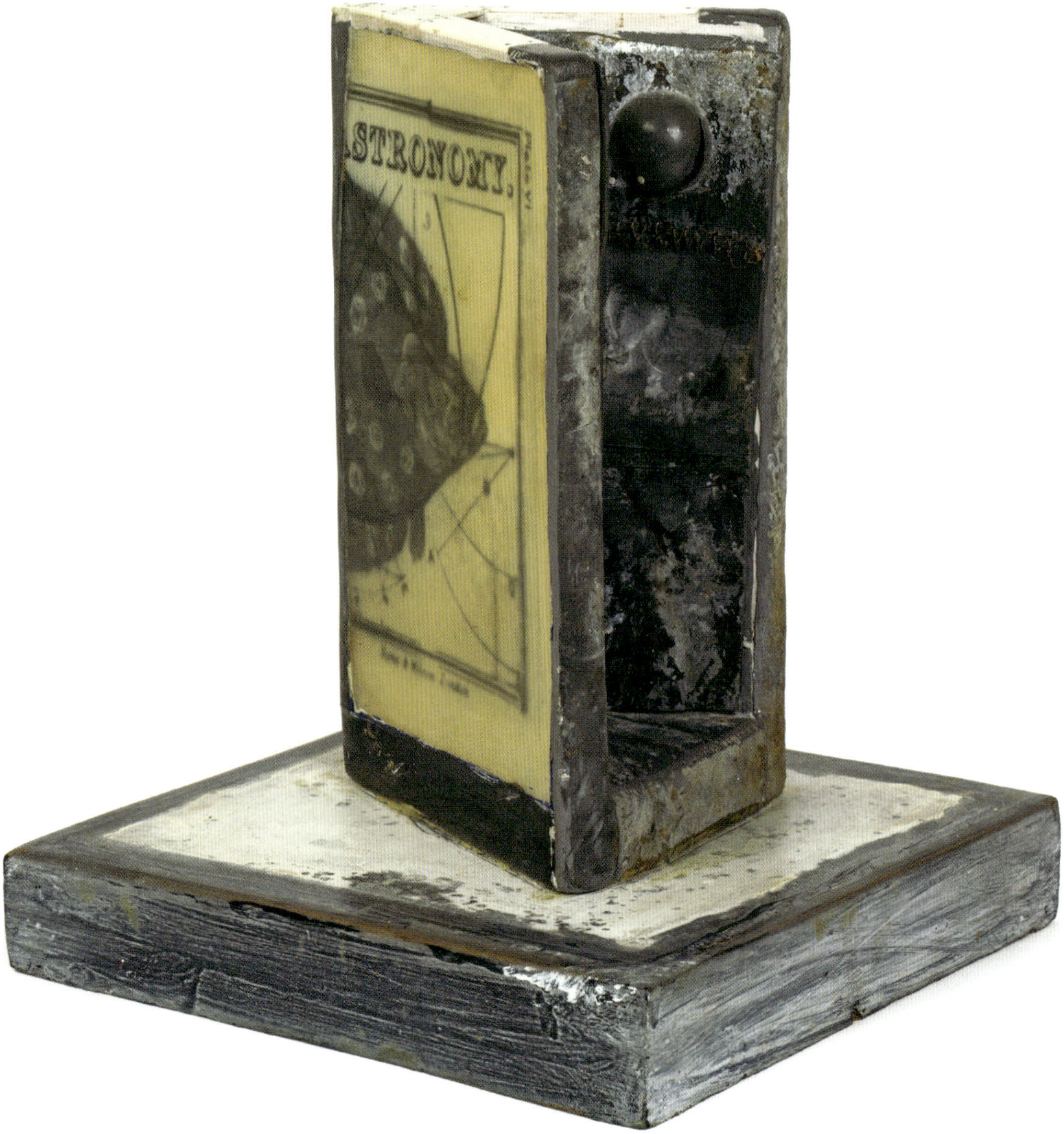

Nautical Astronomy · *2007, mixed-media sculpture, 26 x 22 x 24 cm* · *Ian Mayes QC; photograph Antonia Reeve*

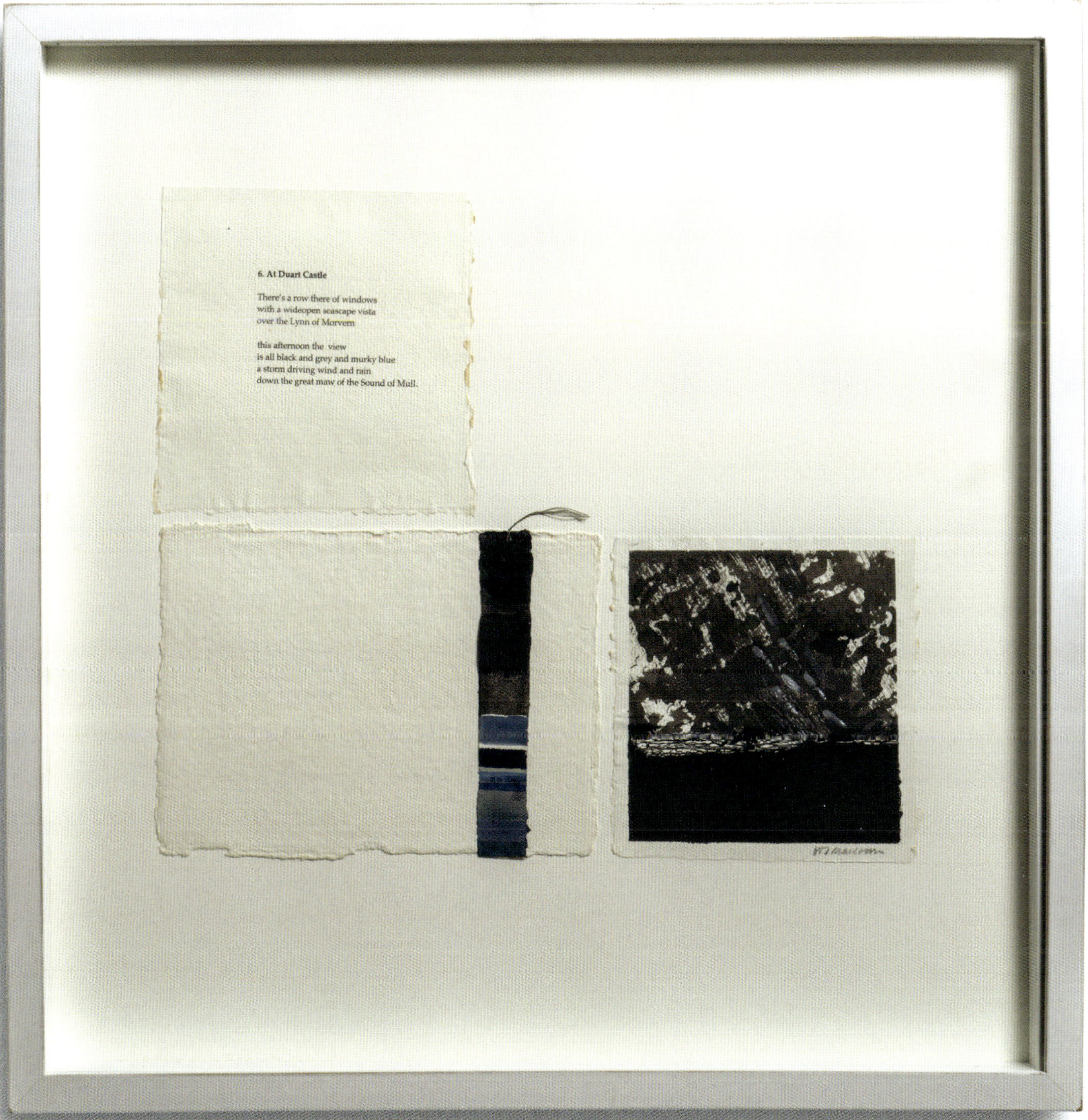

The Island Road: At Duart Castle · *a series of 7 images in collaboration with poet Kenneth White, 2013, text and watercolour, 53 x 53 x 4 cm* · *private collection; photograph Antonia Reeve*

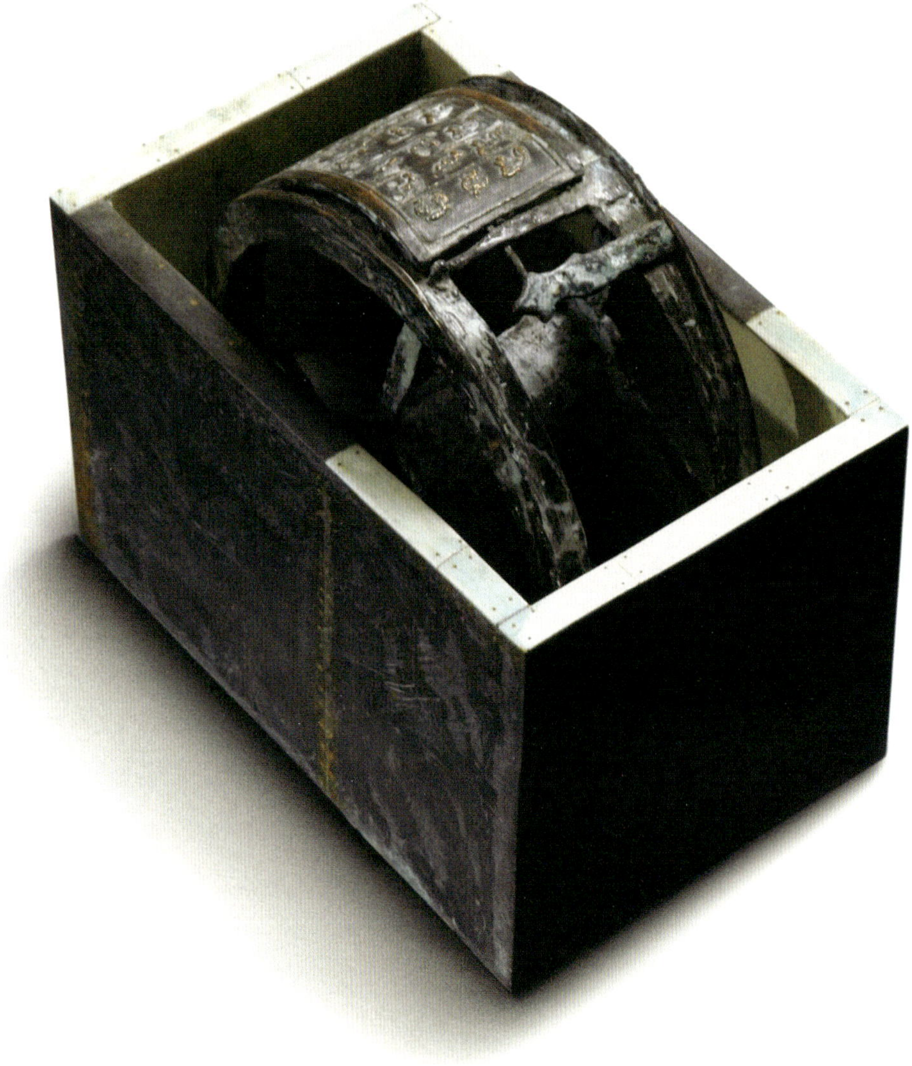

Time Wheel · 2008, wood, bone and bronze, 25 x 26 x 18 cm · private collection

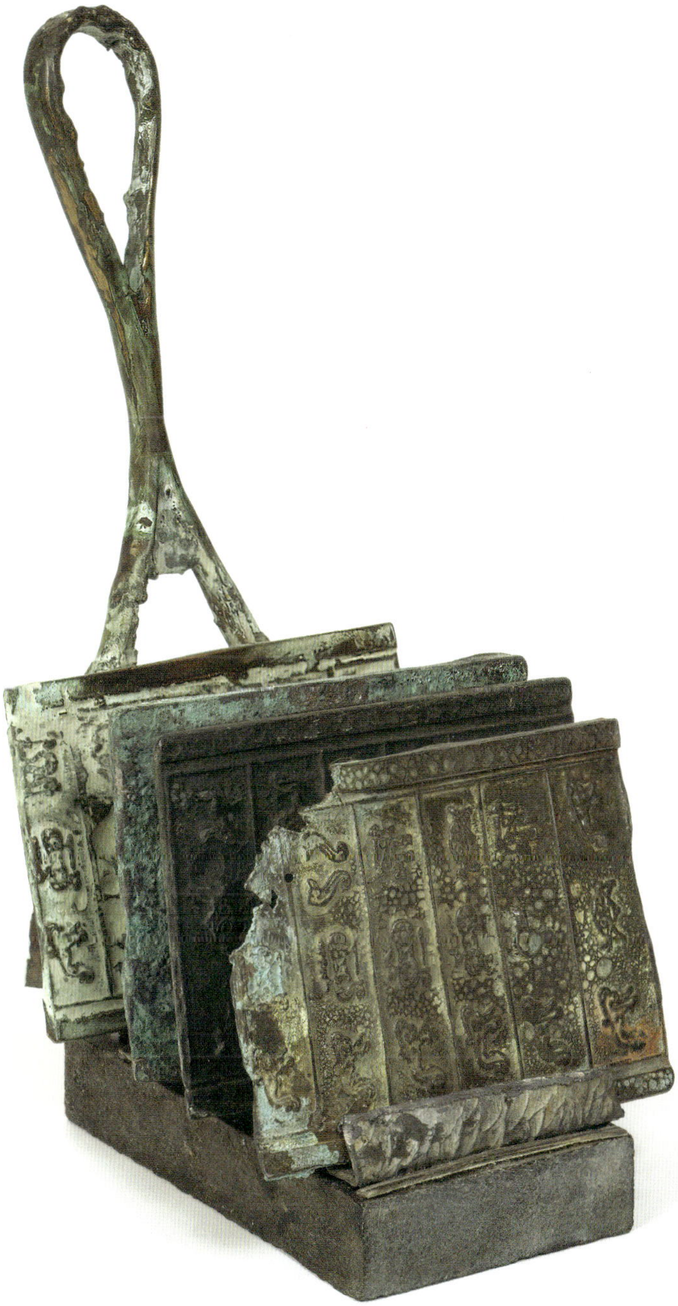

Time Wheel Library · *2008, bronze, 20 x 10 x 16 cm* · *private collection; photograph Antonia Reeve*

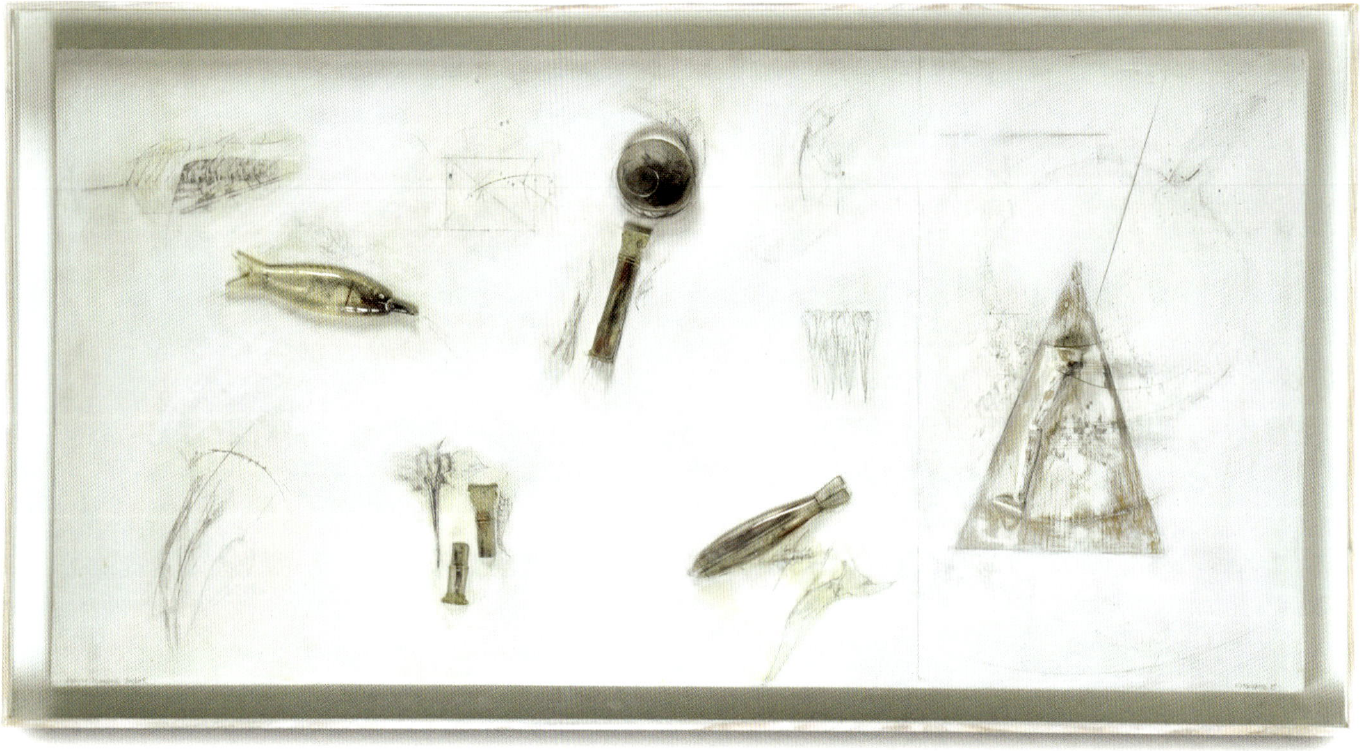

Portrait of a Polymath — D'Arcy Thompson's Daybook · *2008, mixed media on board, 60 x 124 x 4 cm* · *University of Dundee Museums*

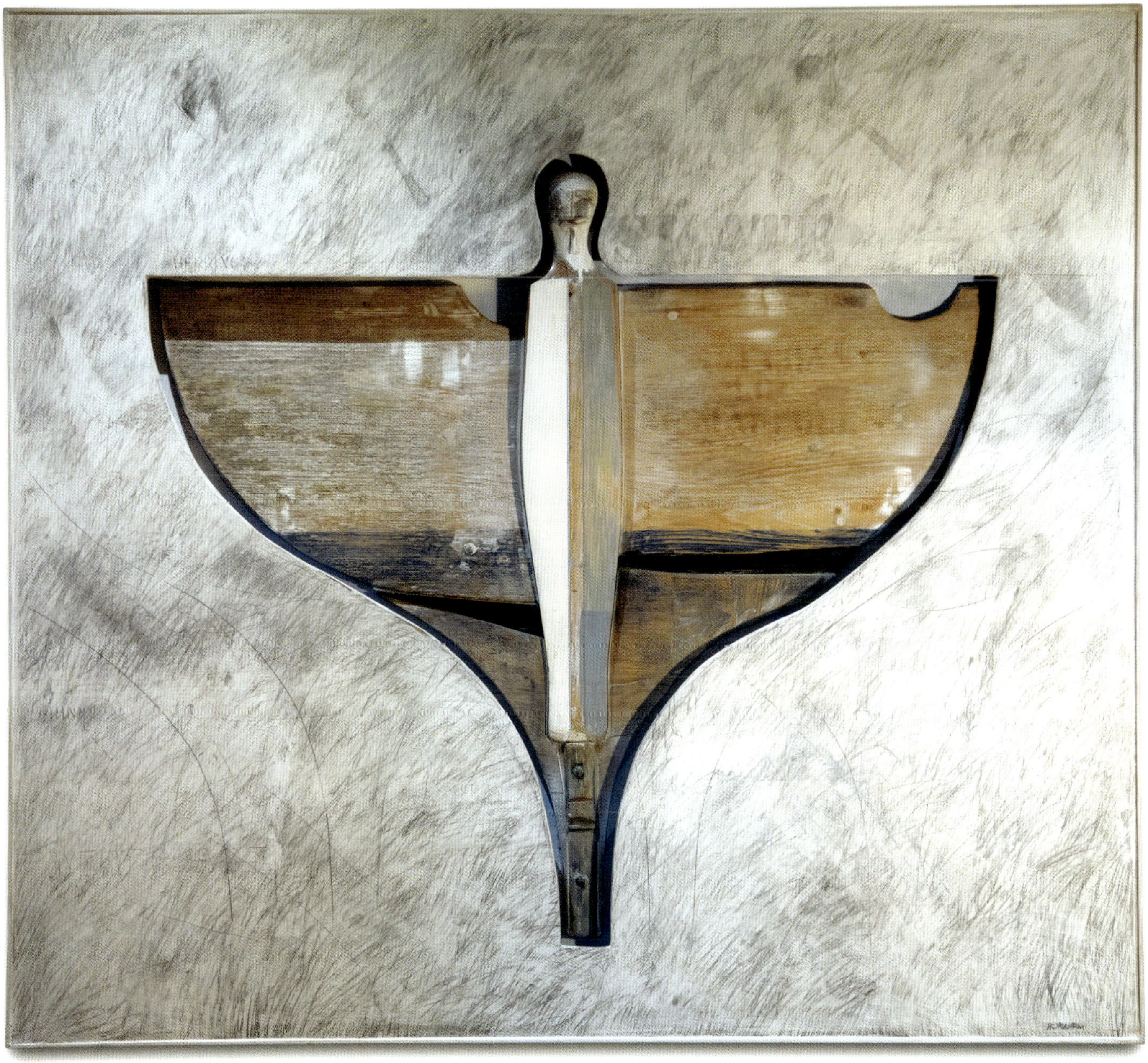

Fhir a Bhata/The Boatman · *2012, mixed media and found objects, 109 x 123 x 7 cm* · *private collection*

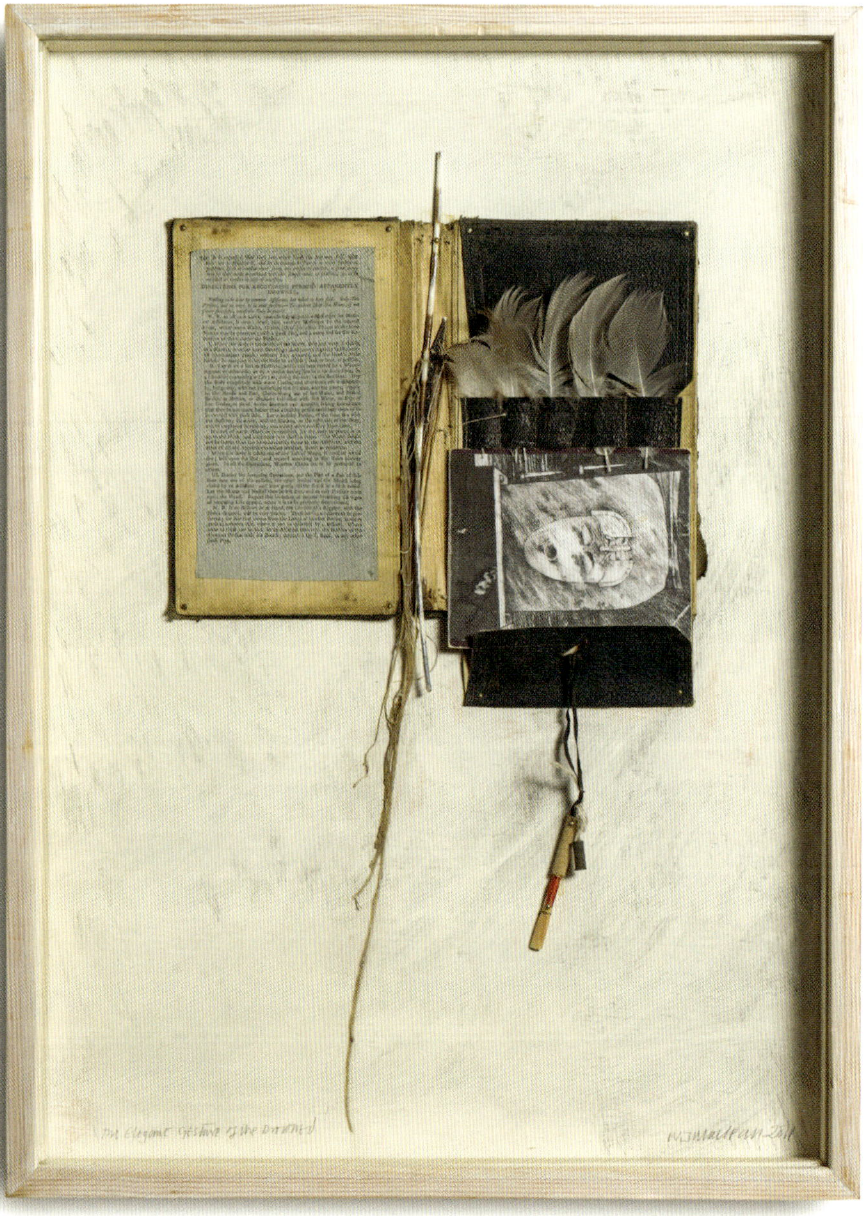

The Elegant Gesture of the Drowned *· 2011, mixed media and found objects, 62 x 44 x 7 cm · private collection, photograph Antonia Reeve*

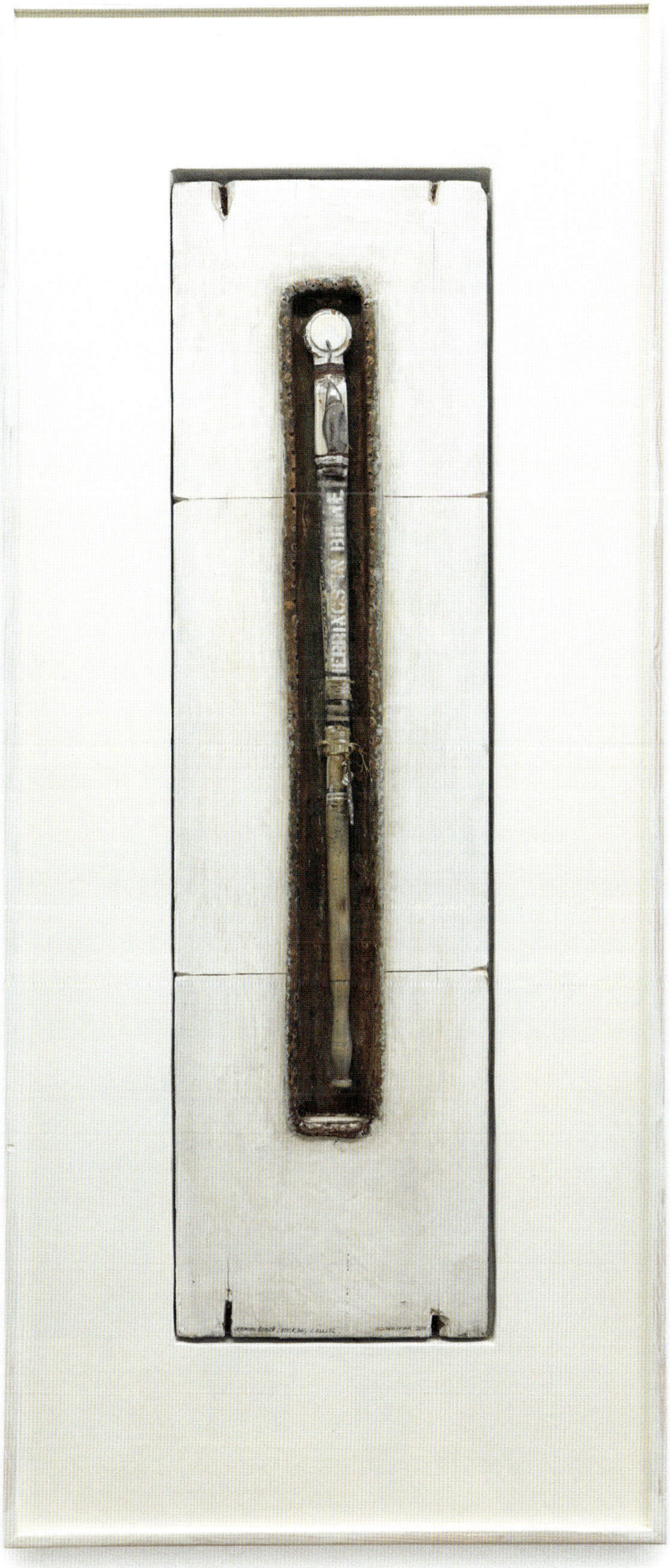

Shamanic Board, Herring Caller · *2011, mixed-media construction, 142 x 63 x 7 cm* · *private collection*

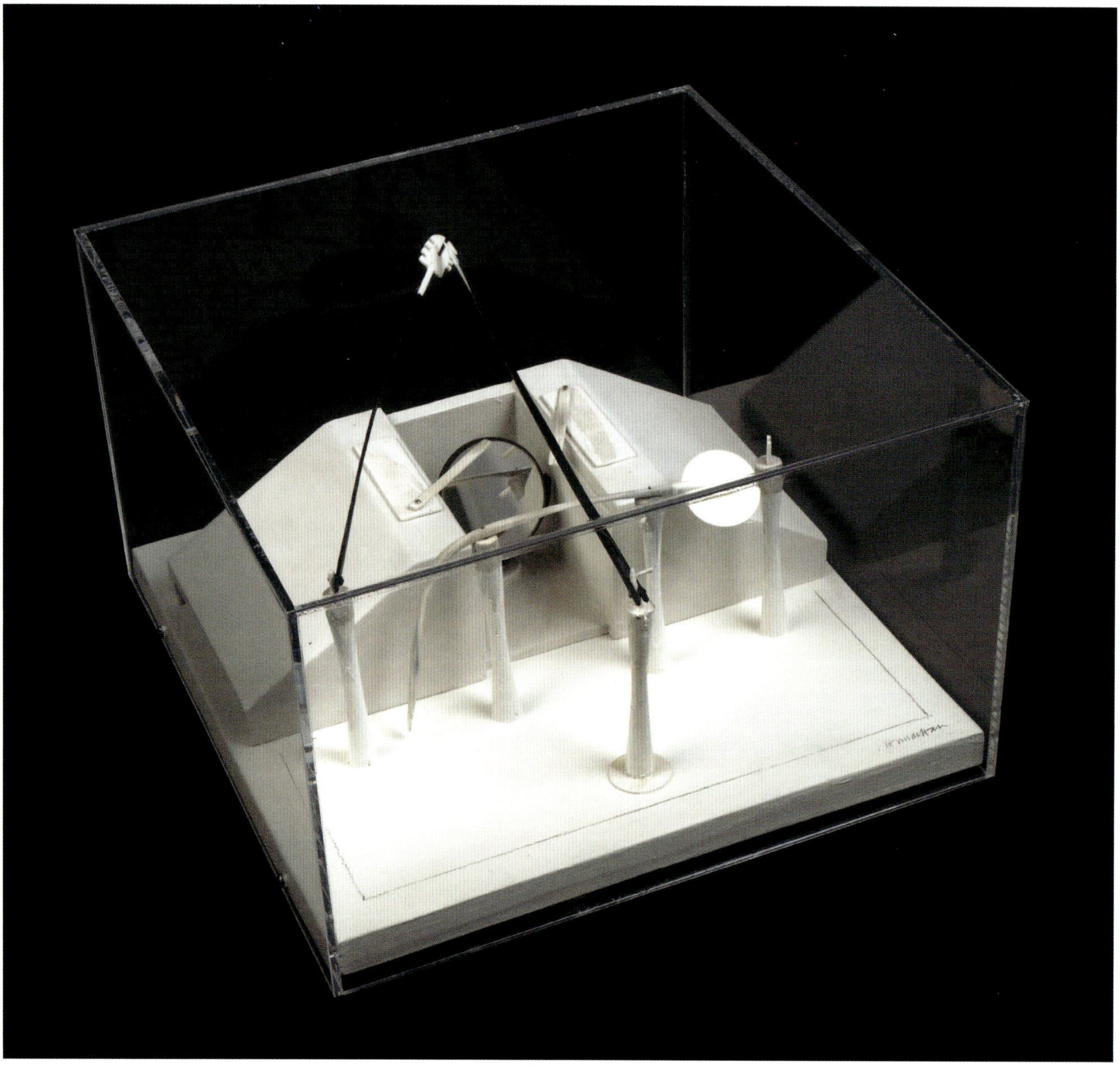

Mariner's Museum No. 1/Fictitious Sun · *2013, mixed-media sculpture, 30 x 30 x 20 cm* · *private collection*

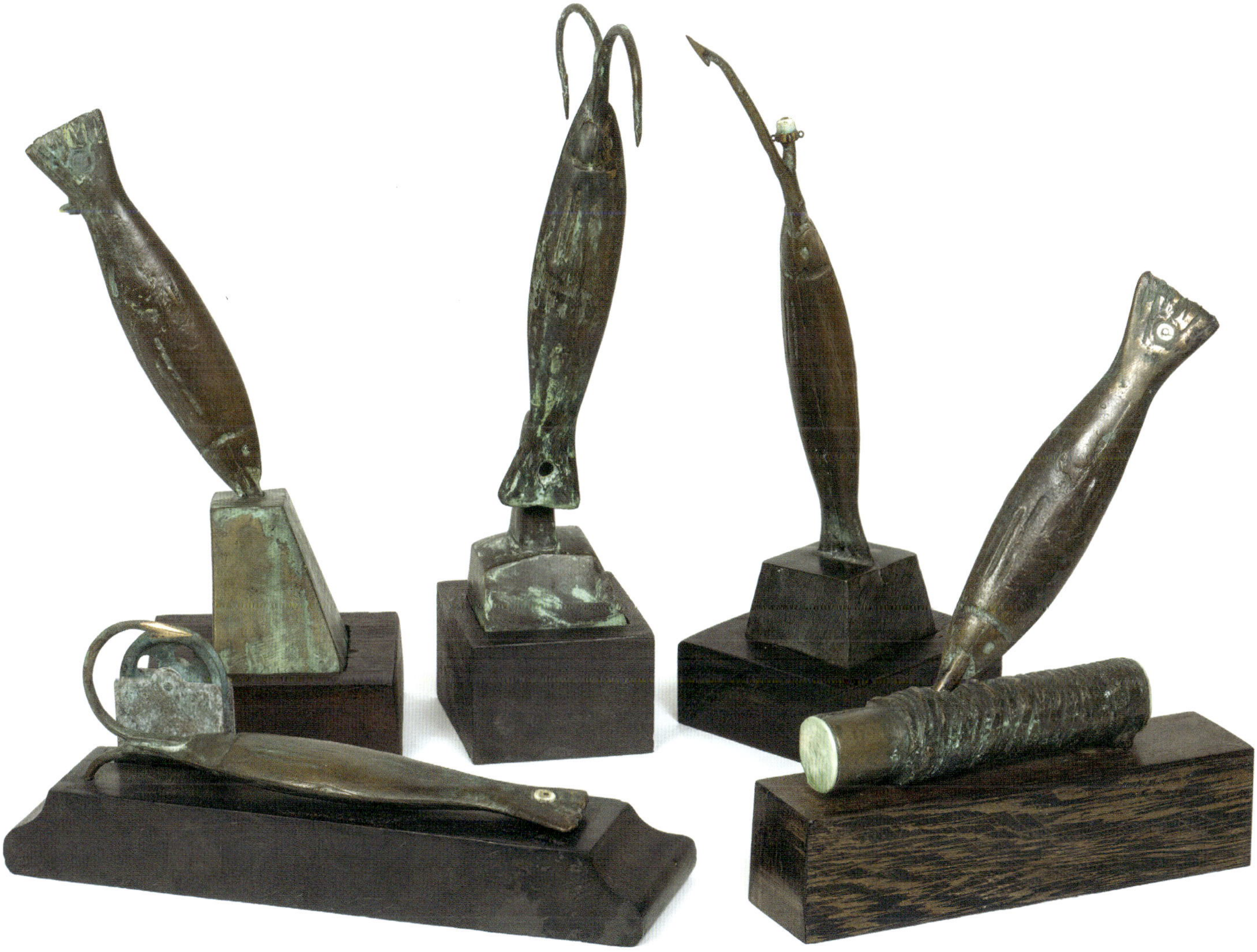

Newfoundland Series · *2004–2015, bronze, bone, slate and found object, various dimensions* · *private collection; photograph Antonia Reeve*

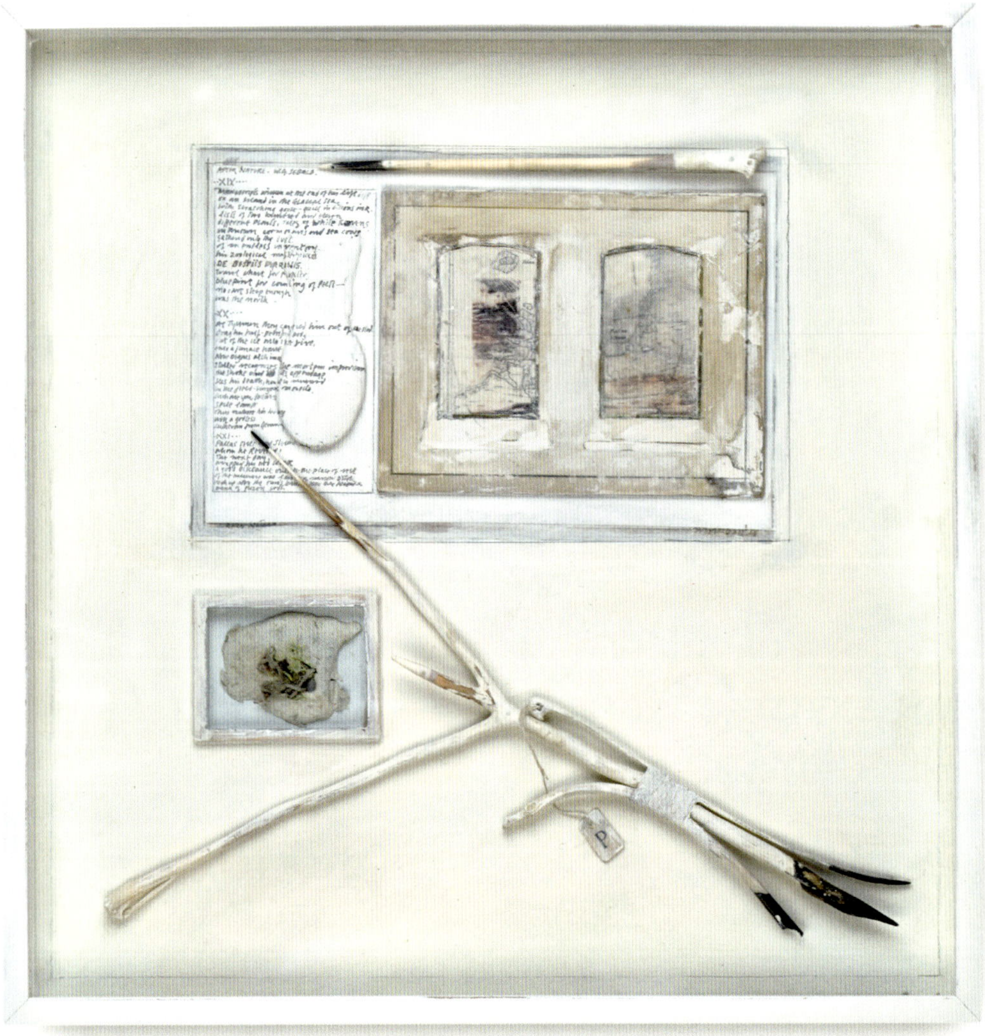

De Bestiis Marinis (for Simon Lewty) · 2014, found objects and mixed media, 52 x 52 x 5 cm · private collection

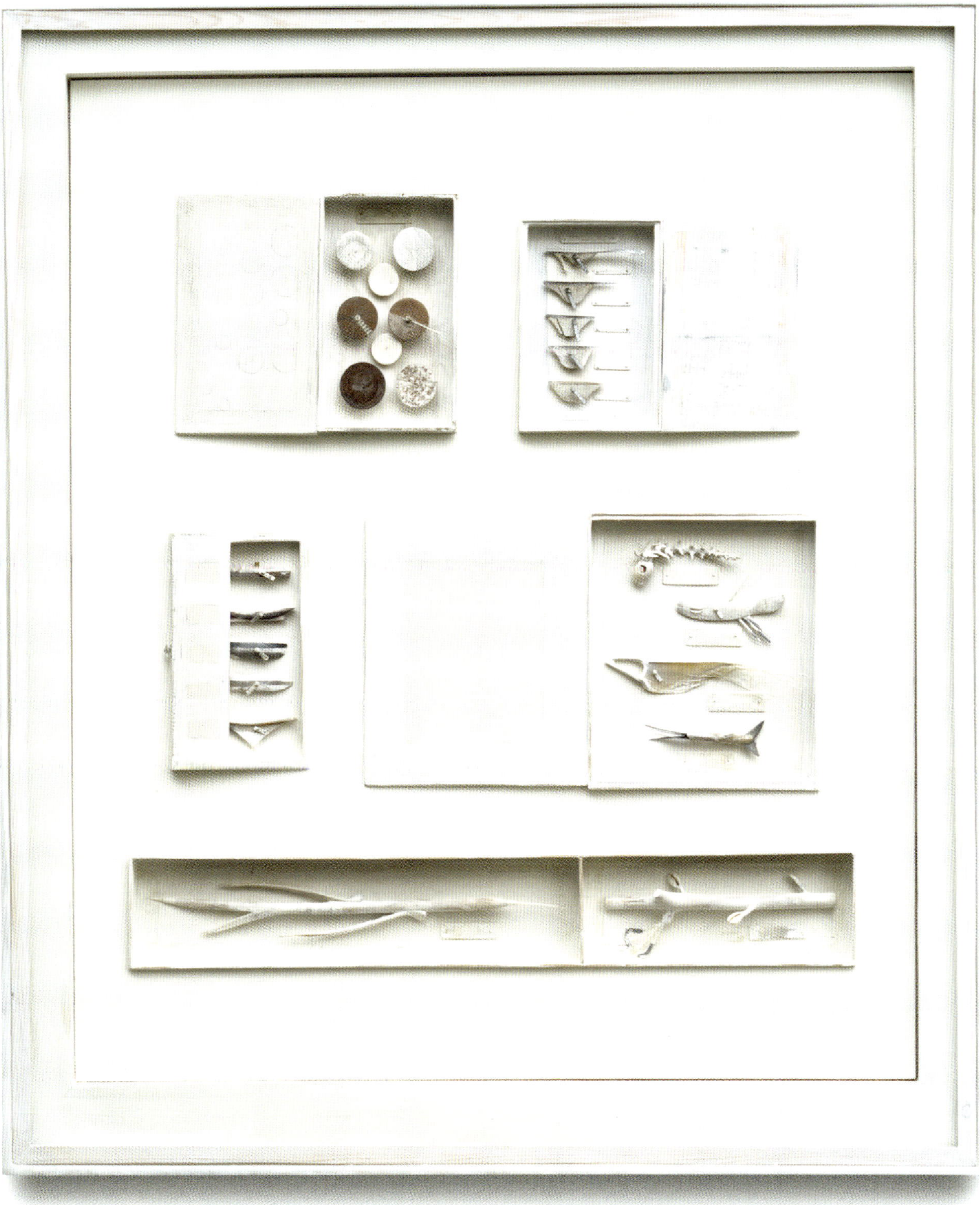

Mariner's Museum/Taxonomy of Tides · *2014, mixed-media construction, 123 x 108 x 9.5 cm* · *private collection*

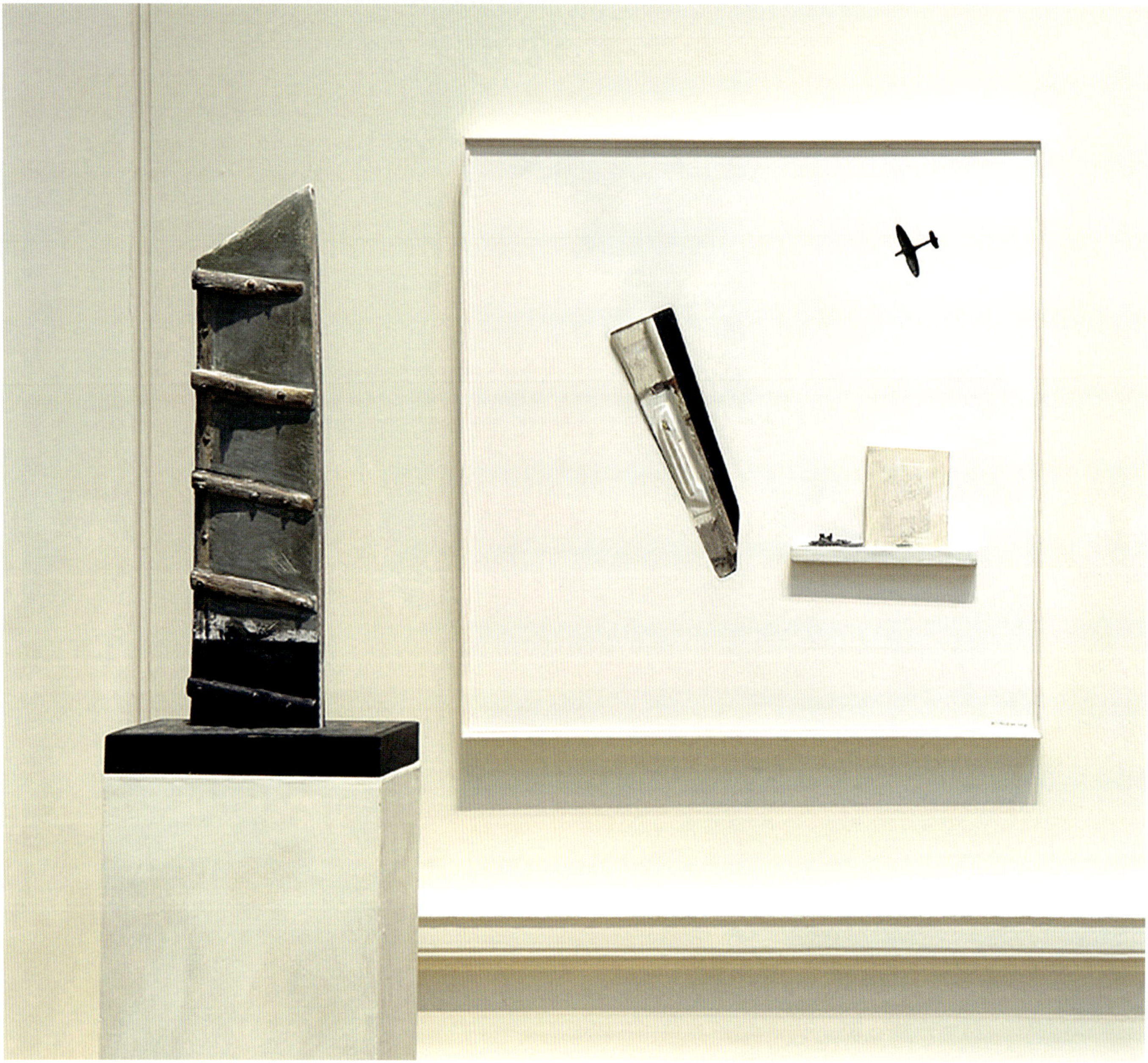

A Candle for Lübeck · *2014, 2 part work: mixed media and found objects* · *Galerie Herold, Hamburg and private collection*

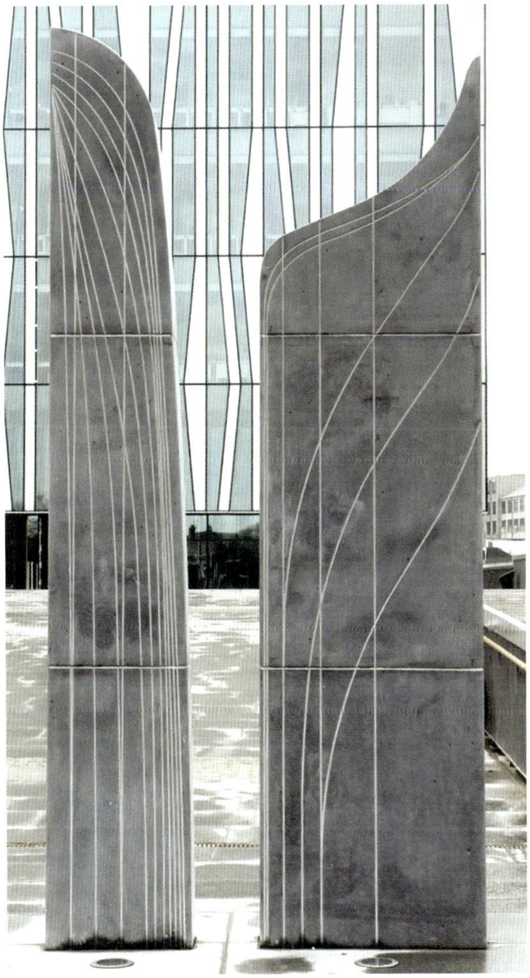

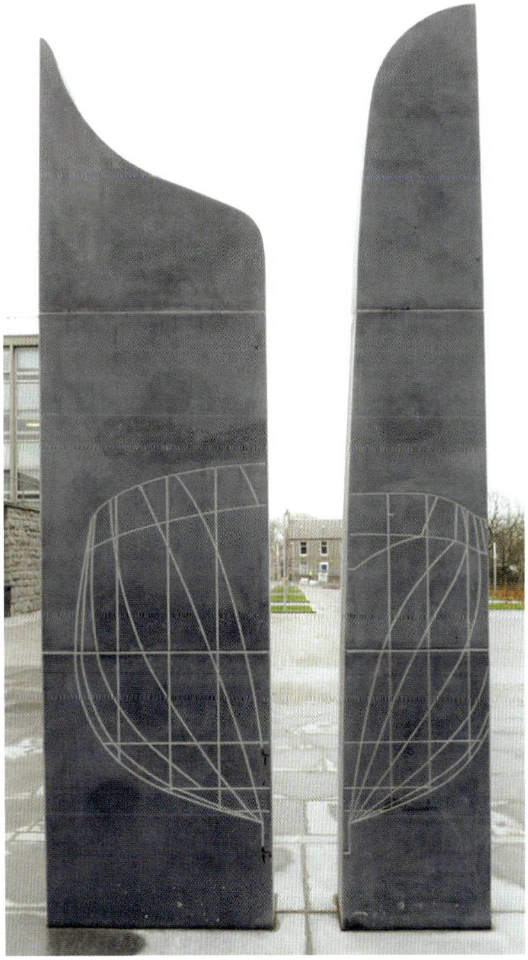

Waterlines · *University of Aberdeen; in collaboration with Marian Leven, 2012* · *photographs Kate Sutherland*

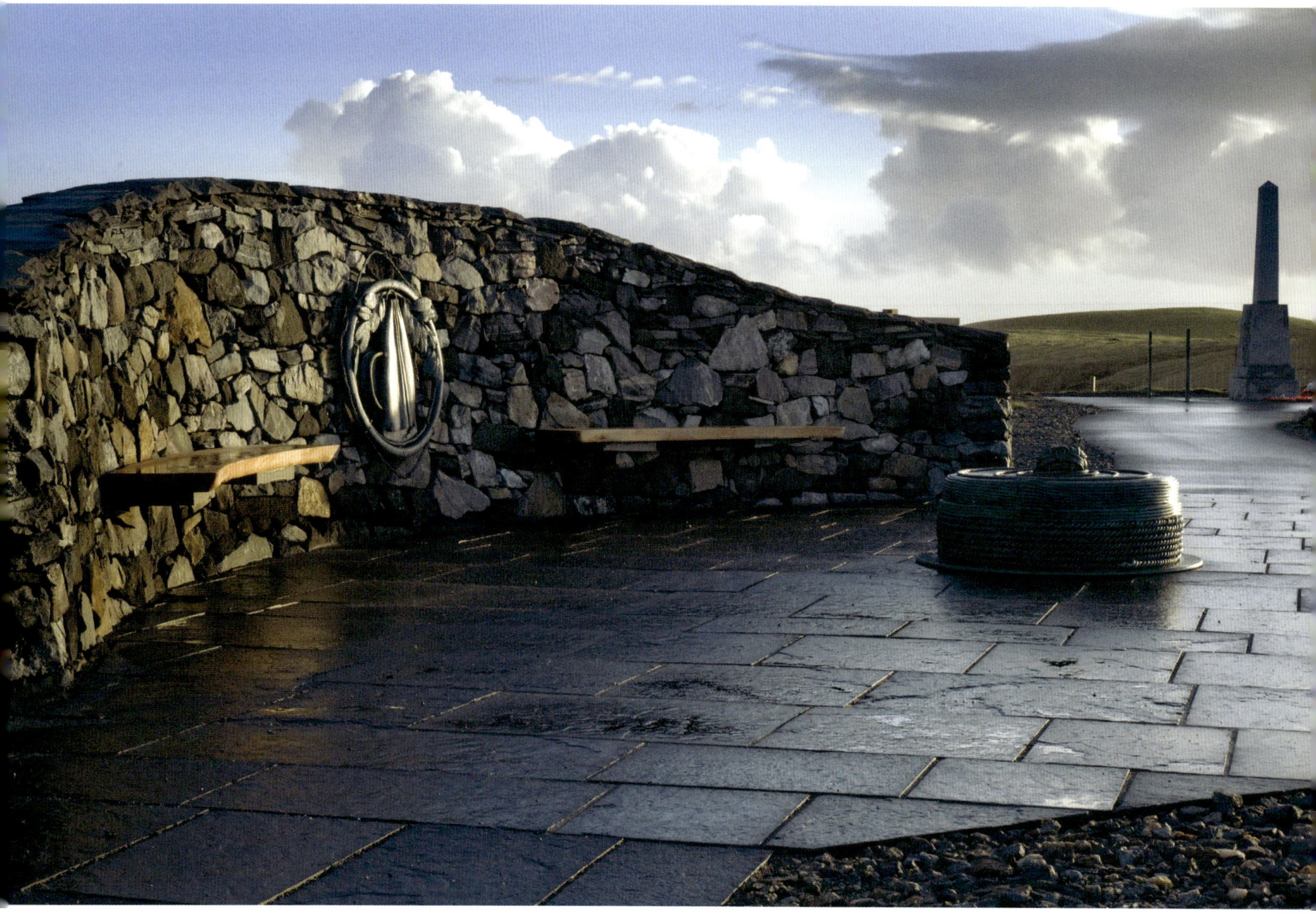

Iolaire Memorial · *Isle of Lewis; in collaboration with Marian Leven and Arthur Watson, 2018* · *photograph Robin Gillanders*

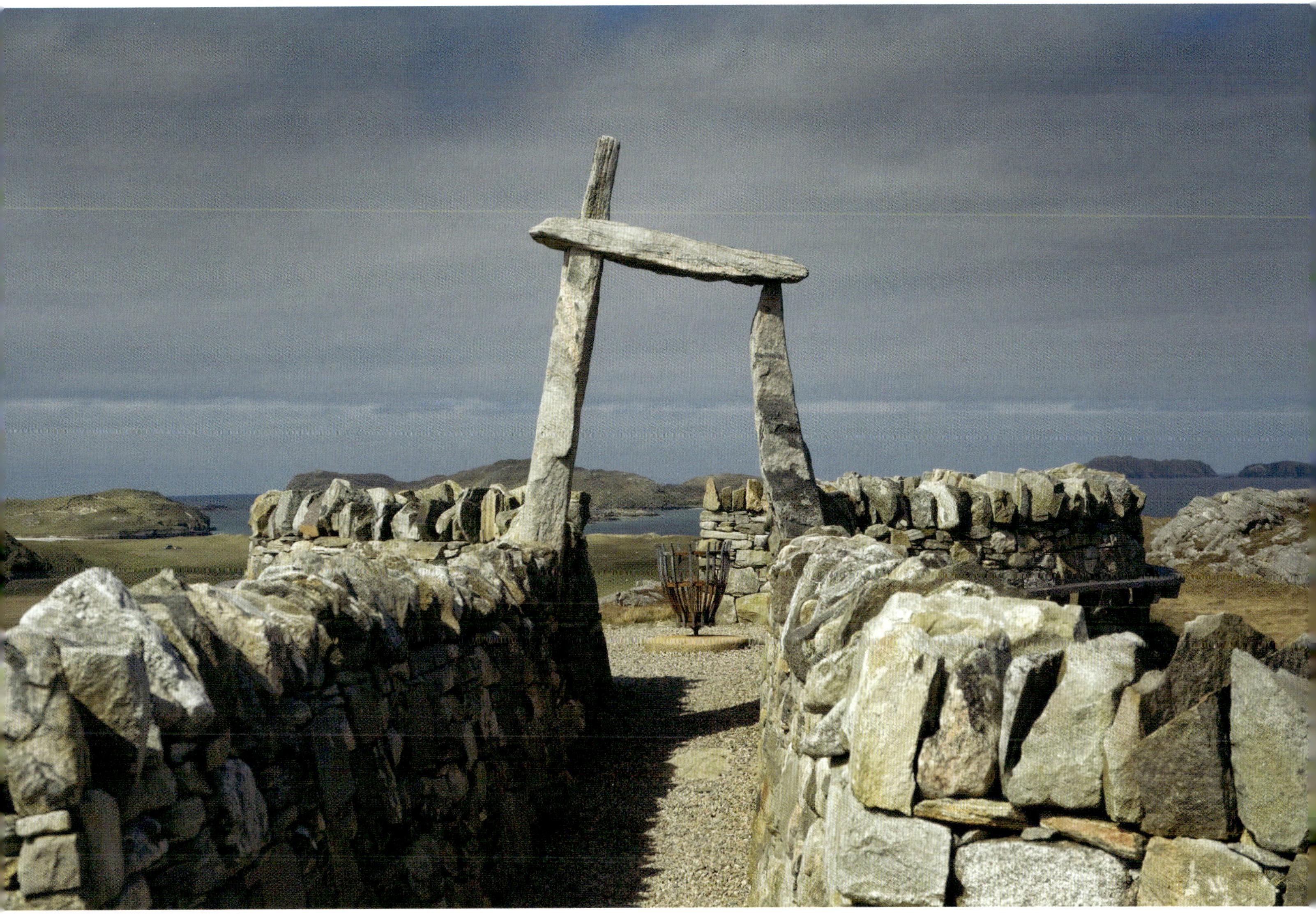

An Sùileachan Memorial · *Isle of Lewis; in collaboration with Marian Leven, 2013* · *photograph Robin Gillanders*

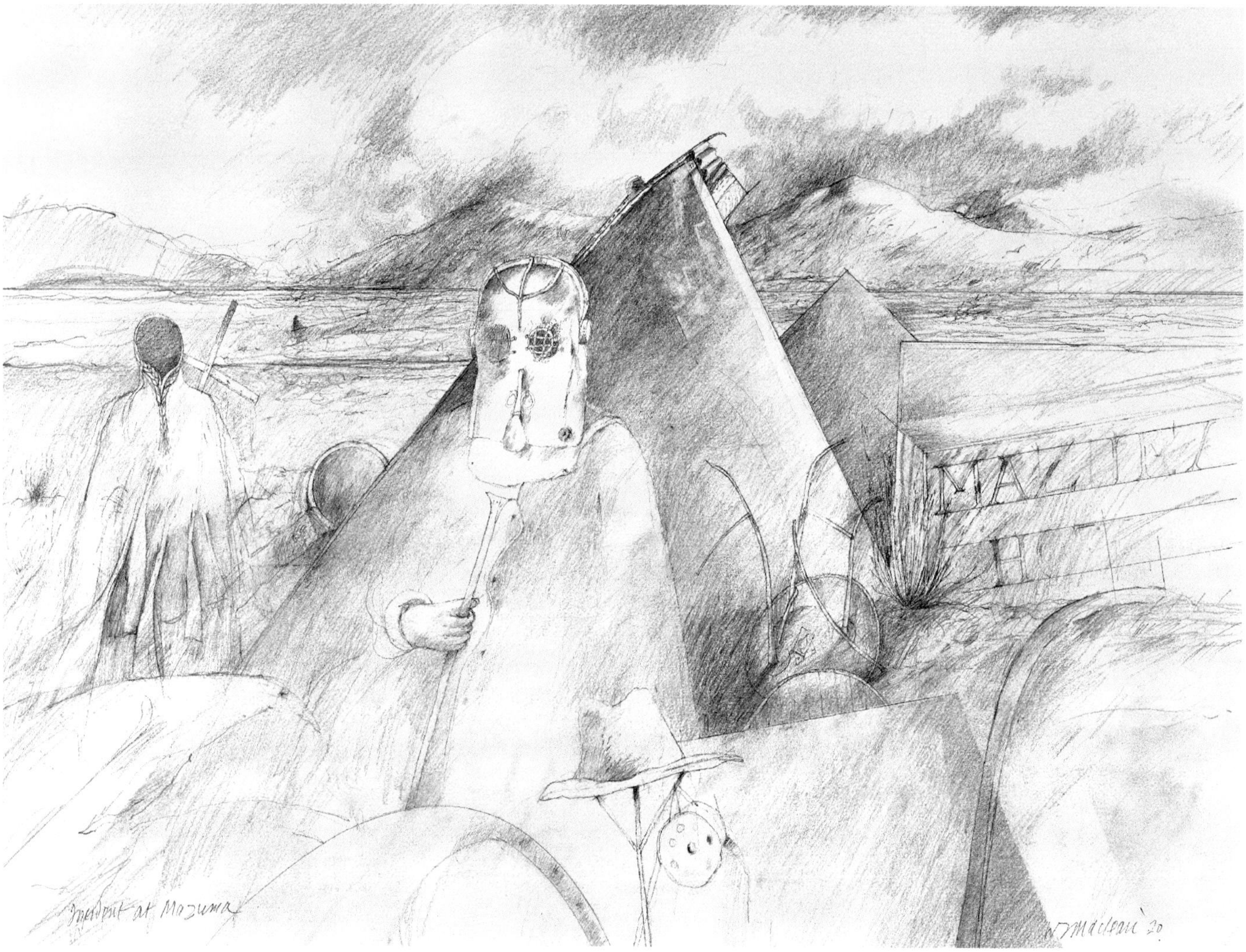

Incident at Mazuma II *· 2020, graphite on paper, 63 x 82 cm · private collection; photograph The Fine Art Society*

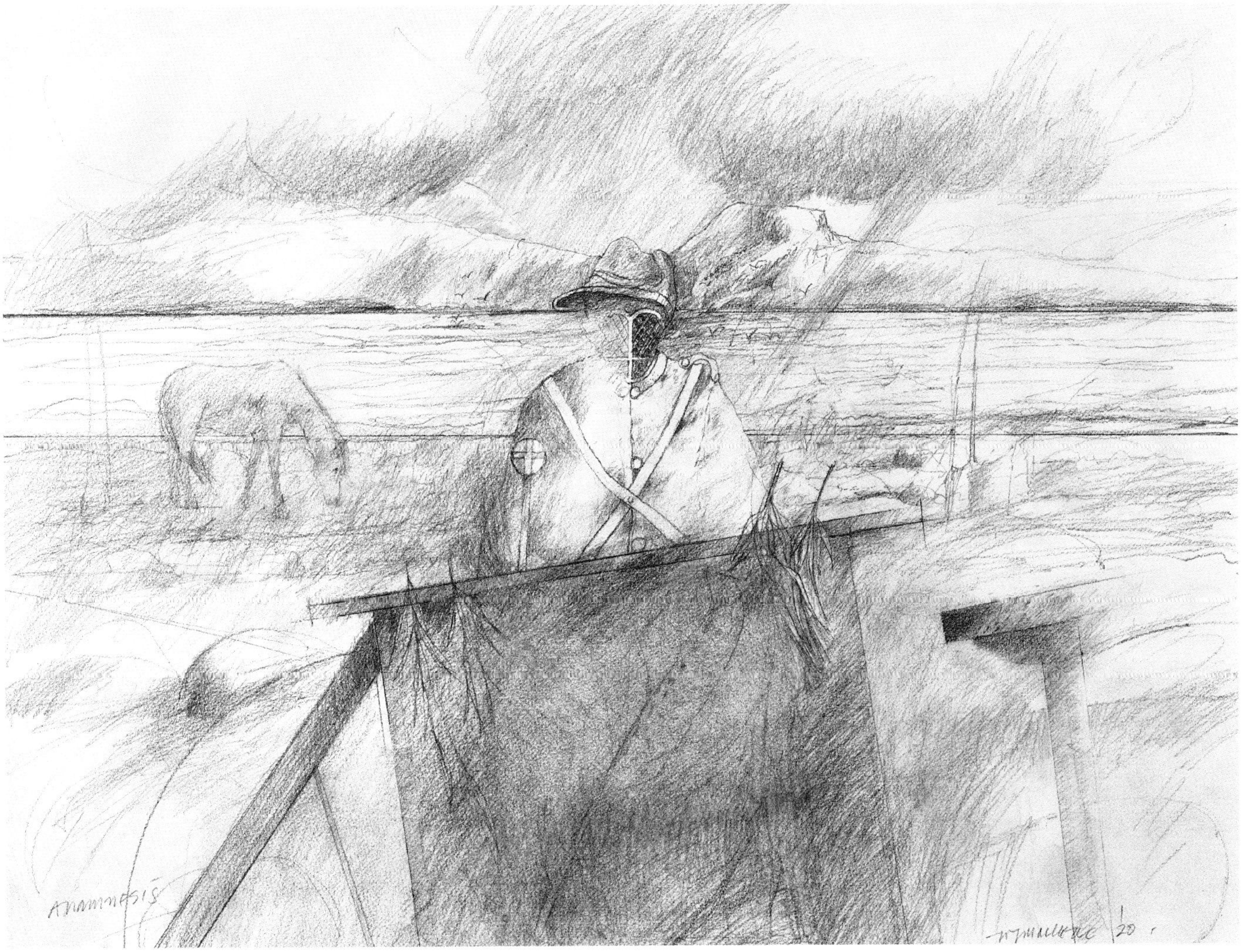

Anamnesis **Murdo Macleod** · *2020, graphite on paper, 63 x 82 cm* · *private collection; photograph The Fine Art Society*

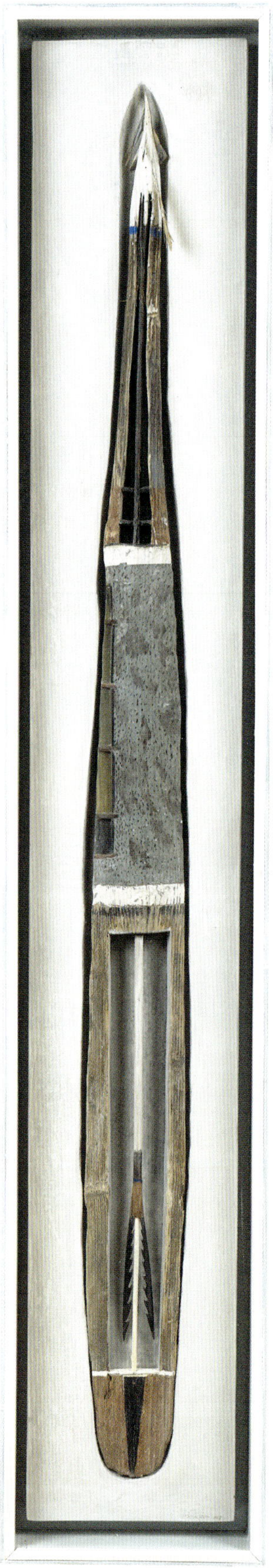

Baleen Zoomorphic · *2018, mixed media and found objects, 158 x 28 x 9 cm* · *private collection*

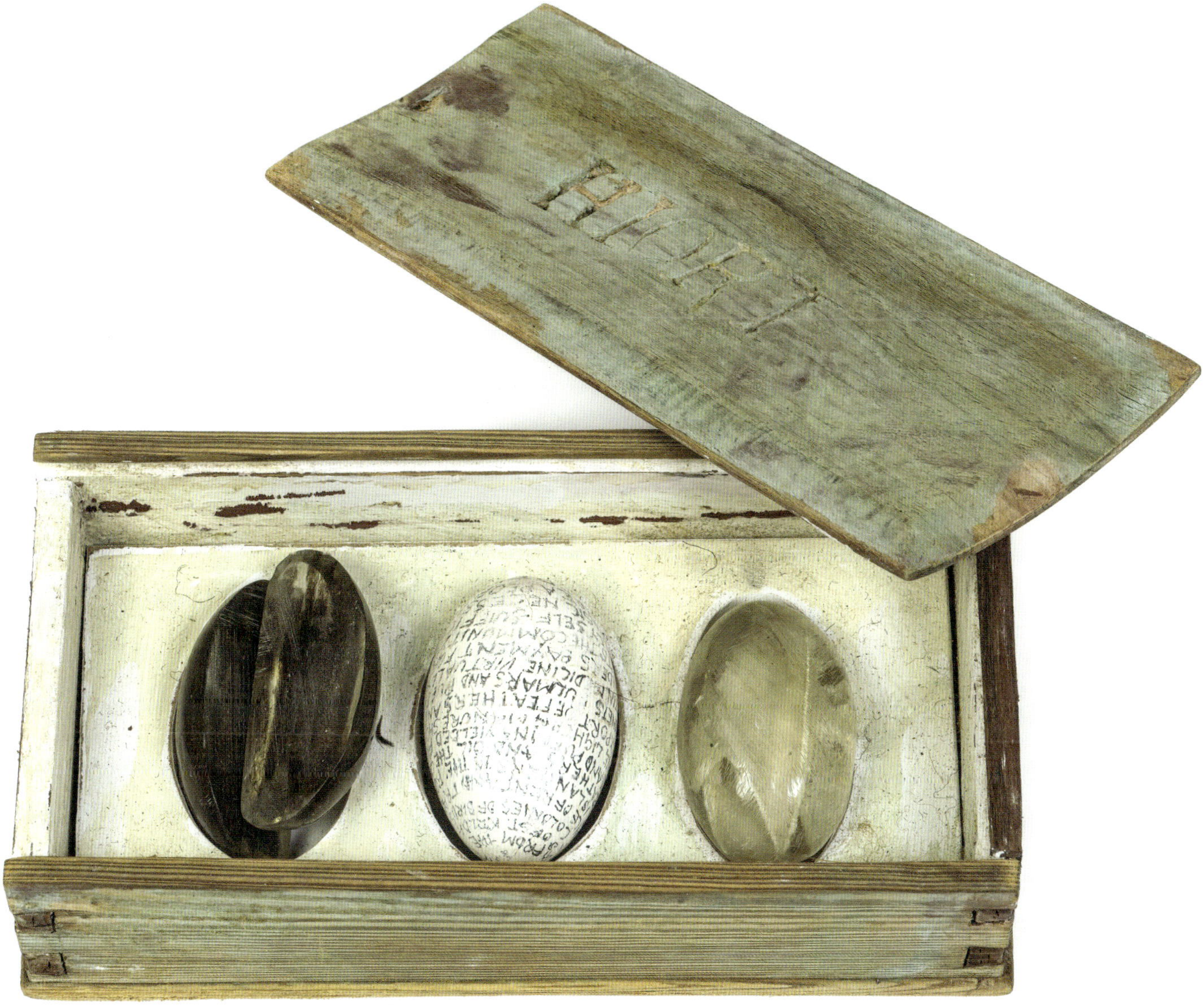

Hiort Box · *2020, mixed media and found objects, 7 x 25 x 12 cm* · *private collection; photograph Antonia Reeve*

Will Maclean

EXHIBITIONS

Note: for exhibitions spanning more than one year or appearing at more than one venue, only the year in which the main/first exhibition began is given.

Key solo exhibitions

1968 · New 57 Gallery, Edinburgh.
1978 · *The Ring Net* (documentary exhib.), Third Eye Centre, Glasgow; Richard Demarco Gallery, Edinburgh; Leeds Art Gallery; Inverness Museum and Art Gallery; Campbeltown Public Library; Tarbert.
1979 · Compass Gallery, Glasgow. Gilbert Parr Gallery, London.
1983 · *Will Maclean: Constructions, Small Sculptures and Drawings*, Richard Demarco Gallery, Edinburgh.
1984 · Kirkcaldy Museum and Art Gallery. Downing College, Univ. of Cambridge.
1986 · *The Ring Net*, Scottish National Gallery of Modern Art, Edinburgh.
1987 · Claus Runkel Fine Art, London.
1990 · Runkel-Hue-Williams, Old Bond Street, London.
1991 · Cyril Gerber Fine Art, Glasgow.
1992 · Retrospective exhib. (accompanying Duncan Macmillan's book, *Symbols of Survival: The Art of Will Maclean*), Talbot Rice Gallery, Univ. of Edinburgh; Art Space, Aberdeen; Kelvingrove Art Gallery and Museum, Glasgow; also Wick, Thurso, Inverness, Kingussie, Stornoway.
1995 · *Will Maclean: Voyages*, Art First, London. Éigse Carlow '95: Festival of the Arts, Ireland.
1998 · *Atlantic Messengers*, Art First, London.
1999 · *Will Maclean: Cardinal Points*, North Dakota Museum of Art, Grand Forks; McMaster Museum of Art, McMaster Univ., Hamilton, Ontario; Art Gallery of Newfoundland and Labrador, St John's, Newfoundland. *Landmarks-Seamarks*, Bourne Fine Art, Edinburgh.
2000 · *Seaways*, Art First, London.
2001 · *Driftworks*, Dundee Contemporary Arts; Pier Arts Centre, Stromness, Orkney; Art First, London.
2004 · *Will Maclean*, Ferens Art Gallery, Hull. *New Work*, Art First, London.
2005 · *North Sea Archives*, DKFA Projects, New York, with Art First, London.
2006 · *Sea Room*, Pittenweem Arts Festival.
2007 · *Works with Poets*, Stanza Poetry Festival, St Andrews.
2008 · *Will Maclean: Different Meridians*, Art First, London.
2011 · *Collected Works 1970–2010*, Fleming-Wyfold Art Foundation, London; *Lead and Line*, Art First, London.
2012 · *Reliquaries*, Dept of Art History, Univ. of St Andrews.
2014 · *Gleaned and Gathered*, Art First, London.
2015 · *Will Maclean: Veering Westerly/Fiaradh Gun Iar*, An Lanntair, Stornoway; Iona Gallery, Kingussie; St Fergus Gallery, Wick; Inverness Museum and Art Gallery; An Tobar, Mull.
2018 · *Will Maclean: Narratives*, Fine Art Society, Edinburgh.
2022 · *Will Maclean: Points of Departure*, City Art Centre, Edinburgh.

Key group exhibitions

1970 · *Four Figurative Painters*, Demarco Gallery, Edinburgh.
1972 · Will Maclean/Ian McLeod, New 57 Gallery,

Edinburgh. Group show at Demarco Gallery, Edinburgh.
1975 · *Six Coastal Artists*, Saltire Society, Edinburgh. *A Choice Selection*, Fruitmarket Gallery, Edinburgh. *200 Years of Scottish Painting*, Marjorie Parr Gallery, London.
1976 · *The Need to Draw*, touring exhib. *Inscape*, Fruitmarket Gallery, Edinburgh.
1978 · Scottish Arts Council Travelling Gallery, opening exhib. *Painters in Parallel*, Edinburgh College of Art.
1981 · *Art and the Sea*, Third Eye Centre, Glasgow; venues in England and Wales.
1982 · *Inner Worlds*, Arts Council of Great Britain, touring exhib. *Artists' Boxes*, Xavier Berg Gallery, London. *Artender '82*, Bilbao, Spain. *Mises en Boite*, Belgium.
1984 · *Scottish Contemporary Art in Washington and London: Will Maclean/Barbara Rae*, Leinster Fine Art, London, and V.N. Gallery, Alexandria, Virginia.
1986 · *Contemporary Art from Scotland*, Leinster Fine Art, London. *As an Fhearann* (From the Land), An Lanntair, Stornoway, Isle of Lewis; Royal Museum of Scotland, Edinburgh; other locations across Scotland and Canada.
1987 · Will Maclean/Italo Scanga, Simon/Neuman Gallery, New York. *Scottish Contemporary Art*, Clare Hall, Univ. of Cambridge. *Round the Scottish Coasts*, Peacock Printmakers, travelling exhib.
1988 · *Modern Masters I* and *Modern Masters II*, Claus Runkel Fine Art, London. *Clean Irish Sea*, in assoc. with Greenpeace, Dublin City Gallery; Cardiff; England; Germany. *The Stevenson Collection*, Warwick Arts Trust, London.
1989 · *Scottish Art since 1900*, Scottish National Gallery of Modern Art, Edinburgh; Barbican Gallery, London.
1990 · *Boxes and Totems*, England & Co., London. *Boites et Reliefs*, Galerie de la Gare, Bonnieux, France. *Scotland Creates: 5000 Years of Art and Design*, McLellan Galleries, Glasgow.
1991 · *Will Maclean: A Night of Islands*, Runkel-Hue-Williams, London. *Virtue and Vision: Sculpture and Scotland 1540–1990*, National Galleries of Scotland at the Royal Scottish Academy of Art and Architecture (RSA), Edinburgh. *Art in Boxes*, England & Co., London.
1993 · *The Line of Tradition: Watercolours, Drawings and Prints by Scottish Artists 1700–1990*, National Galleries of Scotland at the RSA, Edinburgh.
1994 · *Worlds in a Box*, City Art Centre, Edinburgh; Graves Gallery, Sheffield; Sainsbury Centre for Visual Arts, Univ. of East Anglia; Whitechapel Art Gallery, London. *Scandex 1994: An Exhibition of Contemporary Scottish Sculpture*, Aberdeen Art Gallery; Sølvberget library and Kulturhus, Stavanger, Norway; Konstens Hus, Luleå, Sweden; Kemin Taidemuseo, Kemi, Finland. *Calanais: The Atlantic Stones*, An Lanntair, Stornoway, Isle of Lewis; Galerie du Faouëdic, Lorient, France. *Found in Scotland*, Art First, London.
1996 · *Will Maclean and Jake Harvey: Constructions and Sculpture*, Art First, London.
1997 · *Colmcille*, Glebe Gallery, Donegal, Ireland.
1998 · *This Island Earth*, An Tuireann Arts Centre, Portree, Skye. *New Small Sculpture from Scotland*, Morioka Hashimoto Museum of Art, Japan.
1999 · Print commission, *A Tayside Inventory*, with poet John Burnside and Mary Modeen, for Dundee Contemporary Arts. *Scotland's Art 1600–2000*, City Art Centre, Edinburgh. *Transistors: Small Sculpture from Scotland*, Royal Museum of Scotland, Edinburgh;

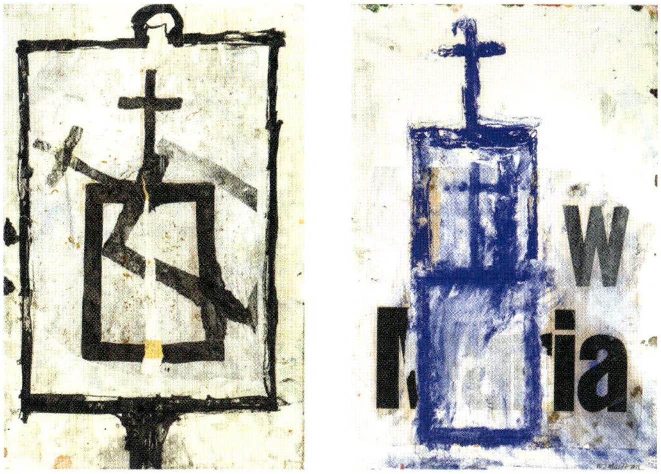

Studies for Casa Berti *(No. 1 and No. 2)*
1992, collage and acrylic on paper, 56 x 43 cm
private collection; photographs Antonia Reeve

Trondhjems Kunstforening, Norway.
2000 · *Expressions: Scottish Art 1976–1989*, Aberdeen Art Gallery; Dundee Contemporary Arts.
2001 · *St Kilda: Islands of Isolation*, Taigh Chearsabhagh Museum and Arts Centre, Lochmaddy, North Uist.
2002 · Kilkenny Arts Festival, Kilkenny, Ireland. *An Leabhar Mòr na Gàidhlig/The Great Book of Gaelic*, Gallery of Modern Art, Glasgow; other locations include City Art Centre, Edinburgh; Ulster Museum, Belfast; USA (from 2010).
2003 · *Insider – Box Art*, Oriel Davies Gallery, Newtown, Powys; Southampton; Canterbury; Derby; Rugby; Aberystwyth.
2004 · *Shared Space*, Compass Gallery, Glasgow. *Glasgow's Art: Selected Works from the Collection 1940–2000*, Gallery of Modern Art, Glasgow.
2005 · *The Scottishness of Scottish Art*, Fleming-Wyfold Art Foundation, London.
2006 · *Simon Lewty/Will Maclean: Charting a Decade, 1995–2005*, Art First, London. *Consider the Lilies: Scottish Painting 1910–1980*, McManus: Art Gallery and Museum, Dundee; in assoc. with National Galleries of Scotland, Edinburgh.
2007 · *Fonn's Duthchas: Land and Legacy*, Inverness Museum and Art Gallery; Kelvingrove Art Gallery and Museum, Glasgow; National Museum of Scotland, Edinburgh; Museum nan Eilean, Stornoway.
2008 · *Window to the West: The Highlands and Islands in Art*, Lamb Gallery, Univ. of Dundee.
2009 · *Coastal Connections: Will Maclean/Marian Leven*, An Talla Solais, Ullapool. *A Field Guide to Observing Art*, McMaster Museum of Art, McMaster Univ., Hamilton, Ontario. *The Collector's Art*, Hunterian Art Gallery, Univ. of Glasgow. *Inspired: Scottish Art*, Fleming Collection, London.
2010 · *From the Studio II: Jake Harvey/Will Maclean, New Sculptural Works*, Art First, London. *Window to the West: The Rediscovery of Highland Art*, City Art Centre, Edinburgh.
2011 · Invited artist, RSA exhib., Edinburgh. *Poetry beyond Text*, Dundee Contemporary Arts; Scottish Poetry Library, Edinburgh; RSA, Edinburgh.
2012 · *Seeing in a Wider Sense*, St Andrews Museum. *Scottish Connections: The Art of Marian Leven and Will Maclean*, Galerie Herold, Hamburg.
2013 · *Waterlines* exhib., Sir Duncan Rice Library, Univ. of Aberdeen.
2014 · *The Power of the Sea: Making Waves in British Art 1790–2014*, Royal West of England Academy, Bristol.
2015 · *Modern Times: Contemporary Art from NYC to Sylt*, Galerie Herold, Sylt. *Confluence: Marian Leven and Will Maclean*, Tatha Gallery, Newport-on-Tay, Fife. *The Moon*, Art First, London.
2016 · *Nordic Masterpieces*, Galerie Herold, Hamburg. *Simon Lewty/Will Maclean: Charting a Decade II, 2006–2016*, Art First, London.
2017 · *Between Tides: Scotland's Working Culture of the Sea*, Fine Art Society, Edinburgh. *Paper Matters 2018: Works on Paper; Cut-Outs/Collage/Drawings*, Art First at Eagle Gallery, London. *Ages of Wonder: Scotland's Art 1540 to Now*, RSA, Edinburgh.
2018 · *Fleming at 50: Radicals, Pioneers and Rebels*, Fine Art Society, Edinburgh. *Water, Colour and Life on Earth*, TheArtsBox, Vicenza, Italy.
2020 · *Archipelago*, Academicians' Gallery, RSA,

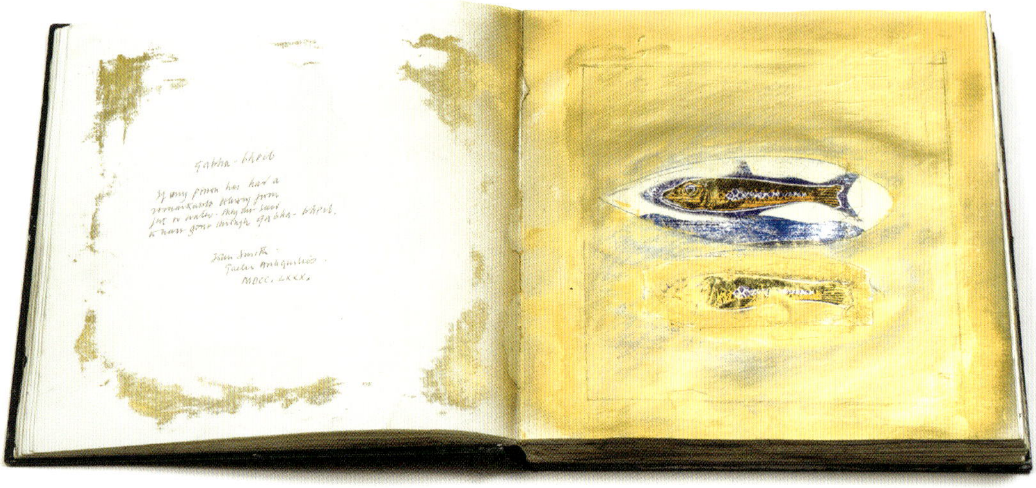

Sketch books: drawing and mixed media on paper
photographs Antonia Reeve

Edinburgh.
2021 · *Owners of the Soil*, Fine Art Society, Edinburgh.

KEY SITE INSTALLATIONS/PUBLIC ART

1994 · Completion and opening of Cuimhneachain nan Gaisgeach memorial cairn, Balallan, Isle of Lewis.
1996 · Completion and opening of two Cuimhneachain nan Gaisgeach memorial sculptures: at Aignish and Gress River, Isle of Lewis.
2006 · Completion and opening of *Crannghal*, with Arthur Watson and Eden Jolly, bronze sculpture for Sabhal Mòr Ostaig, National Centre for Gaelic Language and Culture, Skye.
2008 · Completion of Cairngorm 'viewpoint' commission, with Arthur Watson.
2012 · Completion of *Waterlines* sculpture, with Marian Leven, Sir Duncan Rice Library, Univ. of Aberdeen.
2013 · Completion and opening of *An Sùileachan* memorial sculpture, with Marian Leven, Reef, Isle of Lewis.
2014 · Opening of *Scantlings/Eastward and Westward*, with Arthur Watson, MUSA: Museum of the Univ. of St Andrews.
2018 · Completion of the *Iolaire* memorial, with Marian Leven and Arthur Watson, Holm, Isle of Lewis.

WORKS IN PUBLIC AND CORPORATE COLLECTIONS

Include: Aberdeen Art Gallery; Aberdeen City Libraries; Arbuthnot Museum, Peterhead; Arts Councils of Great Britain; BBC Scotland; British Museum; Carlow Art Collection, Carlow, Ireland; City Art Centre, Edinburgh; Clare College, University of Cambridge; Comhairle nan Eilean Siar (Western Isles Council), Stornoway, Isle of Lewis; Contemporary Art Society, UK; Craft Scotland; Creative Scotland; Dundee City Council; Fanim Hall Collection, Vancouver; Ferens Art Gallery, Hull; Fitzwilliam Museum, Cambridge; Fleming-Wyfold Art Foundation, London; Government Art Collection, London; Highland Council; Hospitalfield Trust Collection; Inverness Museum and Art Gallery; Kelvingrove Art Gallery and Museum, Glasgow; King's College, University of Cambridge; Kirkcaldy Galleries; Lillie Art Gallery, Milngavie, Glasgow; Maclaurin Art Gallery, Ayr; McLean Museum and Art Gallery, Greenock; McManus: Art Gallery and Museum, Dundee; McMaster Museum of Art, McMaster University, Hamilton, Ontario; Mitchell Library, Glasgow; National Library of Scotland; National Trust for Scotland; North Dakota Museum of Art, Grand Forks; Perth Museum and Art Gallery, Scotland; Proventus AB, Stockholm; Rhode Island School of Design, Providence; Robert Gordon University, Aberdeen; Rooms Provincial Art Gallery [Newfoundland and Labrador], St John's; Royal Collection Trust; Royal Scottish Academy of Art and Architecture Collections, Edinburgh; Sahbal Mòr Ostaig, Scottish Gaelic college, Isle of Skye; Scottish Fisheries Museum, Anstruther; Scottish Maritime Museum, Irvine/Dumbarton; Scottish National Gallery of Modern Art, Edinburgh; Scottish Parliament Art Collection, Edinburgh; Stirling Smith Art Gallery and Museum, Stirling; Stoke on Trent Art Gallery; University of Dundee; University of St Andrews; University of Stirling Art Collection; Western Isles Hospital Collection, Stornoway, Isle of Lewis; Westfield State University Collection, Mass.; Yale Center for British Art, New Haven, Conn.

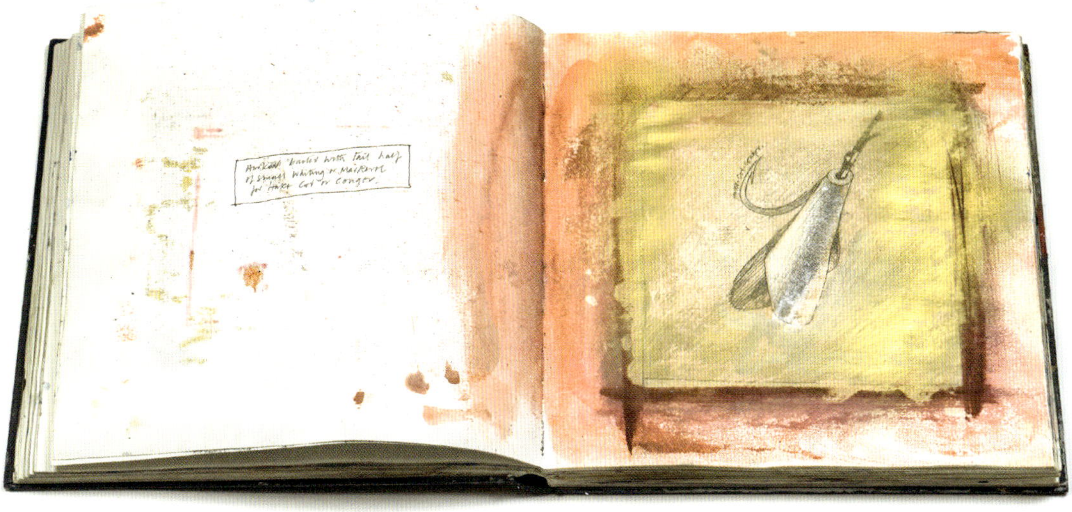

FURTHER READING

Allerston, Patricia, 'The Ring Net: Ring Net Herring Fishing on the West Coast of Scotland; a Documentary Exhibition by Will Maclean', MLitt thesis, Univ. of St Andrews, 1991 (http://hdl.handle.net/10023/7071).

Blair, Lindsay, essay in *Scottish Connections: The Art of Marian Leven and Will Maclean*, exhib. cat., Galerie Herold, Hamburg, 2012.

Blair, Lindsay, 'Paradigms of Transmission: Aesthetic Affinities and Intertextualities in the Art of Will Maclean' in Stephanie Bunn (ed.), *Anthropology and Beauty: From Aesthetics to Creativity* (Abingdon and New York: Routledge, 2018).

Coleridge, Samuel Taylor, *Duan an t-Seann Mharaiche/ The Rime of the Ancient Mariner*, [Gaelic/English bilingual edn, with trans. by Angus Macleod; illus. Will Maclean] (Isle of Lewis: Windfall Press, 2014).

Dubow, Jessica, essay in *North Sea Archives*, exhib. cat., DKFA, New York/Art First, London, 2005.

Gale, Iain, essay in *Will Maclean: Voyages*, exhib. cat., Art First, London, 1995.

Holloway, Richard, 'Introduction' in *Will Maclean: Different Meridians*, exhib. cat., Art First, London, 2008.

Lucie-Smith, Edward, essay in *Scottish Contemporary Art in Washington and London: Will Maclean/ Barbara Rae*, exhib. cat., Leinster Fine Art, London, 1984.

Macdonald, Murdo, essay in *Will Maclean: Collected Works 1970–2010*, exhib. cat., Fleming-Wyfold Art Foundation, London, 2011.

Maclean, Will, with Valerie and William Gillies, *St Kilda Waulking Song*. (Edinburgh: Morning Star, 1998).

Maclean, Will, with Angus Martin, *One Time in a Tale of Herring* [artists' book], Univ. of Dundee, 2010.

Macmillan, Duncan, essay in *Will Maclean*, exhib. cat., Runkel-Hue-Williams, London, 1990.

Macmillan, Duncan, *Symbols of Survival: The Art of Will Maclean* (Edinburgh: Mainstream Publishing, 1992); republished as *The Art of Will Maclean: Symbols of Survival* (London and New York: Art First, 2002).

McGrath, Tom, essay in *The Ring Net: Ring Net Herring Fishing on the West Coast of Scotland. A Documentary Exhibition by Will Maclean*, exhib. cat., Third Eye Centre, Glasgow, 1978.

Moffat, Sandy, essay in *Will Maclean: Collected Works 1970–2010*, exhib. cat., Fleming-Wyfold Art Foundation, London, 2011.

Neat, Tim, essay in *Will Maclean: Constructions, Small Sculptures and Drawings*, exhib. cat., Richard Demarco Gallery, Edinburgh, 1983.

Ness, Kim, essay in *Driftworks*, exhib. cat., Dundee Contemporary Arts, 2002.

Normand, Tom, essay in *Atlantic Messengers*, exhib. cat., Art First, London, 1998.

Patrizio, Andrew, essay in *Gleaned and Gathered*, exhib. cat., Art First, London, 2014.

Reuter, Laurel, 'Introduction' in *Will Maclean: Cardinal Points*, exhib. cat., North Dakota Museum of Art, Grand Forks, 2001.

Woods, Alan, 'Will Maclean' in *Will Maclean: Sculptures and Box Constructions 1974–1987*, (London: Claus Runkel Fine Art, 1987); includes a catalogue raisonné.

Acknowledgements

Will Maclean would like to thank:

David Patterson and the staff at the City Art Centre, Edinburgh, for the invitation to present the exhibition *Points of Departure*. And for their support throughout. Marian Leven RSA, Arthur Watson PRSA and Andy Rice for allowing their work to be included in the exhibition. Prof. Duncan Macmillan, Prof. Murdo Macdonald and Kim Ness for their insightful essays. Clare Cooper, Art First, London; Rainer and Karin Herold, Galerie Herold, Hamburg; and the Provost James Rae Trust for their support in the preparation of the exhibition.

The family of Sylvia Stevenson, a friend and early supporter. Ashley Ferrier; Benjamin Rhodes; Emily Walsh, Jamie Mackinnon and Camilla Riva, the Fine Art Society, Edinburgh; Kevin and Christine Macleod; Lindsay Blair; Malcolm Maclean; Patricia Allerston and Kerry Watson, National Galleries of Scotland, for their assistance and ongoing support.

All photographers and film-makers involved in the book and exhibition. To all the lenders of works, without whom the exhibition could not have been staged. To Paul, Clara, Ann and Ian at Sansom and Co., for their creative talent in bringing this book to fruition.

Finally, to Marian Leven, Miriam, John and David Maclean.